The Rookie Ranger

The Diary of a Wannabe Safari Guide

James Bailey

FASCINATING AFRICA

The Rookie Ranger
The Diary of a Wannabe Safari Guide

ISBN 978-1-0683717-1-4

First Edition
Published by Fascinating Africa

FascinatingAfrica.com

Cover Design by Spiffing Publishing

For Hannah, thank you for taking a chance on me.

And

For our boys, Zach and Archie: Walk with your head held high to show the world your strength, to see the trail ahead and to cherish every step of the journey.

AUTHOR'S NOTE

'I never knew of a morning in Africa when I woke up that I was not happy.' *Ernest Hemmingway, Novelist.*

This memoir is written to the best of my recollection—it's my story and how I understand the events that unfolded. It's not a how-to guide for becoming a safari guide or getting up close and personal with wild animals. If that's your dream, I recommend proper training with a provider like EcoTraining.

Some names and details have been changed to protect privacy. Whilst the heart of these tales is true, I've added a touch of dramatic flair for storytelling. This book reflects my own adventures and perspectives and is not endorsed by or affiliated with organisations such as EcoTraining, Wilderness Safaris, the Zoological Society of London, or the Science Museum Group.

At times, safety protocols weren't strictly followed—don't try this at home! Descriptions of illnesses and medical conditions are based on my observations and are not intended as medical advice. These stories are meant to share my journey, not to endorse or promote anything illegal or reckless.

Lastly, I've taken some liberties with grammar, so you may notice a few unconventional 'ands' and 'buts'. Consider it a nod to the ever-evolving nature of storytelling.

For photos and videos from my time as a wannabe safari guide and related content:

- Instagram: @therookieranger
- Facebook: @therookieranger
- X: jhcbailey
- Website: fascinatingafrica.com

CHAPTER ONE

'I can't remember a time when I was not fascinated by nature. I would say that nearly all children find wildlife interesting. You only have to show a child a snail or a spider to see that he or she is captivated by it. So of those that lose interest with the onset of adulthood, I can only ask: How on earth did you let it happen?' *Sir David Attenborough, Naturalist and Broadcaster.*

Hampshire
9th July 2024

I can pinpoint the precise moment I lost interest in nature. Or at least I know when I stopped being vocal about all things bright and beautiful.

At fourteen, two older boys forced me to watch a home movie of them throwing a rabbit to the dogs. The rabbit died for my persecution and for their amusement. From then on, I stopped championing animal rights, showing my passion for nature and going bird watching for fear of the repercussions.

My love of nature never left me; I kept it hidden,

focusing my energy on different pursuits, namely cricket. I grew up and secured what I believed to be my dream job, Marketing Manager for Durham County Cricket Club. I enjoyed a great setup; I lived with my brother in a house we owned in the party town that is Newcastle-upon-Tyne. Then things changed. A girl asked me if I would ever move to London.

'Absolutely not,' I replied. 'I'm not interested in heading south of Leeds. Well, not unless there's a job going at London Zoo'.

Lo and behold, five months later there was.

I joined the Zoological Society of London in 2004, meaning I no longer needed to keep my geeky love of nature hidden. Far from it, I now had to shout about conservation and wildlife.

Those who knew me in my pre-teen days thought this perfect. I even used to have a zoo in my garden, albeit only consisting of a pond, a bird hide, and a bunch of snails or escargatoire to give them their correct collective noun. An empty pen constructed with entwined sticks stood ready should I one day luck out and find a deer to include in my measly menagerie.

Inside the house, I kept a museum of natural history enclosed in a pine chest of drawers full of shells and dried out crustaceans. There was Ferrero Rocher box after Ferrero Rocher box full of cotton wool to safeguard egg fragments, fossils, and bird nests.

Hally, a stuffed tawny owl named after my godfather, was the prized possession of my museum.

My godfather took it to a taxidermist after I proudly placed its prone body on my parents' Sunday lunch table. *Hally* the owl went with me to London, but eventually, I decided he would be better off as part of the Zoo's education team. Nothing screams weirdo more than a stuffed raptor in your bedroom.

Gerald Durrell's books inspired my enthusiasm for nature, which my Mum further fostered. She would take me on morning walks to look for deer and hares in the Yorkshire valley that lay below our home. These required early starts, but despite rising early we met some friendly people along the way, including one group who later proved to be badger baiters. I had no idea, but Mum played it safe and bade them a good morning.

Eight years had passed since taking the job in London. I'd moved on from the Zoo, completed a three-year stint at the Natural History Museum, before joining the Science Museum as Head of Communications. I oversaw the Marketing and PR for four museums across England. While I enjoyed most aspects of the job, it wasn't perfect. I was no longer working in a field that aligned with my newly awakened passion for nature.

This, along with dealing with a difficult colleague, gradually eroded my confidence—so much that I began to question my own decisions. Today, I believe you'd call it imposter syndrome. Work grew even more challenging as I oversaw two rounds of redundancies in response to cuts in museum funding, a lingering effect of the 2008 financial crisis.

It got on top of me, the stress manifesting itself with my tell-tale sign, a mouth full of ulcers. I made a note in my journal on the twelfth of April 2012. I'd been sat in the Country Bumpkin pub in South Kensington, staring into an expensive pint of lager, yearning for a simpler life. My entry read,

'I can't cope. I'm overwhelmed by it all. I take it personally. I want everyone to get a fair outcome. I need to escape.'

I didn't act on this. I gritted my teeth and distracted myself with touch rugby, running, Heineken six-packs and the London Olympics. It worked—until Sophia, the girl I lived with, broke up with me the night before I was supposed to take her to Paris. I think she feared I was about to propose. For the record, that wasn't the plan—Paris, too much of a cliché.

I deal with problems with action. On this occasion, I did what most men would do and went to the pub. Rather than drink myself into oblivion, I downed several pints and lost myself in countless websites detailing animal volunteering holidays in Africa. That was my plan; I would go to Africa. I would do the type of holiday I liked.

I also needed an immediate plan before returning to the flat. One that would prevent me from appearing desperate and begging her to reconsider.

The plan I came up with was to head to the romantic capital of the world as a solo traveller. Turning this into a halfway decent idea was no easy task. But with a bit more research, the trip now included a rugby match and a visit to the Parc

Zoologique de Paris, making it more my style.

With my future back on track, I trudged up the steep Augustus Road to find a contrite Sophia. She thought it unfair to let me go to Paris alone — although we were still breaking up.

Oh well, she can have Paris, but Africa is mine and mine alone.

London
22nd October 2012

The day after returning from a disastrous trip to Paris, I found myself back at my desk in the Science Museum. It was six thirty-four in the morning, and I had just sent an email to Enkosini, a wildlife charity, offering two weeks of manual labour. By the end of the day, I was fully paid up and committed.

Lapolosa
4th to 11th November 2012

Two weeks on, I landed in Africa. This was my way of getting over Sophia and, more importantly, realising a lifelong dream of working on a game reserve.

The Googling I'd done post dumping led me to Enkosini. Derived from the Zulu word meaning place of kings, it's a Not for Profit founded by Kelsey Grimm, a former banker from the San Francisco Bay Area. I never had the pleasure of meeting her, but by all accounts, she is a remarkable woman. That's certainly what her Dad and Mum told me during my stay.

In 2000, Kelsey worked for a lion breeding project in Free State. Much to her horror, the lions she was raising were allegedly for the canned hunting trade. Such a practice is where lions are hand-reared and then hunted in a fenced-in area. Their upbringing means they're relatively tame, and not as afraid of humans as they should be.

To maximise profit, lion cubs are taken from their mother immediately after birth, forcing the lioness back into oestrus in a practice called speed breeding. The cubs are then bottle-fed by tourists. Ashamedly, I was one of those tourists in the early 2000s, unknowingly supporting this cruel industry. I visited such a place, fed and played with the cubs, and walked with adolescent lions. At the time the experience gave me immense joy, but now, it's an experience I wish I could forget—one I'd rather pretend never happened.

Realising what was happening, Kelsey and her partner, Greg, gave evidence in two High Court cases brought by Johannesburg Zoo against her employer. The action was over the falsely reported death of a loaned lion called Zeus.

Zeus was likely sold for a hefty price; thanks to the recessive white gene he carried. His genetic makeup made him a prime candidate for siring white cubs—a significant prize for any trophy hunter.

The Zoo won a series of court orders for Zeus' return along with his offspring. However, it wasn't plain sailing. According to an online report, the new owner padlocked the gates and fired shots into the air to stress the animals and hinder their collection. During this attempted retrieval the vets were assaulted, the attorney for the Zoo threatened with broken legs, and Greg threatened with death.

Eventually, Kelsey and Greg succeeded in rescuing ten lions with plans to rehome them on their newly established reserve. However, obstacles remained, forcing them to temporarily house the animals at Johannesburg Zoo while they faced yet another legal battle.

By the time of my visit, the lions had been and gone. The authorities seized the cats from Kelsey and Greg, claiming the reserve was an unsuitable environment. It was a great tragedy for two passionate conservationists who had fought so hard.

What the reserve lacked in big cats, it more than compensated for with its breathtaking scenery. The sheer scale of Lapolosa was staggering. Spanning 20,000 hectares, the drive from the main gate to camp stretched seventeen kilometres and even crossed a mountain range. My chalet fully embraced the view, whether I was lying in bed, taking an outdoor shower, or sitting on the open-fronted toilet. After all, who wouldn't want a loo with a view?

Before the reserve was set up, the land had been stripped of wildlife, largely due to the gold rush in the late 1800s, when the area was hunted clean to feed the miners. Once the mines had been depleted, the land transitioned into cattle ranches—eleven of them, to be exact. Our mission was to erase that era from the landscape. The name Lapolosa comes from the Sepedi word for "place of rest," and while the area was indeed tranquil, we quickly found it was far from restful.

The first day was hard graft, a painstaking job of taking down rusty barbed wire fences. The mandatory tetanus jab back in England now made sense as the job came with lots of cuts and blisters. It's a tangible and satisfying thing to clean up the reserve, but not as satisfying as my next job, setting it on fire.

As part of the fire management plan, we burned off two blocks covering six square kilometres. My task? To set fire to the bush. 1.5 kilometres of bush, to be exact. This was exciting but not as satisfying as beating back the flames that tried to turn on us. I say it was fun, but I never lost sight of the fact that it was anything but safe.

Because Lapolosa isn't a Big Five reserve, a trip to Kruger National Park was a must for our African experience. Whilst this was going to be amazing, I secretly wanted to stay at Lapolosa and rip down old fences. On the morning of our departure, we got up at three forty in the morning for our three-day trip.

Despite the heavy rain, we managed an impressive haul of game on our two drives—buffalo, white rhino, steenbok, klipspringer, the fantastically crested African hoopoe, pied kingfisher, giraffe, leopard tortoise, and elephants.

After pitching our tents at Skukuza Rest Camp we visited the commercial area of the complex which included the restaurant and curio shop overlooking the Sabie River. This is where we ticked off the elephant, a herd totalling fourteen descended gracefully to the water. Walt Disney couldn't have done a better job; it was picture perfect.

For the second day in a row, we rose before the sparrows, with my alarm blaring at four forty-five in the morning. The early starts matched my expectations of Africa—the weather, however, didn't. Only the eighties band, Toto, might have appreciated it, surely blessing the rains hammering down on us.

The drive made up for the early awakening and lousy weather. Highlights included leopard, hippo, spoonbill, cheetah, banded mongoose, sable, spotted hyena, lots of elephants, hamerkop, side-striped jackal, and a bedraggled honey badger. The latter cost me a bottle of brandy for the guide as I'd arrogantly said, find me a honey badger and I'll buy your favourite drink.

Siyafunda
12th to 19th November 2012

My first week in Africa flew by. I bid farewell to Lapolosa and transferred to Siyafunda, a volunteer organization that conducted research programmes on the 26,000-hectare Makalali game reserve. During orientation, we were reminded that the camp was unfenced—anything could wander in or through at any time, and yes, this was a Big Five reserve. A torch was required to get from dinner to the bedroom. Not to avoid stubbing my toe, but to shine into the long grass to ensure nothing was stalking me.

During this leg of my journey, I decided to quit my job and become a safari guide. For at Siyafunda, I met two women, both of whom inspired me. Charlotte from London at the younger end of twenty something stood out with her large grey eyes, which sparkled with enthusiasm. Her passion for the work was contagious, and it lit a spark in me too.

Charlotte didn't carry a rifle. If she did, she'd be venturing into *Lara Croft* territory. But she was on her way to gaining her firearms qualifications. I knew this because she showed me a photo of the last time she went to the range. Her left cheek and shoulder were as purple as thunder, the bruising caused by the recoil of each shot fired.

What Charlotte lacked in *Tomb Raider* status she more than made up for in *Top Gun* folklore. The truck she drove bore her name on the driver's door just as *Maverick*, *Goose* or *Iceman* would have on the cockpit of their F-14.

Meeting Charlotte turned my dream of becoming a ranger into something tangible. She'd achieved it, so why couldn't I? All it required was backing up my words with action and taking the plunge. Simple.

The second Siyafunda female to play her part was not the lioness and her four cubs we watched for ninety minutes, although they gave me a memory that will endure a lifetime. It was a German called Mia. Now she did give *Lara Croft* a run for her money with her athletic physique, bush shorts, olive shirt and *Croc Dundee* hat.

Khaki fever took hold of me. Historically, this was reserved for woman falling for men in uniform, which included safari guides. The phenomenon can be traced back to 1914 Britain when women helplessly swooned over men in military dress.

When assigned various duties, I often found

myself paired with Mia. I liked to think she was behind it, just as much as I was. Our tasks were varied. We performed daily checks to ensure the Toyota Land Cruiser was ready for the bush, and recorded sightings and behaviours of pachyderms—a category that included elephants and rhinos.

The physical work in thirty-seven degrees left us hot, sweaty and for me, severely dehydrated on one occasion. The toil was bringing Mia and me closer together, and I enjoyed relaxing over cups of tea and rusks with her and an Australian called Cathy.

Sharing the camp with us were delicate nyala that grazed the lawn around our chairs. While an open camp is great for getting close to gentle antelope, it comes with danger. A leopard had become too familiar with the camp and killed the owner's pet cat. In response, the leopard relocation team, a local charity, set up a trap on the volleyball court, baiting it with an impala carcass.

Later during our stay, we spotted a lioness striding purposefully up the road. She was following the all-too-obvious scent of the dead impala directly to our camp. Upon reaching the clearing behind the workshops, she encountered a scene straight from a wildlife documentary—giraffe, wildebeest and zebra grazing together. After watching them for ten minutes, she slipped silently into the thick bush. The animals gradually grazed their way across the clearing and into the undergrowth before thundering back out—they'd stumbled right into the lioness's path. With this hunt unfolding just behind our camp, we couldn't ignore the reality: we were living amongst wild and dangerous animals.

On the final evening, it was my turn to cook for the camp. Throughout the week, dinner had been more than just a meal. It was a social event, not the routine necessity it had become back home before collapsing in front of the TV. Here, the TV didn't even get a mention. I don't think there was one. It was all about enjoying each other's company.

After dinner, Mia and I talked into the early hours, with a lion roaring to our left and a hyena calling to our right. With the dead impala rotting in the trap, we were certain the lion was making straight for us. Our imaginations ran wild, prompting a hasty—if not entirely dignified—retreat to our rooms.

The two weeks in Africa profoundly affected me; it made me happy. I enjoyed getting my hands dirty. It was hard work, but I loved the daily routine of getting up with the sun and going to bed when I was tired, not when a film finished. The trip reinforced my desire for an outdoor life, away from the hustle and bustle of the city.

London
28th November 2012

Six weeks previously, I'd split with Sophia. Now, we were about to have one of those talks – the 'have we made a mistake, and should we give it one more go' kind. Before I left, we'd arranged to meet in the pub, the Cross Keys in South Kensington, which was our post-work haunt. It was convenient rather than a favourite.

Given the old-fashioned vibe of the pub, Sophia stood out the moment she walked in. She was stunning with her slender physique and long blonde hair. Together we appeared to be the perfect couple, especially as I was not too shabby with my African tan.

B.A. (Before Africa) I'd banked on her throwing her arms around me and sobbing about how foolish she'd been. Now I was worried she would do just that. I didn't want to get back together. I wanted to go back to Africa, work outdoors and hang out with like-minded people —my kind of people, people like Mia.

There was no dramatic showdown or outpouring of emotions. It was all very British—reserved and matter of fact. I was free to go to Africa, but this time, it would be for longer than just a fortnight.

Charlotte was living proof that an African life was possible, and Mia, my partner in crime, was encouraging me to return. However, Mia was the more level-headed one, urging me to take the one-year course to become a field guide. Meanwhile, I was busy researching game lodges for sale.

Mia, rightly, tempered my ambition. Most notably suggesting that it wasn't the best idea to sell my flat to go all-in. But this didn't stop me planning my escape to the most breath-taking continent on planet earth.

I could see no reason not to go. I had no ties beyond family and friends to hold me back, and my job was not secure. The government's ongoing austerity measures had seen to that. If I was going to leave the Museum, I wanted it to be on my terms, not someone else's. From overseeing countless redundancies, I'd learned that losing control was often the hardest part for people. Running away was my way of taking control. At least that's how I justified my decision.

All my life, I'd been the one who talked about what I wanted to do—a dreamer. I liked to frame it as being a creative visionary, an ideas man. But the truth was, I was all talk and no action. That needed to change. I was nearly forty, for crying out loud. I had to go for it. You only live once, and all that.

I'd often discussed such folly with my brother, Johnny, so this wasn't a new idea. During one of our drink-fuelled deep and meaningfuls, I'd dismissed it, likening the venture to career sabotage. When I finally announced my decision, he naturally reminded me of this. Johnny may be three years younger, but his maturity—and my lack of it—makes him many years wiser.

Now I had made my decision. The mother of all to-do lists took shape. The first task was to choose a company that would take on the unenviable task of making me a safari guide.

After trawling through web brochures and comparing notes with Mia, I was no further forward. In the end, I bypassed the websites and found my own source. I messaged Charlotte through Facebook; she'd been through this all before. She put forward two suppliers, one she did her training with, and one called EcoTraining. She recommended the latter. She believed they'd provide more practical experience in the field. Less class time, more bush time.

EcoTraining pitched themselves as the pioneers and leaders in the sector. Being established in 1993 they certainly possessed the pioneer credentials. Whether they truly led was difficult to determine. They operated four camps with traversing rights covering 100,000 hectares. At a multiple of 2.47 this works out at almost a quarter of a million acres. This included a portion in the most magnificent nature reserve in the world, the Kruger National Park.

The clincher for EcoTraining was that all the camps were unfenced. If I chose them, I would live amongst the animals in an unforgettable, immersive experience. I chose them.

26th March 2013

I'd committed—well, at least to the tune of five thousand pounds in down costs. It was time to make it official: time to quit my job.

My boss and I never held formal one-on-ones to go through the motions and tick boxes. Instead, we met casually each morning to review the day's agenda. I guess this was down to his days as a journalist. Roger spent two decades as Science Editor of the *Daily Telegraph* before becoming Editor of the *New Scientist*. Before that, he was the first person, and probably the last, to bounce a neutron off a soap bubble.

Prior to joining as Director of External Affairs at the *Science Museum Group*, I met him at the *New Scientist*. In their swanky Central London offices—by museum standards—he settled me into a large red wing-backed chair and explained how he saw us working together.

'In publishing James, there are two Editor roles, both equally important. There is the Managing Editor that runs the team ensuring that everything that should happen, happens, and that will be your role. Then there's the Editor, the one who has the ideas and gets the glory. That will be my role. How does that sound?'

His proposition came without arrogance or malign intent, and I was fully on board with the setup. It played to our strengths well.

Ian Blatchford, the Director of the Science Museum recruited Roger for his profile and network. And Roger couldn't have got off to a better start. In his first couple of months, he wowed us by arranging for David Hockney to do an iPad portrait of Stephen Hawking in the physicist's brilliantly cluttered Cambridge office. This was something I could never have pulled off myself, not least because I did not know who Hockney was.

Today, I sat in Roger's office for one of our usual catchups. But this time was different—I was about to announce that I was leaving to become a safari guide. As Roger stood at his computer finishing an email, I took a moment to reflect on the magnitude of this decision and everything I would be leaving behind.

I'd sat in his office 1,000 times over but now I was about to leave, or at least start the process of leaving, my mind shifted into absorption mode. The books lining the shelves, many of them popular science editions, demonstrated the meteoric rise in the popularity of science in recent years. Some had been written or co-authored by Roger himself. These ranged from the fun end of the scale, *Can Reindeer Fly? The Science of Christmas*, to the more serious *Supercooperators: Altruism, Evolution, and Why We Need Each Other to Succeed.*

On the walls hung re-prints from the Science Museum photo archive, including an image of the moon landings. This was my favourite because of the pocked detail of the moon surface. There were also the great and good of science from Albert Einstein to Marie Curie, with many in between. The many in between is code for, I don't know their names but feel I should.

Roger dominated the room. At six feet and then some, his presence loomed even larger as he walked on his treadmill, finishing that email. That treadmill had been the topic of another conversation we'd had when I was sitting in the red wing-back chair at the *New Scientist.*

'James, please can you arrange a treadmill for me. I'll pay for it myself, but I'd like a desk where I can walk while I work. I trialled this setup at the *Daily Telegraph* while covering the research of a Brit working in the States. He conducted studies showing that weight loss isn't just about diet and strenuous exercise; it also depends on the calories we burn during our daily activities.'

It was obvious he wasn't joking, and I loved the idea, so I took his request back to my existing boss, and we organised it for him. I think the most sceptical were the chaps from Building Services who assembled the flat pack treadmill ahead of Roger's arrival.

Talk about making a first impression when you

start a new job, it's a first impression that keeps on impressing. It gives Roger a psychological advantage when someone comes to the office. It's also a talking point. Roger will often invite those visiting him to give the treadmill a spin before tweeting their picture. Heston Blumenthal has even succumbed.

He took off his headset and stepped down. At least he wasn't seven-foot-tall anymore.

'James, I'm all yours. What have we got on the agenda today?'

I think my news took him by surprise. Not least because my face was contorting in many directions. There are not many who could say, 'I'm leaving to become a safari guide', without a clown size grin spreading across their face.

Roger was great about it and understood my motivation. As British American author Simon Sinek might say, he got my 'why'—the true sense of purpose this experience would bring me. But there was one problem: he didn't accept my resignation. Despite me making it clear I was leaving; he insisted I sleep on it.

I wasn't racing against the clock just yet. With a three-month notice period and five months still to go until lift-off, there was time to spare.

12th April 2013

I'm short-sighted, not drastically. If I mislaid my glasses, I'd be able to find my way home through rush hour traffic. I find them more a luxury than anything else. They come in handy for driving and for larger than average meetings. To be fair, driving use is more a DVLA diktat than a luxury.

Regardless, I wanted uninhibited vision for Africa. This trip was a big thing for me. I didn't want to leave anything to chance, my eyesight included. For the shooting tests, I wanted to pass with flying colours. When walking in the bush, I wanted to see every detail. Crucially I wanted to do all this wearing Tom Cruise style shades rather than having ones that clipped onto the front of my specs.

With twenty-twenty hindsight, I could have gone with prescription sunglasses. Instead, I followed my flatmate Barnsie's suggestion of laser eye surgery.

Barnsie is a successful chap working in professional sport and had his eyes done. Many of the players he works with have undergone the same procedure. They're cricketers, so eyesight is essential to them. After all, your eyes aren't something you can mess with when you make your living by having a bone-breaking hard ball catapulted towards you at ninety miles per hour.

After an initial consultation, today was the day I followed through with the process. Until the point I was in the chair with the Doctor's knee all but placed on my solar plexus, I hadn't considered that this could be painful beyond the cost.

For those that don't know, and that included me until this afternoon, laser eye surgery is thus. First, it's called LASIK, Laser-Assisted In situ Keratomileusis. The first part involved soothing anaesthetic eye drops. Sweet. Then it was onto the hardcore part of the procedure. A device grasped my eyelids and held them open while at the same time pulling and securing my cornea. At this moment, the conversation between the Doc and me went round and round in circles, something like this,

The Doctor, 'Open your eyes',

Me, 'They are'

The Doctor, 'Wider'

Me, 'They are'

And so on.

Once they were, and he agreed, the next part was relatively easy. A computer-controlled laser emitted a series of nanosecond bursts of light. It cut three precise incisions in my cornea. Rather than cutting out a complete square with a fourth incision, this was left to act as a hinge. The cornea was then folded back.

Even with the eye opened up, it's still not possible to add the lens, nor is there a need. Instead, the inside of the cornea can be shaped by laser to function as a lens and correct the vision. With the shaping done, it was merely a case of folding it back into position for the three edges to seal back into the eye without the aid of surgical adhesives.

With the job done, I donned my *Top Gun* Aviators and headed back to the flat.

Hutton Rudby
11th May 2013

I'm home, my family home in God's country, North Yorkshire. It's a million miles away from the hustle and bustle and stress of daily life, of London life. My home is not the flat in South West London; it's where my family is, my Mum and Dad, and where

I grew up. I imagine that will change over time if I marry and am fortunate enough to have children. But wherever home may be, it should always be where you feel safest.

Am I waffling? I don't even know why I started today's entry with the need to express where I'm at my safest. It may be a result of the wildlife atrocities I've just read about. There truly is evil in this wonderful world of ours.

Two days ago, in a national park in central Africa, 17 Arabic-speaking poachers, believed to be Sudanese, took to a tourist viewing platform overlooking a large clearing in the rainforest at a location called Dzanga Bai, the 'Village of Elephants.'

That day, the Bai transformed from a tranquil garden of Eden into a chaotic scene of death. The opening fire would have shattered the peace. The sound of an AK47 is hard to describe; from what I can deduce, it can be compared to a sledgehammer striking a table ten times a second. Now imagine that multiplied by seventeen, assuming each poacher carried a rifle. It's unimaginable. As bullets rained down on the elephants, the resulting chaos must have been unfathomable.

Witnessing such an event would have been harrowing. The Kalashnikovs would have been indiscriminate, with no carefully aimed shots to minimise the elephants' suffering. Instead, much of the ivory was likely shattered, rendered worthless. It was a senseless, moronic act.

The elephants would have bellowed and screamed, collapsing as bullets shattered their legs while they tried to escape. Those unlucky enough to survive the first shots would have likely laid helpless. They would have endured a long and painful death. The poachers would have hacked off their tusks with pangas with their lifeblood soaking into the African soil.

Poachers gunned down twenty-six forest elephants that day, including four calves. Many escaped. It could have been worse, though saying that feels inappropriate when twenty-six lay dead. Typically, between fifty and two-hundred elephants gather daily to drink the mineral and nutrient-rich waters. How did the trauma affect those who escaped? Do elephants suffer from PTSD? I'm sure they do.

As a safari guide, I'll be able to do something; even if it's a small thing, I'll champion the conservation cause with my guests to spread the word.

London
15th May 2013

It was full steam ahead, pulling everything together for my departure. There were a million and one things to tick off my neurotic list, from vacuum sealing photo albums to mothballing my clothes and cancelling contracts. Packing in the twenty-first century involves much more than self-assembly boxes and bubble wrap; it includes the digital world too. I spent most of my time backing up my rickety old computer on the cloud.

The most pressing task, aside from securing a

student visa, was finding someone to take over my room as Barnsie's flatmate. This wasn't easy. The first person I suggested, according to Barnsie, was too dull. Eventually, I found someone who loved the flat. The catch was, he wanted to move in within six days. But, with the job done, I moved out.

Except for the Hepatitis and Typhoid jabs, the preparations were fun. Gathering the gear and the meticulous planning required gave me a buzz and built the excitement. I wasn't following Doctor Livingstone's footsteps to discover the source of the Nile nor Scott to the Antarctic, but I was planning a once in a lifetime adventure for me.

One item harder to find than a black cat in a coal cellar was a suitable bush hat. Any self-respecting ranger needs a reliable hat. Despite scouring the pricey outdoor shops around Covent Garden, I still hadn't found this essential piece of gear. I was picky—I wanted 'the real McCoy', something *Indiana Jones* or *Mick Dundee* would wear. Leathery, no chin strap. I didn't want to look any more like a Boy Scout than I already did. In the end, I turned to the internet, and The Safari Store in Lancashire became my saviour.

The pièce de résistance was a Barmah Squashy Hickory Suede bush hat of Australian heritage. The morning it arrived felt like Christmas. I was more than a little excited—this was the final piece of the puzzle, the perfect finishing touch for my adventure. And the hat fit perfectly.

'I could do this', I thought. 'No—I am going to do this. I'm going to become a safari guide.'

25th May 2013

The fact I'd given up my job gnawed away at me, especially as the future job market, should I return, was looking bleak. Plus, I didn't hate my job, I did things most people would only dream of. Just five days ago I oversaw the press conference operations for the announcement of Tim Peake's mission to the International Space Station in November 2015.

It was an honour to meet such a humble man. I was also struck by how small he was; I suppose not needing much legroom is an advantage on a long-haul flight. That said, he would grow about three per cent taller in orbit, thanks to the lack of gravity compressing his spine.

These factors fuelled the self-doubt creeping in. A lack of confidence in myself is my biggest weakness, and I need to become stronger and not let it take hold. However, on this occasion, it soon vanished with the reassurance I found in people's reactions when it was finally time to share my news. Some shrieked,

'That's so perfect for you, James, what a great fit' and

'You'd be amazing at that. I'm surprised you've not done it before now — you're always talking about your zoo days'.

I suspected that meant, 'It's so boring when you start every sentence with "When I was at the Zoo".'

To those who congratulated me, I pointed out that their praise wasn't necessary. This wasn't a job I'd interviewed for or something I'd earned through hard work and training. It was simply a case of me paying to study overseas. Their response was always,

'No, congratulations on being brave and following your dream. We all have one, but don't dare pursue it'.

I certainly got what they meant, but this wasn't an impossible dream, and I should know, as I've had many of those. A handful off the top of my head included 'Arena Cricket', which took over my life in the early 2000s. It was to be indoor eight a side professional cricket in Newcastle's 5,500-seater arena. I even got ten of Durham's professional squad to attend the stadium first thing in the morning for a trial on a ply-board covered ice rink.

Then there was 'Monkey Jungle', a ten-acre walk-through monkey zoo in County Durham. I spent a couple of years chasing that dream, but it ultimately came to nothing. I became so obsessed that nothing else seemed to matter. It shouldn't have been a surprise when my girlfriend ended our relationship—unfortunately, on the day we were supposed to move in together. I never got a clear reason for why she called it off. The silver lining being it wasn't me—it was her. Looking back now, though, it might have been me. It probably didn't help that we spent her birthday visiting a potential site for the mini zoo.

Both dreams held potential, but neither reached a significant Champagne moment. I never saw them through. But to become a safari guide, all I needed to do was pay the tuition fees and go.

Others told me that my news had got them thinking about what they could do. My plans inspired and enthused them. Now they wanted to do something rather than just talk about it.

I wasn't on a mission to get everyone to quit their job. There are, of course, many ways to live your dreams. But this didn't stop me from recommending a video featuring an audio recording of British philosopher Alan Watts, 'What Do I Desire?' The abridged version is one minute, forty-three seconds of pure motivation. In short, when giving career advice, he asks one question.

'What would you do if money were no object?'

In the video the students come back with their voices full of passion that quickly fade when they follow up with the inevitable 'but'.

'But there's no money in that.' They say.

His advice is not to worry about the money but simply to identify what it is you want to do and just do it. Chasing the money will leave you miserable, he says. You'll end up doing the things you don't enjoy doing. As we spend sixty per cent of our lives working, we shouldn't want that for ourselves, and we shouldn't want it for our children and their children. This can become the case if we don't break the cycle. Instead, he says we must fill our lives with what we like doing and become masters of it, then the money will follow.

CHAPTER TWO

'For what it's worth: it's never too late to be whoever you want to be. I hope you live a life you're proud of, and if you find you're not, I hope you have the strength to start over again.' *F. Scott Fitzgerald, Novelist.*

London
31st August 2013

I'm rubbish at goodbyes, so British, no emotion, everything bottled up inside. Nothing to show I'm going to miss my sister, Emma, and two nieces who dropped me at the airport. Not seeing the little ones every second weekend will be the hardest thing, they're so much fun and growing up alarmingly fast. I consoled myself with,

'I'm only away for eleven months, that's not even a year.'

I say this, but I have a larger game plan in the back of my mind, to take up permanent residence with one day owning a lodge.

Packing was an ordeal, but I crammed everything

into a huge cricket bag, now known as Baby Elephant, and one carry on sports bag. I was overweight, meaning I had to sort through my hold luggage which I spread across the tiled floor at the South African Airways desk. The weight I took on the plane didn't change, just its distribution from my checked luggage to carry on.

Once airside I found a letter from Emma which she'd slipped into my sports bag. It ended with,

'Please don't stay.'

She'd obviously picked up on my longer-term aspirations. At least she'd not slipped in contraband to prevent me from getting through security.

I was lucky to make the flight. Having disappeared into a world of my own, as I usually do, the last call for BA0057 snapped me back to reality. I dashed for it with my twenty kilogram carry on tossed over my shoulder. This was an undignified way to start the most momentous year of my life.

Johannesburg
2nd September 2013

A new chapter of my life has begun, the African chapter. I touched down at five past nine yesterday morning at Johannesburg's OR Tambo Airport after an overnight flight from London Heathrow. I must admit the name was a bit confusing. When booking the flight, I thought it was a choice between Joburg or Tambo airport.

The airport is in fact named after Oliver Reginald Kaizana Tambo, an anti-apartheid politician and revolutionary who served as President of the African National Congress from 1967 to 1991.

Cousin Alison and her husband Graham gave me a warm welcome in Joburg. They'd given up their entire weekend to run around after me, making sure I was thoroughly entertained and equipped. While I was 5,635 miles from London, their hospitality in Bryanston made it feel like I hadn't left home.

In fact, it felt like I was home—not London or Yorkshire, but home in Africa. While everyone else was doing the Ibiza thing in their twenties, my brother Johnny and I were heading to Cape Town with friends. I knew the Western Cape wasn't the 'real' Africa, but we loved it all the same.

The real Africa is the bush. I first experienced it with Johnny when we visited my mum's cousins in Kenya. We took two trips in the early 2000s, and we were well looked after, going on safari with Abercrombie and Kent, the luxury purveyors, at mate's rates thanks to a family connection who worked there. The luxury was incredible, but what I enjoyed even more was when we loaded up two pick-ups and headed into the wilds of Kenya for a week of camping en famille.

Our mini convoy arrived clad in the oxidised red soil of the savannah at a mud hut village. My Mum's cousin did a deal with the Chief so we could wild camp in a riverine thicket on the banks of a river. The shade of the trees and the coolness created by the water was a blessing given the soaring temperature.

Being African, our hosts had 'mengi' help in the house—'mengi' meaning 'a lot' in Swahili. While the cook, maid and the rest of the staff stayed at home, the gardener joined us on the trip. It seemed like a holiday for him too. The only thing he was asked to do was dig the long drop at the beginning of the week.

The latrine was basic but ingenious. It was located a short walk from camp, and downwind, of course. A canvas modesty blind offered some privacy on the camp side. But the moment of inspiration was an old school chair, complete with a toilet seat and lid.

The week was a boozy affair. By midday, we'd be sitting in director's chairs in the middle of the river, drinks in hand. Our aquatic living room was set up in the fast-flowing parts of the river to reduce the risk of contracting bilharzia, a parasitic disease. As for crocs and hippos, I wasn't entirely sure what our plan was there.

Nelspruit
3rd September 2013

Last night everyone who gathered around the table had a reason to be there. Some ran away, some ran toward something, but the majority knew neither their destination, their purpose, nor their motivation. They were lost.

This was true of me too. Admitting this to oneself is bad enough, but now we were asked to share our dreams and demons with a bunch of strangers we'd just met.

Anton Lategan, Director of EcoTraining, convened us at the Old Vic Travellers Inn for the official start of the course. In usual ice-breaking style we all, one by one, stood up to introduce ourselves and state what we wanted from the experience.

For me, this was easy. I wanted to become a safari guide. I wanted to learn as much as I could over the next five months, get a proper lodge placement and stay on so I could carry on living my dream.

Rather than listening to what people said, I tried to remember names. I'm rubbish at this, especially when they're not your standard fare. I had mastered several, either at the airport guest house last night or on the journey to Nelspruit. The easy ones included Carmen, Ulrica, and Ben.

Carmen was the first person I met at the backpackers in Joburg, mainly because I recognised her from Facebook. Charlotte had connected us when she noticed we were both joining the same intake at EcoTraining. Carmen came across as a lovely girl, but she was just that—a girl, only 18. Despite her age, she seemed mature, though she was still twenty years my junior. While that felt like quite a gap, I wasn't the oldest in the group. That honour belonged to a forty-three-year-old South African named Cliff, who, thanks to his size and the presence of another Cliff, was at once dubbed Big Cliff.

A handful matched my age of thirty-eight, a few ranged in their early thirties, then some in their mid-twenties and plenty of nineteen-year-olds. Our mixed bunch included one Swede, one Swiss, five English, four South African and two from America. Thirteen of us made up group 7E. I'm presuming this name came from being the seventh year of the professional field guide year-long course and the fifth intake of 2013.

Once we'd shared, it was over to Anton for a pep talk.

'At EcoTraining, we will get you as close to the earth as possible. Nature will get into your hearts and minds. We will show you places, share experiences, take you away from technology and immerse you within beautiful surroundings so that nature takes over your soul. We will teach you to respect nature and work in harmony with it. You will learn how a natural system is sustainable when man does not interfere, how it can clean itself and regenerate. You will reconnect with nature and take the EcoTraining philosophy forward.'

He paused and looked at two or three of us individually before starting again.

'You will be in a privileged position to do this as a qualified field guide. A guide is a leader, a guardian of nature, an interpreter, and an honest host to visitors. A guide should stand for the highest standards of ethics and care for nature and people, in the wilderness and in their own community. Guides are the key to sustainable tourism, as they passionately take a stand for conservation.'

Anton carried on for some time and once the briefing was finished, we switched to the tried and tested method of ice breaking, alcohol. Ben and I clicked as soon as we met, so we stuck together at the bar. He is six foot four, into rugby, American football, has a *BSc in Biology* and has already worked on a lion project.

As a group we drank many a Castle beer as we got to know one another. There's a chance that the friendships we formed tonight will be the enduring ones for the course.

After the luxury of my single occupancy double at the guest house the previous night, it was now on to backpacker dorms and time for earplugs. I'm not sure what an elephant sounds like when it snores, but one of my roommates certainly gave me a fair idea.

Due to this literal elephant in the room, I got little sleep. This left me tired, and as such, I felt vulnerable about what lay ahead. Because of this it suddenly became incredibly real during our rifle competency briefing and test today.

The briefing was a wake-up call—one that terrified me. It laid bare the realities of what I would be doing and the risks of living in the bush. There was talk of being prosecuted for manslaughter if a guest was killed because one of us did not stop a charging elephant in time. There was also the possibility of meeting armed poachers. If you took everything the instructor said at face value, it seemed likely we'd either leave Africa in a body bag or after serving a prison sentence.

After being deemed competent on paper, we then had to prove we could shoot straight on the range. It was hot and dusty, with everyone cowering under the shade of a scraggly thorn tree. Give me a month or two, and I should be able to name what species of tree was sparing us from chronic sunburn.

CHAPTER THREE

'The best friend on earth of man is the tree. When we use the tree respectfully and economically, we have one of the greatest resources on earth.' *Kahlil Gibran, Writer.*

Selati Private Game Reserve
4th September 2013

Despite the five-hour journey from the Old Vic, our transfer dropped us at the gates of Selati Private Game Reserve while it was still morning. We'd had a brutally early wake-up call. From what I understand, though, early starts are just part and parcel of what's to come.

The last thirty minutes of the journey were technically through the bush. We made our way along the slick tar road with the two-metre-high electrified game fences of Selati on one side and Makalali on the other. Makalali was a surprise as it's where I did my volunteering the year before.

The trees were the typical African acacias I'd seen in films and documentaries. A flick through the crisp, untouched pages of the one-kilogram *A Field Guide to*

Trees of Southern Africa revealed that there was more than one acacia these trees could be. In all, the book detailed fifty-four.

The bush on the reserve side of the fence line was thick. All I could see were trees, miles and miles of trees. Now and then a giraffe head or a baby mountain jutted above the tree canopy. From my earlier trips, I knew the latter as kopjes, the perfect place for a sundowner.

We were met at the gate by a volunteer in an old, battered Land Rover with an even more battered trailer on the tow bar. There wasn't enough room for all of us, so they relayed us to camp in shuttles.

Once there, we were introduced to our two South African instructors, JP and Margaux, who, at a guess, are a little younger than me. We gathered in the thatched open-sided building. This is the place that will host our lectures; mealtimes; meetings and study. The only place we'd spend more time was in the bush.

They took this opportunity to introduce us to the vuvuzela of South African Football World Cup fame. The long monotone note created when the plastic horn was blown would signal a reason to come to the deck, whether it be for food, class or an emergency.

JP delivered our briefing and orientation gravely. I suppose we fell under his responsibility, and if anything happened to us, on his head be it. He reminded us that anything could and would come through the camp. To hammer his point home, he gestured to the volleyball court.

'There, a lioness chased down, killed, and ate a

warthog. There's probably no better example I can give to show how real the danger is.'

Our hosts were a double act, and now it was Margaux's turn. She wasn't here to scare us with stories of dangerous game; instead, she put the fear in us with a whiteboard showing the schedule for the next 30 days. It was packed solid, with no rest days in sight.

More alarmingly, Margaux introduced us to the honesty bar—a chest freezer on the deck, complete with padlock. If, by morning, the tally chart didn't add up, the bar would be locked until the outstanding balance was paid.

After signing our lives away via indemnity forms, the moment we'd all been waiting for arrived: who would be tenting with whom? Ben and I made a pact over drinks at the Old Vic that we would tent together if we needed to share.

It turned out we didn't have to share. Or at least, I didn't. Being a mature student, I got my own tent—apparently, we're too set in our ways to share. Ben, still a 'mere child' by comparison, was paired with Pieter, an Afrikaner fresh out of school. I briefly considered offering to take Ben in, but he didn't seem upset. What Ben didn't know was that Pieter was the snoring elephant from the backpackers. I kept quiet—Ben would be alright.

In human geography terms, the camp followed the layout of a linear village along the banks of the Selati River. Right at the centre were the deck and kitchen, both substantial structures with thatched roofs. Next to the deck was what I imagined would become the heart of our being—the campfire. Opposite was the office, housed in a military-style tent.

The layout effectively split the camp into two parts, with one half reserved for women and the other for men. This wasn't to discourage tent-hopping; it was simply to provide separate male and female ablution blocks.

The ablution blocks were well designed. They had four of everything: four toilets, four showers and four sinks. Canvas curtains provided privacy in the showers and toilets, closing with hooks when occupied. Banks of milk crates, cable tied together, created shelving for wash bags.

The camp was interlinked by a network of dusty paths edged with stones collected from the river. From the centre the trail stretched out in four directions, north led down to the river, south wound its way towards the garage with east and west leading to the segregated accommodation. Each end of the easterly and westerly paths was anchored by an instructor's tent. Their tents looked comfortable and even included en-suite facilities.

Our army green dome tents were more spacious than expected. For me this was probably because I'd struck lucky by not having to share. Inside, a mattress lay on the ground, accompanied by a pillow, and blue pyjama sheets with fraying bobbles. Additionally, there were two black milk crates, like those used for shelving in the shower block. These versatile plastic crates offered endless uses, limited only by one's imagination. Currently, one serves as my laundry basket and the other as my bedside table.

A laundry service was included in the course fees. All I had to do was to put my crate out on the given day each week. Oh, and wash my socks and jocks by hand as the camp staff don't do smalls.

Neatness is not my strong point, but this must change. The most important rule after not being killed by a wild animal is to keep the tent tidy. Why? So, you won't get killed by a wild animal. Floordrobes were a big no-no, as such a mess would make it difficult to remove any snakes that may have slithered through the tiniest of gaps where the three zips of the tent's door met.

My tent is a decent walk from the main camp. Still, Cliff number two, this one from California, hence his newly given name of California Cliff, must walk past mine and then a further 200 metres. I'm uneasy with the prospect of my journey after dark, but Cliff must be beside himself with his.

After beers at the campfire, I headed to bed via the ablutions block. With the hyenas calling nearby, the fresh elephant dung outside my tent and the telemetry picking up the collard lioness on the far side of the bone-dry river, I was a tad nervous. Once in the stooped safety of my tent, I unfurled my sleeping bag with a thorough shake to ensure nothing crawled or slithered into it during the day. All was in order.

Before falling asleep, I tentatively took one last trip to the bathroom. I went, torch in hand, scanning for reflecting eyes of lions and leopards or the dark outline of an elephant. My trip majored on stressy. In the pitch black, animal noises were the only thing to break the silence. The fear peaked as I approached my tent, rising with each step. Like a scene from a horror movie, I kept thinking, *almost there.* With my heart racing, I was now at my most vulnerable, bending over to unzip the door.

5th September 2013

I slept soundly until a snort jolted me wide awake at three-thirty. The culprit? An elephant, casually feeding on the tree next to my tent. As you might expect, this was more than a little unnerving.

After this false start, the day started a few hours later with a four-hour bush walk. There was no big game but plenty of time to concentrate on grasses, trees, lichens, bushcraft, and Stone Age tools. As fascinating as the stone tools were, I didn't think that each one proffered as an example could have been the real deal. If it had, then Selati in the Stone Age would boast the same population as present-day London.

In the afternoon, Margaux took us on a game drive. While it was a drive and not a bush walk, we spent most of the time out of the vehicle crouched in the dust. Margaux circled markings in the sand with her red bushwillow tracking stick.

'What is this?' she asked.

Not a lot, I thought. It was little more than a scuff mark in the sand. People chimed in with guesses which were based on the size of the circle.

Hippo? Giraffe? Rhino? Zebra? Elephant? Once all the enthusiastic guessing died down, Margaux said,

'For those that guessed rhino, you're right, but

what type, black or white?'

This stumped everyone. It turned out to be a white rhino. We could supposedly tell because of the three toes that a rhino has. The front one and the side two on the white rhino are of similar size. The identification is then completed by the heel of the imprint, being shaped like a W. W for white.

The black rhino has one large front toe and two smaller toes of equal size. This explanation makes naming tracks sound easy. But it's far from easy. I still couldn't see the W but got the general idea when Margaux used her stick to trace it.

From what we've learnt so far, tracks can be obscured in a host of ways. Wind and rain can affect them, and animals might walk through them—including my fellow students. There could be scuff marks from a wounded animal dragging its foot, or from a leopard or lion hauling its kill.

Further down the road, we found a wake of white-backed vultures picking and tearing at a dead waterbuck. The carcass, relatively fresh and stinking due to its stomach contents being spilt over the sand, was now our focus. Is this not weird? Most normal people don't obsess over dead bodies unless they're starring in an episode of CSI.

We finished with sundowners at the weir. The appearance of a herd of elephants was a grand spectacle, made even more special by Ulrica's reaction—she had never seen an elephant before. Despite such a moving sight, the darkness and prospect of dinner forced our return to camp. On the way, we parked up in the dry riverbed, shut off the lights and let the pitch-black night swallow us whole. Margaux had brought us here for one reason, and it didn't disappoint. In the inky darkness, we were treated to a fantastic show put on by fireflies doing their frenetic dance. The little light blasts of the bugs surrounded us. While up above, light-years away, their dancing was complemented by an unspoilt view of the Milky Way.

7th September 2013

This morning's drive was crammed with highlights. For me, this included aardvark tracks and a white rhino sighting. We wouldn't have seen the rhino if Margaux hadn't followed up on the signs, freshly scattered dung and its spoor. Knowing it was in the area; we kept our eyes peeled on both sides of the track as the Landy crawled slowly along. We were finally rewarded when we spotted its hulking but surprisingly well camouflaged bulk in the thick bush.

After a biome lecture and then further study California Cliff and I went running. I've done plenty of running in many places around the world, but this was hard. All my fitness must have vanished. It certainly didn't help that it was approaching thirty degrees, and we were running on a sandy riverbed.

The instructors told us that the midday heat of the African sun offered the best time to exercise. The premise suggested predators would rest in the shade of a thicket. Still, we felt grateful to Joosta, one of the three newbies who had joined the group. Our group was now known as 7E plus three. If anything appeared, she needed to shout 'FREEZE'. After all, the golden rule in the bush is, *whatever you do, don't run*—not even Usain Bolt could outrun a dangerous animal. Similarly, if the animal were not acting aggressively to begin with, we could trigger its instinctive nature to chase through the act of running. After all, throwing a ball for a cat or a dog usually gets it to pounce and fetch. I, for one, didn't want to be pounced on, or fetched.

The evening's walk was a buzz. We tracked a herd of elephant through the bush and kept making incremental advances towards them. In the end, we were thirty metres away. Watching these animals on foot was mind-blowing. The power they show when they wrap their trunks around a tree, shake it and then push it over is not just humbling but scary. JP explained that by shaking the tree, the elephant weakened the root ball making it easier to knock over. The elephants want the roots because they're the most nutritious part of the tree at this time of the year.

On my way to bed, I caught the flash of an eye in the blueish beam of my LED torch. The reflection sent my heart into overdrive, as I half-expected a leopard to come crashing through the bushes. How stupid but relieved I felt to realise it was a genet—a small mammal from the same family as the meerkat.

8th September 2013

Today, I was dressed in khaki and driving a Land Rover across an African game reserve. It was my first go as a wannabe guide. The experience was challenging, and it only got tougher when scanning for game—searching for tracks and trying to identify trees.

To ensure the best chance of spotting something, it's recommended to look to the distance towards twelve o'clock before dragging your gaze back to your feet at six o'clock. Once that move is complete, you whip your eyes up to three and scan across to nine, right to left. Because westerners read left to right, going in the opposite direction slows the process down, offering a better chance of seeing something.

After a hearty breakfast of bacon, fried eggs, pancakes and a fruit salad, my group was on firewood duty. We took to the Landy to fetch a trailer full of hardwoods such as acacia and mopane. There was no need to cut down any trees; the elephants already took care of the felling for us. We then finished the job with pangas and bow saws. Care had to be taken not to lose a limb when swinging the panga, not to grab hold of anything venomous and to keep an eye out for dangerous game that could appear from nowhere.

9th September 2013

Despite the morning drive's aim being birding, there was plenty of mammal action, including white rhino and a group of giraffes at the waterhole. The latter prompted some debate over their collective noun. The two favourites were a *tower* and a *journey*. Our proper focus should have been on observing the giraffes for the biological marvel they are. It was mind-boggling watching them drink. According to Margaux, they only drink every few days as most of their water comes from the plants they eat. This prevents them having to get into this vulnerable leg spreading address daily.

I'm not the only one fascinated by giraffes. NASA has done research on the blood vessels in giraffe legs to get inspiration for human spacesuits. This is because of the giraffe's ability to protect its brain from sudden changes in blood pressure when it lowers its head to drink. To do this, it has valves to stop the backflow of blood and elastic-walled vessels that dilate and constrict to manage flow.

That afternoon we ventured out with JP on a bush walk. When we were nearing the end, he suggested we find our own rock in the riverbed and take fifteen minutes to enjoy the sunset in complete silence.

Solitude suits me perfectly, well within reason. I enjoy my quiet time, my me time. I sat on the riverbank in the dappled shade of a weeping boer-bean tree. I closed my eyes and listened to the sounds, which both relaxed and frustrated me. The frustration grew when I couldn't identify a bird call, and many remained unknown to me. Despite this I fell into a daze of tranquillity as the disappearing sun danced on my eyelids.

We are fortunate to have the instructors we have. In the guiding world, or at least the guide training world, JP and Margaux are a power couple, think Bill and Hillary Clinton without Monica Lewinsky. They have twenty-three years' experience between them, and this is at a relatively young age. It was my job to extract maximum knowledge from them so I could make the most of this crazy experiment of mine.

They're passionate about the small things, the intricacies that make up the delicate parts of the ecosystem. It wasn't just the mega-fauna for them. JP appeared far more excited by the birds of the veld than he did walking through it searching for lion or elephant.

Despite Margaux's first role in the sector as a lion researcher in the Kruger, she too wasn't blinded by the storybook characters. Her true love lay with the big trees, particularly the sycamore fig, which she called the Queen of Trees. She was passionate about tracking and wanted to become a master of the art form. She was certainly on the right path—I reckon she could out-track most nine times out of ten. Margaux possessed a natural-born talent.

JP himself was well travelled; he'd worked all over the world as a cultural guide. He first got into it by accident when he met three Swiss tourists at a backpackers. One of them was taken ill and medivacked home along with their partner. This left one, a girl who asked JP to show her around South Africa. He took her up on her request but accepted no payment. He enjoyed the experience and went onto pursue a career in guiding.

It was another chance encounter that got him into birding, birding in a big way. The encounter came while hitchhiking back from a Cape Town museum when a chap picked him up and took him into the bush. This trip to the forest didn't happen straight away. Only naïve teenagers in horror movies would agree to a stranger taking them to the woods on meeting them beside the road. JP wasn't naïve and gave the man a false telephone number to throw him off the scent. However, fate intervened, and some weeks later, the same guy and his wife walked into the restaurant where JP was working. Not long after that, JP joined him in the bush and the rest, as they say, is history.

It was almost a different story. Earlier in his life, JP spent three months bed-bound after breaking his back while surfing. I know little about this story as I wasn't told by either Margaux or JP, but it appears to have left him driven and grateful. He is a total book worm and determined to excel in his chosen career. He sees merit in studying towards the next qualification and the next one after that. He scours all the books looking for facts that no one else knows. He wants us to do likewise, to discover what he calls, killer facts. I'm not sure this tip is to help us become better guides or because he doesn't want to get bored out of his mind by rookie guides repeating the same facts, drive after drive, day after day.

10th September 2013

I'm enjoying the bush walks and find myself picking up dung and pulling it apart to see what story it tells. We're lucky to walk each day, and that along with the game drive means we're spending a minimum of six hours in the field.

This morning as we finished our pre-walk briefing, a lion's roar echoed from the other side of the riverbed. From that point on, we pursued it hotly through the bush for an hour. I, for one, had no idea what we'd do when we caught up with her. I guess a game of tig was not in order.

JP tracked her by ear. Leading us towards the lion's roar or the alarm call of an animal she'd spooked. We moved at pace, almost at a run, to keep up with her.

We narrowed it down to a small block; but we didn't see her. At one point, JP was convinced we walked straight past her. We weren't playing tig; it was hide and seek.

It was a jam-packed day of sightings. During the afternoon game drive, I sat on the tracker seat. This is a small foldable seat perched on the bonnet of the vehicle where the tracker, with their legs dangling in front of the left headlight, sits. Aside from driving the Land Rover, this—with its unprotected proximity to the animals and uninterrupted view of the road ahead—is my favourite place to be.

Our first sighting was a breeding herd of elephants, always fascinating to watch. It was even better from my front-row seat. Next, we spotted a young bull elephant, which Margaux shouted down before he could cause any harm.

Without fail, afternoon drives and walks end with sundowners. On arriving at this evening's location, we settled into our little groups and caught up over a cold drink. California Cliff disappeared down the track to find a bush to water. This manoeuvre nearly spelled disaster for him. As he finished his business, he almost got caught on his zipper when a lion, not far off, let out a thunderous roar. Once everyone and 'everything' was accounted for, we sped off in the Landy, spotlight in hand, in search of the lion.

Earlier today, between lunch and study time, I walked to the far end of camp and swept the path smooth. This was me being a total geek. I wanted to catch the tracks of animals that visited overnight to have something to show my 'guests' when guiding tomorrow. I was confident I might be in luck. After dinner, Margaux took out the telemetry device to reveal a lioness at their end of camp. JP felt the situation grave enough to take his rifle to bed with him. We, on the other hand, were left to walk back to our tents with our eyes wide open. Our adrenaline was pumping as our torches swept the bushes ahead.

11th September 2013

During the pro-field guide course, the instructors simulate what it is like to work in a lodge. This means long hours and seven days' work, five weeks in a row.

However, we're really tested with nine weeks on, one week off.

When we first arrived, we were put in pairs to act as a duty team – this covered all camp chores and guiding. I'd been paired with Big Cliff from Port Elizabeth, now Ben's tent mate. It turned out that Pieter was the snorer of the backpackers. Who knew?

Cliff and I were up at four-fifteen to prepare the coffee station before waking the guests—our fellow students—at five o'clock. The forty-five-minute head start was to boil two large stainless-steel kettles on the gas burners. They took an age to come to the boil, and not having hot water ready for tea and coffee when people arrived on deck was the worst offence.

With the water boiled, we poured it into three large green Stanley thermos flasks that retained heat incredibly well. We laid these out alongside enamel mugs, which were placed upside down, as well as UHT milk and tins of tea and coffee. We also made a light snack available: cereal, fruit, and rusks. The main breakfast—a massive fry-up—would follow our morning activity.

Taking the actual game drive was challenging. There was so much to think about and remember. I had to use the radio correctly, avoid hitting guests with low-hanging branches, know which branches I could drive over, look for tracks, scan for birds, spot mammals, pick out different trees, navigate the terrain, listen for alarm calls, and steer clear of driving through elephant dung. The latter is so important given how many insects that could be killed by doing so. One study found an incredible 4,000 dung beetles arriving at a fresh pile of elephant dung within fifteen minutes of it being deposited.

All of that was before I even arrived at a sighting. Then it was about stopping in just the right place—in the sun during the morning chill or in the shade as the day heated up. Stopping was tricky, and doing it quietly was even harder with the age of the vehicle. But as I learned on the go, I soon found myself freewheeling into sightings, the mark of a real pro.

Despite the abundance of impala on the reserve, they took a long time in coming. The first sighting was poor, and I couldn't say much about the antelope as they weren't doing anything. Guiding is all about context, not just regurgitating facts. The second herd was better, and I grew in confidence as people asked me questions.

Our lectures covered a range of 'ologies, from ecology and geology to meteorology and archaeology. The zoology component was broad rather than species-specific. Learning about individual animals was our responsibility, done in our own time.

For today's drive, I'd prepared five mammals, five birds and five trees, of which I could use impala, warthog, guinea fowl, elephant, and lots of trees. For the elephant, it was only its poo I got to talk about—the glamour of guiding.

The group gave me decent feedback at the coffee stop, which helped me relax and grow in confidence post break. Despite this I made a bad call in trying to find a leopard from an alarm call that Margaux heard rather than following the lion's tracks which she'd spotted. I missed both signs and never found the leopard.

I also came unstuck on my dust trap; I'd tried to be clever. I got a few tracks which I identified with help from the team. But we were all baffled trying to work out an obscure one.

At dinner JP said he'd been up to the dust trap and seen one track which he was excited about, the track of a Tokoloshe. None of us had heard of it, well, at least not in our group. We didn't even know if it was a mammal, bird or invertebrate.

When JP described it, I realised he'd got me. It turns out a Tokoloshe is a short man of hip height with a withered grey body, scraggly hair, long fingers, big pointy ears and a skull gouged with a red-hot poker. This hole is formed when the being is first created, it's the source of its power, which includes becoming invisible when it drinks water.

The Tokoloshe comes from Zulu mythology and is considered an evil spirit. Its origin was an explanation of why people died as they slept in their rondavels at night. This phenomenon of unexplained deaths only affected those that slept on the floor, with those sleeping at height appearing to be out of reach of the evil spirit. The scientific explanation was that the fires they slept around created carbon monoxide, which is heavier than air. This meant the colourless, odourless, and tasteless gas sank to the bottom and poisoned people in their sleep.

The Tokoloshe is also known to rape woman and bite off the toes of those sleeping. But there is protection against such a monster. Legend has it that placing a brick under each foot of the bed affords protection to the potential victim as they are then out of reach.

So why was this spoor in my dust trap? Well, that's because Ben let on to JP about my plan.

13th September 2013

As we turned in last night, the entire camp was buzzing with the prospect of sleeping in until six o'clock. Whilst that may have been the plan, there wasn't much chance of it happening. The camp is home to various pairs of crested francolins. This partridge-sized bird starts a prolonged, raucous reveille at five o'clock each morning, without fail and without relent.

Even before the duetting francolins started, I woke several times throughout the night. Most notably when Doc, my tent neighbour, got up at three-thirty to visit the loo. Unfortunately for Doc, he never made it out of his tent. As soon as he poked his head out, he saw something staring right back at him. Thinking better of it, Doc settled in for the long and uncomfortable night that comes with a full bladder.

On our way to the rifle range, we got stuck behind a white rhino. I don't think anyone could begrudge such a traffic jam given the perilous position rhinos hold on earth thanks to prolific poaching. In 2007, poachers killed twenty rhinos for their horn. The following year this surged to eighty-three and last year, poachers slaughtered 1,004. Instead of feeling elated by seeing such majestic animals, I always feel sorrow given the status that has made them famous.

Once at the range, there was plenty of sitting about, waiting our turn to step up to the firing line. California Cliff and I passed the time by working on our bird call knowledge. We had most success when making up innocent and not so innocent mnemonics for each call. I mastered four calls, so only another seventy-six to nail before our basic birding test.

Finally, my turn came to take to the range. On being handed the rifle with the bolt back, JP said,

'Rifle safe'.

I was nervous about being handed such a powerful weapon, and I definitely didn't want to drop it. I took it firmly from him and checked it by inserting my pinkie into the breach to ensure there wasn't a round up the spout. There wasn't, so with a nod to JP, I repeated his words back to him.

'Rifle safe'.

With safety goggles and ear defenders on, I walked up to the shooting point with the rifle in my right hand, held horizontal to the ground with a forward tilt of the barrel.

I now needed to run through the drills. First, I cycled the ammunition to ensure none of the rounds were misshapen to cause a jam. To do this, I placed a round into the breach and then pushed forward the bolt into its closed position. The rifle was now live and would go off if the trigger were pulled. I then gently pulled back the bolt to eject the unspent round before putting it back into the pouch on my belt. I repeated this for each of the rounds in my bandolier.

Once complete, I then loaded the rifle for real. I

pushed each of the five rounds into the magazine with my thumb. With the last round in place, I held it down in the magazine with my right thumb. My left hand then pushed the bolt over the top. Before I closed the bolt, I used my little finger to check there was no round in the barrel. With the bolt closed, the rifle was completely safe. This is called stage two. This negates the need for a safety catch, which is not a failsafe, as it could easily be snagged on a branch when moving through the bush, rendering the rifle unsafe. If I need to arm the rifle, then I work the bolt to bring a live round into the firing position.

I'm not hunting. There is no need for the stealth provided by a safety. The noise of a bolt being worked will not be an issue, as if I needed to do that then all hell would have erupted.

The laws of physics say that every action has an equal and opposite reaction. This was certainly the case when, on JP's command, I pulled the trigger. This ever so light depression of my index finger set off a chain of events.

First, the firing pin was released, striking the primer on the base of the round. This created a spark igniting the propellant in the casing. The exploding charge created a build-up of gas, propelling the bullet down the barrel towards the target. The detonation was so intense in the confined space that not all the energy escaped. This drove the bullet forward. At the same time, the opposite force slammed the butt of the rifle into my shoulder.

Wow. The kick and heat produced shocked me.

We were shooting a .375 calibre rifle. So-called

because of the diameter of the bullet. This projectile is 0.375 inches in diameter, that's 9.5 millimetre in new money. A .375 rifle, providing it is packed with heavy enough ammunition, is the minimum calibre to stop thick-skinned dangerous animals such as elephant, buffalo, and rhino.

Firing the rifle was an adrenaline rush that got my heart racing, a condition that is not conducive to shooting straight. However, the sharp, sour smell of the spent propellant provided a surprisingly calming effect. My first shot of five would have given the buffalo pictured on the target a fright, but then I found my aim. I scored thirty-eight out of fifty, probably average. The main takeaway for me is that my breathing needs some work.

We finished the day in true bush style, a braai in the Selati riverbed. EcoPride, the lion NGO that operates on the reserve, joined us. Excited by the fresh faces, a few of our group got stuck into the beers. I wouldn't fancy having their heads in the morning. I was some way behind them in the beer stakes. Even so, after a number of beers, I felt fearless walking around camp. Too brave. I must remind myself not to become complacent. I needed to remain vigilant and respect the wild animals that I was living with.

14th September 2013

Margaux gave us a bonus sleep-in today. An extra hour in bed after last night's river braai was welcome. No hangover for me, but my head felt cloudy. A long shower would have cleared things up, but elephants dug up and disrupted our water supply.

My sleep last night was broken. First, the cackle of hyenas interrupted it, followed by the deep-throated rumble of a lion. It was a night I wasn't prepared to venture out of my tent. My solution? A piece of Tupperware I'd brought from England.

Back home, it kept my morning cereal fresh and crunchy. For this trip, it kept my electrical odds and ends dry and in one place. Or at least that was until early this morning. Now it served as my chamber pot for number ones.

An embarrassing decision but the right one given the fresh leopard tracks through camp. These tracks were a reminder I was a long way from home. This was someone else's territory, and they had the edge on me in every way - strength, speed, stealth, vision, power, and instinct. As a species, we think we're smart, but when laid bare in the wild, we're mere prey.

JP left for another EcoTraining assignment today, which means we won't be seeing him until our assessments at the end of November. With JP gone, a new instructor arrived. A wild-looking man with scraggy blonde hair, a chestnut-coloured weather-beaten face, and a wrist full of beads. Graham Cooke, a founding father of EcoTraining, wasted no time in assessing our knowledge by taking us out on a walk. He fired question after question at us with the focus being on trees and grasses. There were no easy points.

If I wanted to know anything and everything about leopards, then Graham is the man. At twenty-two, he raised two six-week-old leopard cubs as his own while working at the world-famous Londolozi Lodge. His story was co-written by author Fransje Van Riel who used Graham's diaries as well as spending countless hours with Graham in person, over the phone and via email. The book, *My Life with Leopards,* follows the story of Boycat and Poepface.

The sibling cubs arrived at Londolozi to star alongside Brooke Shields and Martin Sheen in the 1992 film, Born Wild. With the film finished, Graeme took them to a ram shackled secluded camp on an island in the south Luangwa Reserve in Zambia. Here Graham spent two years habituating them to the wild.

Graham saw himself as their mother and guardian, just as devoted as any mum, offering them unconditional love. Although this was half a lifetime ago for him, even today the cubs continue to affect him deeply, and they will for the rest of his life. There's not one day that goes past that he doesn't think about his nervous daughter or his easy-going son. Memories are prompted daily by the physical scars he carries on his body from playing rough and tumble with these apex predators. Living day in, day out with these cubs for the best part of three years, he was able to gain unparalleled insights into leopard behaviour, particularly their vocalisation.

This experience has shaped the man he is today, half-human, half wild cat. His human development has centred around not taking anything that you love for granted. His wild side pays little respect to convention. It manifests itself in a growl or two that I imagine would be understood clearly by a leopard. Graham is fun and approachable, but he gives nothing away. He is a private person. He carries the heavy emotional baggage that his experience has burdened him with. No spoilers here, read the book.

Given neither California Cliff nor I could hold the rifle steady yesterday, we pimped our usual fitness session by adding some rocks to the equation. Our goal was to build strength in our arms by running up and down the riverbed carrying these makeshift weights. Our prison-style exercise regime took place under the watchful gaze of a lone nyala. The presence of this male antelope was both reassuring and inspiring. It was a magnificent-looking animal with rusty-coloured socks, a shaggy grey coat and vertical white stripes. Its white mane ran along the length of its spine. But its real beauty was in its face. Adam Ant styled white markings ran across the bridge of its nose from eye to eye. Above these sat spiralled horns of seventy centimetres, each with a yellow tip.

18th September 2013

It's incredible what you can accomplish by rising early. By nine o'clock, we had completed our first exam, which left the entire day to do with as we wished. We tried a hybrid game of rounders and baseball, which was blasphemy to my toy cricket set we used. The game was a write-off. No one could agree on the rules, and with tempers in the camp running high, all the signs were there for a *Lord of the Flies* meltdown.

Come the afternoon there was one thing we could all agree on, a game drive. We parked up in a large clearing, grabbed a sundowner and settled into pockets of conversation around the vehicle. The sunset bird song provided the soundtrack for our night out. This fell silent or at least fell into insignificance with the strained groaning of a lion's roar reverberating from a thicket. He or she couldn't have been further than 500 metres away.

We hastily packed the cool box and clambered on board the Landy. Margaux raised EcoPride on the radio, who guided us to a nearby watering hole where we saw him. A big male crouched down; front legs bunched up with his bum in the air. What a privilege to watch him lap up the water with his pink sandpaper tongue. On having his fill, he strode off in search of female company.

We followed him as far as we could but lost him when he went cross-country and disappeared into the thorny bush. Margaux guessed where he would turn up, so we drove straight there and waited. Before long he appeared from behind the vehicle and completed a full circle of us, which was unnerving in our open-topped Land Rover.

We savoured our share of him. Leaving him to his night, we headed back to camp. On the way, we passed a member of the anti-poaching team patrolling on foot with his semi-automatic rifle strapped across his chest. We warned him about the big male prowling down the road, but he seemed unperturbed.

29th September 2013

I woke with a jolt at three-forty-five to what sounded like a firework going off. It was the elephant, right outside my tent, snapping branches. I lay cocooned in my sleeping bag, fully alert given the adrenaline flooding my veins. I could hear his every breath, his mastication of the bark and even the grains of sand shifting under his weight. This is becoming the norm, which is fine—though it might have been easier if I weren't on wake-up duty forty-five minutes later.

Once Big Cliff and I had organised coffee and rusks, I carried out my vehicle checks. There's a basic checklist. First up is to pop the bonnet and check the essentials—oil, brake fluid and coolant—replacing them where necessary. Then I check the contents of the Landy. The list includes: spare tyre with a double check that it's fully inflated, backup fluids, tyre jack and spanner, first aid kit, spotlight and a toilet roll in case any guests—or a guide—gets caught short. A clear-out of any rubbish is next. Items are often secreted away in the seatback pockets; there's usually an apple core or a blackening banana skin. The last duty is to kick each tyre, ensuring they're one hundred per cent. On this occasion, I got halfway before discovering a flat. Changing the tyre delayed me, but at least I caught it before everyone turned up.

The drive left me disappointed. I felt I wasn't sharp with my facts, meaning I lost confidence early doors. For me, no matter what I do, I need to feel confident. If I lose it or doubt myself, it becomes a vicious circle that can spiral out of control. This lack of confidence made me more serious and less enthusiastic than I should have been, which was clear in the feedback at the end of the drive.

On reflection, I felt that during the drive I was noticing field signs without even thinking about it. I'm certainly feeling like a guide. In fact, Ulrica snapped me in action on her SLR. I was perched on the driver's seat with the brown bush behind me. In full flow, I gesticulated, wearing my Indiana Jones hat and sporting a beard.

The lousy weather, particularly the wind, meant we ditched the afternoon activity and watched a film. Our cinema set up was rustic. To amplify the sound, we placed the speakers in a large cooking pot, which worked relatively well.

Nowadays, we take so much for granted with DVD players built into our laptops. I remember Dad setting the cine projector up in the sitting room to show *Tom and Jerry* for our birthday parties. As technology advanced, we'd hire a video player from the village Post Office along with a film. It's not that I was born in the dark ages; it's just that technology moves so fast.

The choice of film was interesting. It was a fictionalised account of the true story of two man-eating lions that dragged people from their tents while they slept. *The Ghost and the Darkness,* released in 1996, featured Val Kilmer and Michael Douglas. A project was started in March 1898 to build a bridge over the Tsavo River in Kenya. It was part of the construction of a railway line linking Uganda and the Kilindini Harbour on the Indian Ocean. Lieutenant-Colonel John Patterson led the project.

Two mane-less male lions terrorised the camp, raiding the campsite at night to eat the workers. They killed 135 in total. The lions found the campground easy pickings despite the thorn fences workers erected as barricades and the fires they set to deter them. The lions continued to come, and hundreds of workers fled, meaning construction of the bridge ground to a halt.

Patterson tried in vain to hunt, ambush, and trap the lions. He eventually succeeded and shot the first lion. It measured three metres from nose to the tip of the tail; it was so big it took eight men to carry it to camp. The second lion returned again and again despite being wounded many times by Patterson's rifle for twenty more days before it was slain. With the man-eating lions now dead, the workers returned, and they completed the bridge in February 1899. Both lions are on permanent display at the Chicago Field Museum after being bought in 1924 for $5,000, that's $68,000 in today's money.

If that wasn't enough to put us on edge, Graham's story certainly was. While we gathered around the campfire, Graham told us how a chorus of frogs saved his life. During his time guiding he became stranded in the bush and needed to walk back after the sun had gone down. When he walked past a small pool, the frogs stopped calling. Once he'd passed it, they started again. As Graham walked further on, the frogs stopped. Something else must have walked past the pool. Realising something was amiss, he climbed a tree. From his perch, he saw a lioness walk below. He was being stalked.

1st October 2013

An animal bounding down the track with what sounded like asthma interrupted my sleep at ten o'clock. It didn't carry on past but stopped for a good sniff around my tent. I'm not sure if it paused to catch its breath or because it was curious about me. Shamelessly, I couldn't muster the courage to sneak the zip up for a peek. My curiosity fell victim to my imagination. I wish I had, for when I got up this morning, aardvark tracks littered the path. I've never seen an *earth pig*.

Not long after the aardvark visited, the elephant was back. Of the 30,000 hectares that make up Selati, one elephant zeros in on my tent night after night. This is usually a fun experience; the type I came to Africa for. But last night he kept me awake for an hour and a half ahead of today's assessments. I did not sleep with him munching in my ear, which I found marginally less annoying than someone eating an apple on a train.

For some, the chewing could cause such an intense emotional response that they'd abandon their tent to escape the torturous noise. These would be people with misophonia, which translates as hatred of sound. For people with this condition, the part of the brain, the anterior insular cortex, that joins their senses with their emotions is overly active. There can be many trigger sounds from a clicking pen and knuckle crunching, but the most common ones are related to food such as slurping and crunching. I don't feel unreasonable over my annoyance with a masticating elephant.

Despite all seven to eight tonnes of him standing just a metre from where I lay, I wasn't worried—until he gave my tent a solid feel. This made my heart race. Can I now say I've been felt up in my sleep by an elephant?

He, or perhaps other elephants, kept waking me throughout the night. At one point, the thunderous crash of a falling tree echoed like a gunshot across camp.

Today was disappointing on two counts. First, the field observation test didn't go well, I could have performed considerably better than I did. For the test we headed into the bush and walked around with Graham pointing out different field signs and asking questions about them. What track is that? What is its foot structure? What is its digestive system? How long is its gestation period? What type of social structure does it have? What is that bird call? What is that tree? What is the medicinal use of said tree, and what is a cultural belief of it? What is that grass? Who flung that dung? What disturbed that soil? What rock is that and what three minerals does it consist of? What other antelope are related to that group?

The second disappointment was my trip to

Hoedspruit. To get a permanent job in a lodge, I need a PDP, Public Drivers Permit, and I can't get that unless I have a South African driver's license. First up, my theory test. I've been cramming for this in the middle of the night using an incomplete driving manual. I passed two of the three sections but failed the 'sign' element by one mark. I did relatively well considering half the pages missing were those that detailed the road signs. I will have to go through the whole thing again. The ironic thing is that I drove myself to the test and then back to camp in my rented car.

To cheer myself up, I undertook some retail therapy and bought a camera trap. Back at camp, I set it up outside my tent. By doing so, I've guaranteed no visitors to my tent tonight.

CHAPTER FOUR

'Almost everything will work if you unplug it for a few minutes, including you.' *Anne Lamott, Novelist.*

Karongwe Game Reserve
3rd October 2013

The drive from Selati to our new camp, Karongwe, took two and a half hours from gate to gate. On either side of the transfer was a fair amount of waiting, followed by the slow, bumpy navigation of the reserve's twisty roads.

On our arrival we found the camp set on the banks of a dry Karongwe River. In the rainy season, it can fill quickly to act as a tributary for the Olifants River.

The camp set-up is more robust than that at Selati. Within the main communal area, there are three raised decks, and a further building acts as the visiting instructor's quarters and the camp office. We're accommodated in ten A-style framed walk-in Meru tents which hail from Mount Meru in Tanzania. There's enough space in here for a pair of proper beds with duvets. The Tokoloshe will not get me now. Unfortunately, there's still no door to the tent, meaning I must bend over to pull up the zipper. I know, first world problems.

The downside of coming to Karongwe was the prospect of sharing one of the ten tents. So far, I've avoided it, but yesterday upon arrival my luck ran out. Saying that I've got it pretty easy, I've been paired with Ben.

7th October 2013

It's been a quiet couple of days on the animal front, well for my group it has. For Group A not so much, they saw leopards mating the other morning. We've not seen a leopard full stop. We also lost an evening and morning game drive to a night out at the bush bar, Mahlahlah to watch the rugby. The bar is a game lodge in between Makalali and Karongwe that's open to the public every Saturday night. It acts as a magnet to bush folk from miles and miles around. It's okay, not great, but it's the only thing.

The most unnerving thing about the bar is that the clientele goes at the booze hard with knives and sidearms hanging from their belts. Once they've had their fill, they jump into their vehicles to drive home, no doubt having to weave through elephant and buffalo as they go. Not something you'd see back in the UK, but they seem to cope fine.

Taking eighteen adult students, who spent over a month in bush isolation, to a bar was a wild experiment. A thesis on animal behaviour could have been written. Several people felt rough and a little silly the morning after the night before. I wasn't one of them, which is both impressive and surprising.

Doc and I were on duty today, so we got up in the dead of night. After doing the wake-up call from tent to tent I started back toward the kitchen. On my way I caught two eyes in the beam of my head torch and then a second set. They belonged to a pair of spotted hyenas. I called Doc so he could look. The hyenas edged a little closer and closer again, growing in confidence each time. Still, if we made a sudden movement, they would back off. We left them to it as we figured they would move on of their own accord. Moments later, I came out of the kitchen to find one standing right in front of me. Now the situation turned serious. The hyena's jaws, which could exert a bite pressure of 800 kilograms per square centimetre, hung level with my crotch.

8th October 2013

With a new camp came new instructors. Massi, or Massimo, to give him his proper name, was based at Karongwe full-time. He had been bigged up to the girls as the Italian Stallion because of his heritage, striking looks, and tousled dark hair. I got the impression that they weren't disappointed.

Then there was Henry, who was closer to my age. In fact, he may have been a few years my senior, but it does not matter when you're middle-aged. The first thing you notice about Henry is his huge, warm personality—magnetic and engaging. His energy fills the room. His genuine interest in others instantly puts you at ease. Then, you notice the slight limp. Back in 2003, he suffered a broken pelvis when an elephant gored him with its tusk. Thankfully, there was no internal organ damage. He received immediate medical help from a guest. On the back of his experience, Henry places great emphasis on the wilderness having healing powers. These powers have helped him along his own personal journey back to physical and mental wellbeing.

Henry was our instructor today, and despite all his experience, he said game drives don't get more special than the one this morning. For me, this was a once in a lifetime experience. The only thing better would have been to play cricket at Lord's.

On responding to a sighting of a cheetah hunting, we arrived to find she'd made her kill, a common duiker. Her tan-coloured coat with solid black, round spots blended perfectly into the landscape. The area was in an apocalyptic state. A bushfire had been through a week before and left the area charred. The only colour came from a ruddy coloured termite mound and the golden sand road. We parked up and watched jealously as guests from a lodge walked onto the scene. Luckily, after fifteen minutes, they moved on, and we finally had the cheetah and her four cubs to ourselves.

We left our vehicle to sit within fifteen metres of the sighting. As the morning passed, both we and the cheetahs moved around until at one point only three metres of sand separated us. While we watched them, they completely stripped the carcass clean, leaving only skin and a bone as evidence with one cub trotting off with the head as a plaything.

We spent two hours with the cheetah family. The greatness of the experience came not from how close we were, or even that we were on foot, but from her and her cubs' complete acceptance of us. Despite the grey sky and the chill of a winter morning, I've never felt so warm. Sitting in the fine African sand, surrounded by wild animals running freely around me, I felt like part of their world. For that one moment in time, I was at complete peace.

Hoedspruit
14th October 2013

We all looked different today. Not because we bundled up like Michelin Men to combat the temperature that plummeted to twenty-four degrees centigrade. No; it came down to the lack of khaki, not a stitch could be seen. Instead, we dressed in our civvies for the fifty-kilometre trip down the R527 to town, where we enjoyed a rare day off with access to Wi-Fi and pizza.

If we dressed to fit in, then it would not work. We should have kept to our usual garb. Every man, woman, child and dog walking the streets of Hoedspruit sported safari taupe from head to toe. I'm not sure what else we expected as this is safari country and Hoedspruit sits bang in the centre. Game viewers buzzed up and down Main Street and various units of anti-poaching operators in their camouflaged fatigues stocked up on smokes and supplies.

Hoedspruit lies directly west of Kruger National Park, seventy-kilometre from the Orpen Gate which represents the closest public entrance to the parkland. There are several private game reserves much closer including Klaserie and Timbavati that open to the national park itself. No fences separate any of the concessions with the animals being able to traverse at will. These and the other private reserves mean Hoedspruit has the largest conservation area in the world that's under private ownership.

The first official landowner in the area, or more accurately, the first white landowner, was Dawid Johannes Joubert, who registered his farm in 1848. That same year, a cloudburst caused a major flood of the river, during which Joubert lost his hat. For him, this was a significant incident, given the importance of hats to the farming way of life. To replace it for the much-needed sun protection, he couldn't pop to the shops or order a new one online. To mark his loss, he named the river Hoedspruit, Afrikaans for Hat Creek.

I must appear anti-social to my classmates, as all I wanted to do was hang out on my own. This wasn't a reflection on them—well, not all of them—but after being cooped up together for so long, I needed a break. Regardless I am probably semi antisocial. Without fail the psychographic testing I've been through at various points of my career states I have an introverted disposition. This doesn't mean I'd rather be marooned alone on a desert island. No, it's a case of needing the opportunity for some downtime where

I can re-charge with no one wanting to chit chat.

My 'James Day' meant hopping from café to café to find the best internet reception for Skype calls across the world. I spoke to my folks in Yorkshire, my sister in London and my brother in the Caribbean.

I enjoyed listening to the latest adventures of my nieces, and hearing that my bro had run the Chicago marathon. I'm proud of my family and miss them.

However, the emails I received disappointed me a little. I got plenty of them, but they tended to be short, more of a conversation. I felt nostalgic for the long letters I used to exchange at school and university. I still have many of them gathering dust in the attic. They're full of detail but with that comes the occasional paragraph of cringe-worthiness, especially those written during my adolescence.

I ended up at Sleepers Restaurant, which is in the old railway station. This station should never have been built in this spot. It was a mistake by the train driver. As passenger travel became popular, the transport railway required passenger stations to take advantage of the new trend. One of the five major stops along the Selati Railway was to be Hoedspruit. Unfortunately, the train driver unloaded the steels in the wrong place. His instructions were to 'stop after the third bend by the large knobthorn tree'—advice that wasn't as clear as it could have been. Instead, he stopped on Berlin Farm, not Hoedspruit Farm. His error didn't become clear until much later, by which time Hoedspruit had already developed around the new station.

Karongwe Game Reserve
15th October 2013

After a day full of study, barely leaving camp, I thought I'd struggle to find a highlight. But there was one—and it was a memorable one at that. We found a boomslang, incredibly well camouflaged in a tree next to the campfire. The boomslang is a slender green snake with large black eyes. Their venom is haemotoxic, so if you were to be bitten, you would, after twenty-four hours, haemorrhage internally. A blood transfusion would be required to save your life.

16th October 2013

With the morning activity behind us, we packed up the vehicles to head to our sleep-out spot, thirty minutes from camp in the middle of a dry riverbed. Once set up, the afternoon was ours to do as we wished. People used the time in many ways; some dug a big, pointless hole. Others carved wood, while some engaged in a poo fight. Throwing and spitting impala and kudu dodo is a thing out here.

Once the dung was flung and the hole filled in, we split into our usual groups for a challenge. Using a sycamore-fig base plate, red bushwillow drill and dry elephant dung, we made fire by friction. Taking it in turns, we created large blisters on our palms and, after twenty minutes, a fire finally sparked to life. Not a bad effort, but to do it alone would have worn palms red raw.

My luck is pretty rubbish. I drew the two to three o'clock sentry shift again, this time with Ben. The fullish moon illuminated my vigil. There was plenty of activity on our watch to remind me we were in the wild. A small bachelor herd of elephants fed on the riverbank, hyena calling, lions roaring and audio of two leopards mating. At one point, an elephant wandered out onto the riverbed while his companion dozed off, his loud snoring giving him away.

During the next shift, the elephants crossed the riverbed behind the Landy and walked past where Duncan lay. The Swiss man lay sprawled on the sand, completely unprotected, with just two metres between him and the elephants. I was farther away, but I can assure you, a seven-tonne elephant appears humongous and incredibly imposing when it is towering over a mere human lying exposed on the bare ground.

18th October 2013

I was up at six o'clock, which constitutes a significant sleep-in for this guiding life. With a self-study day ahead, I worked steadily through until nine o'clock in the evening, pausing only for food, exercise and a few visitors. There'd been the opportunity to go for a revision drive to the dam. I declined the offer as it seemed a bit of a skive. Staying behind turned out to be the right choice, as we had unexpected guests. The elephant herd returned, and they came straight through camp, stripping trees and hoovering up the jackal berry fruits around the campfire. Seeing them amongst our tiny human possessions highlighted size and underlying strength. But they weren't bru Their delicate tiptoeing around director chairs demonstrated this.

One bull was a dream to watch with his tail swinging from side to side over his ample grey buttocks as he waddled down the interlinking dust paths. When he turned back on himself, we enjoyed a fabulous view from the safety of the deck.

His mammoth tusks were in perfect symmetry and relatively unblemished. We'd pay thousands for a set of teeth like that. But I guess people do. An African elephant is killed every fifteen minutes, so its ivory tusks can be sold at £1,200 a kilogram to be carved into jewellery and ornaments. Man's hunting of elephants with big tusks over the past hundred years has led to a reduction in their average tusk size. This is because the *Big Tusker* gene is being steadily wiped out. Evolution in action!

25th October 2013

Today was our EcoTraining assessment drive, and it didn't get off to a promising start—there was no coffee or rusks. The drive itself went well, and I loved taking people out. I had so much to talk about, I stopped three times before leaving the turning circle. I guess my guests must have thought, what a geek or something more derogatory. Well, if they didn't then, they certainly would have when I tried calling a bird in by doing an impersonation of a pearl spotted owlet.

Swadini
3rd to 10th November 2013

Despite the chance for a lie-in, the camp was up by five-thirty. With little to do and our hire car not arriving until ten o'clock, we had some downtime before heading out on leave.

Everybody was heading in different directions. Some returned to Selati to do a week's survival course run by JP, a few went sightseeing, and the rest back to see their families. Ben, Ulrica, and I spent the week at a chalet in Swadini, a resort in the Blyde River Canyon Nature Reserve. We didn't have any grand plans other than, study, exercise, and something different like horse riding, although the latter never materialised. To me this all sounded great, well until Ulrica piped up in the back of the car.

'Will people think James is our Dad?'

The resort may be dated, but it's hard to grumble after spending two months under canvas in the bush. Now, we enjoyed running water, an electric kettle for tea on demand, doors, a firm bed, and blackout curtains—all luxuries. I really can't stress enough how luxurious a door feels after stooping to enter and exit a tent for a prolonged period.

In the week off I didn't manage the revision I'd hoped despite the *FGASA* finals looming at the end of the month. I did, however, pass my driver's theory test, which came as a relief. What really got my goat was not being able to book my practical there and then. Why not? I'll tell you why not—they only take bookings for a future date on the fifteenth of

November. That means I'll have to get time off from my tracking course, hire a car and drive into town. There were no exceptions. I was told that this is how it's done and that was that. I respectfully asked to see the manager to discuss the predicament with him, but he walked off half-way through my plea. This is a wonderful country, but the admin and attitude sucks.

Being out of a Big Five reserve meant I got lots of running without fear of being predated. The scenery around the resort stunned me with its sheer rock face of red sandstone climbing vertically some 500 metres to within touching of the clouds. The river added to the tranquillity, gently tumbling around boulders. At the same time, animals, such as wildebeest, kudu, vervet monkeys, baboons, duikers, bushbuck and warthogs, roamed freely. When I wasn't marvelling at the wildlife showcase surrounding me, I checked the dusty substrate ahead for leopard spoor. With abundant game and excellent cover, this area provided the perfect habitat for Africa's most adaptable apex predator.

Towards the end of the week, I organised the Swadini half marathon around the 1.8-kilometre loop of the resort. As the winner, I was chuffed, but there wasn't much competition as I was the only participant. It proved a punishing run as I started at eleven-thirty in the morning. By the time I'd finished, the temperature had climbed to thirty-seven degrees centigrade.

Ben left Ulrica and me for twenty-four hours to visit the EcoPride conservation project back at Selati. He planned to do his placement there if he liked it. As he headed off, dressed in khaki, it felt like we were sending him off for his first day at school. Maybe I was their Dad after all.

With this in mind, Ulrica and I made our way to the laundry to do our family chores. A washing machine is a luxury, so we wanted to make the most of it. I'd forgotten the washing powder, so I dashed back to the cottage. As I rounded the corner to the stable-style back door, an enormous baboon launched itself over my right shoulder. In what could only have been a minute he'd been through the bin, opened and eaten Ben's marshmallows and left a stink in the house.

Luckily, Ben was so full of stories from his trip that we never touched on the thieving baboon or the missing marshmallows. His highlight was coming face-to-face with a lion when the EcoPride team led him into thick bush for a closer look at the male. Not the smartest move, but at least the lion was never in danger—they weren't armed.

CHAPTER FIVE

'Education is the most powerful weapon which you can use to change the world.' *Nelson Mandela, President of South Africa.*

Selati Private Game Reserve
11th November 2013

The constant *good-lord-deliver-us* of the fiery-necked nightjar, along with a duetting pair of African scops owls, filled the night air, reminding me I was home. Well, home away from home—I was back at Selati, where my bush adventure began two months earlier. This time I found myself in my original tent, now with a tentmate. Luckily for my sanity, it was Ben.

First up in our month of courses and assessments is tracking. This course will not be easy, as you either get it or you don't. You can work and try as hard as you like, but there is no substitute for primeval instinct. I'd love to have the gift, but I'm not blessed that way.

For the assessment, it's as much about not getting the track wrong as it is getting it right. For every wrong answer, you lose points. For example, an obvious level one track is worth one point. But, if you incorrectly identify it, you lose three points. Conversely, if you get a level three track correct, you get three points, while an incorrect answer drops just one. A cleverly constructed and punishing assessment.

For the afternoon, I took the wheel of the Landy. It was my first time driving with a professional tracker in the hot seat, and what a difference he brought.

Innocent, a twenty-two-year-old tracker from Londolozi, was our instructor and a demigod of bushcraft. He could spot the direction of a centipede's track from a hundred metres. And, translated into English, his name was perfect: Innocent Ngwenya—Innocent Crocodile.

Our sundowner stop was Galon Dam, where I pulled up under the apple leaf tree. As far as tracks go, it doesn't get better than a water hole with its dusty outer ring and inner circle of mud.

A few sips in, we heard the snort of an impala. We reacted fast with half the group in the vehicle by the time of the second snort, the rest by the third. If a predator was causing the impala to alarm, it fell to me to deliver the sighting. I looked over my shoulder and called out,

'All in?'

Without waiting for a response, I pushed down on the accelerator and let the clutch go. We lurched forward, causing Innocent to juggle his stick. With Mr Crocodile clinging precariously to the tracker's seat, I raced to the next block to see what spooked the impala. Most likely it was a leopard, and most of us hadn't seen one yet.

I killed the engine so we could listen. We heard another snort. This time it was to the left. I put the truck in reverse and sped backwards. My urgency took us past the turning, but having soon corrected, we were off again.

As we pulled into the clearing, we saw a large male leopard bolting across the ground. I called it in over the radio before going off-road in an attempt at a second sighting. Nothing. We circled back to his initial location where we found him lying up next to a rock.

Once again, we lost our leopard, but this time Innocent anticipated his next move. We drove straight to the dam. After twenty minutes, he strode in. What a view of him, such a jaw-dropping, powerful animal. Half an hour later, he disappeared. This time we went to the sodic site where we expected him to appear. And he did. Eventually he slunk off and we called it a night.

If I ever question why I'm here, or why I'm doing this, I simply need to remember today. Oh, and the morning with the family of cheetahs.

15th November 2013

As duty guide, I was up stupidly early for wake-up call. I convinced myself this extra time would sharpen my senses and focus my mind. Not the case. As I knelt in the dust over the first track at five-thirty-five, I made an elementary mistake. I was minus two and it wasn't even six o'clock.

Some of my esteemed fellow students, who will remain nameless, did not help my mood by being ogres and bores during the assessment. We should do all future tracking exams under these guidelines:

1) Don't whine when you make a silly mistake. No one else cares unless they made the same mistake.

2) We're trying to name footprints in the dust, why would adding yours help?

3) If it's an obvious giraffe track and they're obvious, ID it and move on. The longer you dwell on it, the less it looks like a giraffe.

For our afternoon assessment, we returned to Galon Dam. After a while, EcoPride pulled up in a cloud of dust. A researcher announced their telemetry had pinpointed a lioness resting just twenty metres behind us in a thicket. Moving quickly but calmly, we climbed back into the Landy and drove a few kilometres down the road to resume the exam.

I was last to go on one track. It was a tough one, level three, so important that I took my time and thought about it. As I knelt precariously on my dodgy knee, I couldn't concentrate, not because of the pain, but because all I could hear were shouts of,

'Hurry! A lion's coming down the road.'

Not that anybody could see the lion, they now had him on telemetry too. Inevitably I made a rash decision on the track which didn't help my overall score.

The tracking assessment was done and dusted. I don't think I did well. The early feedback is I'll get level two. They award level four to those with an unbelievable one hundred per cent.

It's been a privilege to have been taught by Innocent this last week. His life story is incredible. He's a standout tracker in the business, but he started out as a poacher. This is a real-life story of poacher-turned-gamekeeper.

Innocent was born in poverty, extreme poverty, with many brothers and sisters. His parents separated when he was young, not the done thing in Shangaan culture. So much so his grandmother asked his father to stay away, and he did.

In a newspaper article, this young, wise man talks about his earliest memories and how 'hunger disturbs your brain'. He recalls how he would do anything to survive—anything for food.

He started off catching small birds, using the traps he'd shown us as part of the course. He was doing it to feed his mother, brothers, sisters, and himself. I understand the need for subsistence poaching and have sympathy for his predicament. However, I don't condone it and would place the blame on the Government for failing to feed their people.

At nine years old, having been encouraged by the older boys within the village, he'd crawl through the perimeter fence of Manyeleh Reserve. Now he was poaching, not only for food but for money. He was snaring leopards, and his pack of dogs were making the kill.

At sixteen, Innocent found his estranged father, Lyson. He'd tracked him to Ngala Game Reserve, where he was working as a ranger. The two of them hit it off straightaway and shared a small room on the reserve. During this time, Innocent's metamorphosis took place as his father taught him the importance of preserving wildlife.

The pivotal moment came when his dad enrolled Innocent in the Tracker Academy—the same organisation that had provided our course over the past few days. It was established to provide unemployed people with new skills. Innocent took to tracking like a duck to water. During his final exam, he inadvertently showed up his instructors whilst achieving maximum marks. He had insisted that an almost unrecognisable track was from a duiker, not a steenbok. He wouldn't drop the matter and was ultimately proved right.

17th November 2013

As my tent shook, I felt around on the upturned milk crate for my alarm clock. It read four o'clock. It wasn't the bull elephant shaking my world awake, but the morning call.

Today marked the beginning of a week-long introduction to trails guiding and orientation under two instructors, Massi and Rhodes. Rhodes was new to us and the eager one, keen to make the most of every bit of light the day offered, which explained the early wake-up call.

Yesterday on their arrival in camp we kicked off with introductions, quickly followed by the first lecture. This was everything you need to know on orientation, including a theoretical and practical guide to GPS. It turns out there are twenty-four satellites crisscrossing in medium Earth orbit, that's roughly 12,500 miles above our heads. Each one circles earth twice a day, and of these twenty-four a GPS receiver needs to lock onto a minimum of four satellite signals to provide a reliable position.

The Global Positioning System was originally a military tool. However, this changed after a Korean Air Lines Flight, number 007, made a navigation error and flew into Russian airspace. On 1st September 1983, the Boeing 747 was shot down with all 269 lives on board being lost. To avoid any such disaster happening again, President Ronald Regan ordered that the US Military's GPS, known as NAVSTAR, become available for civilian use.

As soon as it was light enough to do so, we walked out of camp. A big part of the course, over and above learning to navigate, is to practise handling a rifle while walking. The rifle is not loaded; they will not let us loose with a loaded weapon without a great deal more training.

By the afternoon, it was my turn to lead. The difference between leading was like night and day compared to simply walking in line. The concentration was exhausting. You must stay alert, constantly scanning for anything life-threatening.

The mental strain was compounded by the blazing sun, a heavy pack, and the weight of the rifle burning my arm. At least that's my excuse for missing the five-metre-tall giraffe just seventy metres away.

A hot and humid afternoon combined with my first walk as pseudo lead left me shattered. When we came in sight of the Landy, my mind switched from dangerous game to the icy drinks that were waiting for us at the truck. Could Rhodes sense this? I don't know, I hope not. Regardless, he stopped us to gather around him.

'Ladies and Gentlemen' he started,

'We can all see the truck over there on the bank, only 200 metres away. It's been a long hot walk. We were up early, and I'm sure you're thinking about the cold beers in the cool box. But note this one stark fact, most accidents with the Big Five happen within 300 metres of the vehicle when both guide and guests become complacent.'

On arriving at the vehicle, we didn't dwell long over those chilled sundowners as the thunderheads had darkened the sunset. If the rain arrived, getting stuck was a real possibility, and we were a long way from home.

The expected rain was forgotten when we discovered a female white rhino feeding in a clearing. As we free-wheeled into the sighting, we sent a flurry of red-billed oxpeckers skyward, disturbing them from their last morsels before heading to roost. Like many of our sightings, the repetitive refrain of the Cape turtle dove—*work harder, drink lager*—provided the background music. The scene reached perfection when the African sky was lit by sheets of lightning in the distance.

It turns out Rhodes knows what he's talking about. On returning from their walk, Ben's group climbed aboard their truck to discover a lion laying up only twenty metres away as they drove off. That's close by any wild animal standards but considering a lion at full tilt runs at 22.5 metres per second they were fortunate to arrive home safely.

I've a lot of time for Rhodes, he's a gent, and I feel I can relate to him. He gave up his career of some twenty-seven years to follow his dream of working in the bush. I'm presuming he had a successful career within finance, which has allowed him to pursue this folly of fancy. Before his corporate life, he was fighting a bush war with the Rhodesian Light Infantry.

I like the structure and adventure that a military life could give. Still, I'm not sure I'd have been happy about the moments of excitement I'd have seen in the British Army. Deployments for my generation would likely have included Northern Ireland, Kosovo, Iraq, and Afghanistan—far removed from the 1990s army recruitment ads, where a chap named Frank skied and windsurfed his way around the world.

When Rhodes isn't instructing, he's leading trails on the Makuleke concession through his company, Shangani Trails. The name comes from his Zimbabwe heritage and is Shona for 'to walk on the sand'. This reflects his belief that, 'The only way to enjoy and truly understand the bush is to be able to walk through nature, experiencing the smell, sounds and sights undisturbed by all external, artificial noises.'

22nd November 2013

Duty day for me, I was up at three-thirty to set up the morning coffee and to prep the vehicles. After a week of theory and practical work, assessment day finally arrived. Before this trip, I didn't know north from south. The only time I used the points of the compass was to say that I came from the North East. As for navigating, the most challenging I had it was to read the London Underground map to know which line to take and where to get off. Actually, to be fair, that's not as easy as it sounds.

Today I was being tested on my orientation skills. An OS map of contours, water pumps and comms masts replaced the tube map. The sat nav was replaced by the sun and a compass.

My situational awareness will be the most important part of the assessment. This includes walking with my head up, smelling and listening for the Big Five, route choice, and looking for signs. These could be tracks, browsed branches or droppings of varying sorts. I also had to be aware of wind direction and, critically, oxpeckers. If you miss either the sight or sound of these little birds, it's goodnight Vienna as far as the assessment is concerned.

My walk could have gone better. I got so wrapped up in finding my way to the target point I missed a giraffe, again. How do I keep missing these living totem poles? An exam then followed the practical. With the final paper handed in Rhodes and Massi then locked themselves away to mark the exam. I passed. With flying colours in fact. I guess I'm my own worst critic and giraffes matter little.

23rd November 2013

Shock and awe best describe our instructor, Jeremy's, approach to the four-day wilderness medicine course which kicked off today.

Jeremy's focus was on prevention rather than cure. The first day was emotionally draining. He wanted to make sure we didn't get ourselves killed or maimed out here. To ensure this, he shared photographic and video evidence of what happens when people break the rules or are stupid. In this evidence, there were many contenders for the Darwin Awards—those that have 'contributed' to human evolution by selecting themselves out of the gene pool by their own actions.

One man lost his lower jaw to a pet hyena while feeding it mouth to mouth. Given the jaws of spotted hyenas are capable of crushing bone, this was the worst idea since Eve said to Adam, she was feeling peckish.

A video showed a man shooting his friend square in the chest to see if the bulletproof vest would work. It didn't, and he died. There were also: mauling's from lions, goring's from buffalo, gunshot wounds, human remains, open cavities from wild animal attacks and someone shooting a hole through the peak of his cap when checking his rifle.

It wasn't just about prevention; it was also to steel us for what we might encounter. Statistics from South African National Parks show there's an injury on a game reserve every three hours and a death every fifteen days.

It didn't seem right to be viewing the videos. However, if it helps to prepare for emergency situations and prevents us from becoming complacent, then so be it.

The content proved too much for some, prompting them to lie down on the cold concrete floor of the toilet block. However, a small number of the group seemed a bit too fascinated by the images for my liking. I'm not suggesting they got off on it, but there was a sick perversion in their interest.

The unexpected benefit of being camp bound today and for the three days to come is not having to pull on my heavy, smelly boots. But I'm sure within twenty-four hours I'll be climbing the walls with cabin fever desperate to get back on reserve.

28th November 2013

The beauty of life in the bush lies in the ability to get things done by rising with the sun. We finished our two-and-a-half-hour *FGASA* exam before breakfast. This wasn't an insignificant exam—it was the qualifying test to become a safari guide. With the theory behind me, I moved on to the practical: the assessment drives. I need to pass both to qualify.

An air of excitement filled the camp ahead of the first drive. I was originally set to take it, but California Cliff wanted to get his done first, so we swapped. The vehicle was packed and ready fifteen minutes before departure—something almost unheard of. Cliff summed up the experience perfectly.

'It's like doing stand-up in front of your friends who'd heard all your material before, but there's one lone critic sat at the back.'

It was the lone critic, the assessor, who proved to be Cliff's downfall after a clash of personalities.

29th November 2013

It's rare I turn down a drive, but today I prepared for this afternoon's assessment instead. I felt guilty not supporting Carmen on hers, but she filled her vehicle regardless.

I was also on duty, so I cracked on with camp life. This included taking the Landy onto the reserve to escort the gas delivery vehicle back to the main gate. After a week of being camp bound, it was gold dust to drive through the reserve to warm up the senses.

By the time of my assessment, the truck was sparkling—or as much as a battered old ride could be. I'd done my checks and felt relaxed. That is until my faux guests arrived. Like Carmen, my truck was full to bursting with JP as the assessor. I also welcomed what you'd class as a VIP on board—Margaux joined us too.

It's treated as a regular game drive, but it's not. There are few paying guests that want or need twenty trees pointing out and explaining to them. Despite having to tell stories about trees and wax lyrical about rocks, I pledged not to stop until I found something with a heartbeat. A bold and painful move, but ten minutes in it paid off. A giraffe.

The trickiest part of any drive is the elephants. Especially here, these aren't ordinary elephants, they're Selati elephants that in the past have been hunted by man. And I was about to bump into a herd of them.

It wasn't a sixth sense that foretold what was coming; the evidence lay in the footprints on the dirt road ahead. Some were oval, others round, varying in size, but all bore a mosaic pattern. Each print was unique to its owner, with the sand shaped by the cracks, forming interconnecting miniature mountain ranges. All the tracks shared one characteristic, a little flick of sand at one end. This showed the direction of travel. The elephants—a breeding herd—were clearly heading in the same direction as us.

I couldn't avoid them as that would have looked weak, plus I didn't have time to detour. But I hoped they would have disappeared into the bush by the time we caught up with them.

This wasn't about a lack of confidence. Since arriving in Africa, my confidence has grown in leaps and bounds. The knowledge I gained from the course, my passion for wildlife, and my purpose here created the perfect recipe for a more confident James. My peers often say I come alive when I don my safari hat and talk bush. No, this was purely about maintaining a healthy respect for elephants in their natural environment, where they occasionally face the threat of being shot at by humans.

Rounding the corner, it was apparent I couldn't avoid these elephants, even if I wanted to. Their pungent odour hung in the warm evening air. Discarded branches, stripped of their bark, lay strewn across the floor like Lego bricks across a playroom. Dark patches marked where urine had pooled and soaked away in the sand. Four or five boluses made up a pile of half-digested vegetable matter. The dung was fresh.

I didn't need the coveted *FGASA* qualification to know we would catch up with the eles. And there they stood. Suddenly, things turned tense. We were in the middle of a breeding herd. There wasn't much I could do, and I certainly wasn't going anywhere, so we sat back and watched. The finale of the encounter came when a large cow, standing three metres at the shoulder, stared down at us. With a flap and crack of her oversized ears, she moved on, having realised we were the good guys.

I took off once she and the rest were clear of the road. It was a race against the clock to get back within my allotted time. As I neared camp, I spotted a wasp dragging a paralysed baboon spider across the road. Due to the elephant negotiations, I'd already been given an extra fifteen minutes. Still, JP stopped the clock, as this sighting was too rare to ignore.

Back at camp, I got the nod—I'd passed, pending some homework on birds, elephant social structure, and an astronomy test on the next clear night.

Hoedspruit
3rd to 8th December 2013

After a month of assessments, I spent a week off doing little besides making the most of being in a town, albeit a small one. This meant access to the

Internet, an electric kettle, pizza, a proper bed, hot showers and chilled pints of lager in tall, somctimes frosted, glasses. And of course, doors!

I didn't study as much as I'd hoped during my time off. Whenever I tried, the sun on my face and the hypnotic *dooth dooth* of the sprinkler kept winning the competition between shut-eye and *Smithers' Guide to Mammals of Southern Africa.*

While being off-grid, I've missed coverage of many world events. Still, there was one that would have reached me no matter where I was: the passing of Nelson Mandela at ninety-five, or Madiba, as his clan name goes. It was a sad day for South Africa, the continent, the world, and democracy. The imagery played repeatedly in bars and restaurants was of him, wearing a Springbok jersey, presenting the Rugby World Cup to Francois Pienaar in 1995.

The coverage of his death was widespread and glowing. The Times's obituary reported that...

'Nelson Mandela called himself a troublemaker and a humble servant to his people. He was, in fact, the preeminent political leader of his age, tearing down the evil of apartheid and almost single-handedly laying the foundations of a free South Africa.'

And against this evil, he showed unbelievable absolution. Fergal Keane wrote for BBC Online:

'To the wider world, he represented many things, not least an icon of freedom but also the most vivid example in modern times of the power of forgiveness and reconciliation. Back in the early 1990s, I remember then President, F W de Klerk, telling me how he found Mandela's lack of bitterness "astonishing".

'His fundamental creed was best expressed in his address to the sabotage trial in 1964.

'"I have fought against white domination, and I have fought against black domination," he said.

'"I have cherished the ideal of a democratic and free society in which all persons live together in harmony and with equal opportunities. It is an ideal which I hope to live for and to achieve. But if needs be, it is an ideal for which I am prepared to die."'

CHAPTER SIX

'When it comes to mastering a skill, time is the magic ingredient.' *Robert Greene, Author.*

Mashatu Game Reserve
9th December 2013

Today we travelled to Botswana for our week-long Advanced Rifle Handling (*ARH*) course at Mashatu. If I'm to become a Trails Guide, I need to pass this course, but success is alarmingly rare.

Having arrived at the Pont Drift border crossing, our driver wished us farewell and pointed us in the right direction. The usual route involved a rickety cable car across the Limpopo, but today, with the mighty river parched, we opted to walk rather than risk the gondola. The apparatus looked critically endangered, soon to be extinct in the wild. Though the river lacked water, it was filled with fine sand, making the trek slow going with Baby Elephant on my back.

We had been told to prepare ourselves for how breathtaking our new camp would be, and we were not disappointed. The location exceeded all expectations;

the place was truly wild. En route, we drove through a herd of a hundred elephants. The camp, nestled in woodland on a floodplain, was rustic in nature. The paths were little more than game trails. A reliable torch was essential for navigating the 175 yards back to my tent.

We were oversubscribed on the first night, so Jenny and I shared a tent. I didn't know her well—certainly not well enough for this arrangement. I didn't want to let myself down by snoring, needing to pee or accidentally breaking wind. As a result, I got little shuteye, but Jenny seemed to sleep well, snoring and farting all night long. I am, of course, joking.

11th December 2013

Yesterday's focus was on dry drills with dummy rounds to work on technique. This develops muscle memory so that when the proverbial hits the fan, everything happens on automatic.

We've lucked out with two of our instructors, Sean Patrick, who is co-author of my go-to reference book, *Game Ranger in Your Backpack*. While the book is not high end in terms of extensive scientific detail, it is crammed with amazing facts in a digestible format. And then there's Bruce Lawson, the most experienced Trails Guide and instructor in South Africa. Bruce has been guiding since 1992, and a Trails Guide instructor since 2007. During this time, he has accumulated 10,000 logged hours walking in Big Five areas. He is without a doubt an expert in his field.

Bruce's life story would make an inspiring tale of

triumph over adversity, and I hope that one day he will write it up to share. Amongst his many achievements, Bruce completed a 12,000-kilometre walk from Cape Town to Cairo with no vehicular support. This earned him the title of Captain Morgan Adventurer of the Year. He has also been a South African paratrooper, a medic and a researcher in Antarctica. He spent eight years as Director of the Field Guide Association of Southern Africa. Everything he has achieved is astonishing. Especially since he was told he would never walk again after being involved in a car crash as a child. Subsequently as a young adult, he fell during a rock climb and broke his back.

Today, Bruce took us to the makeshift range in Secret Valley to shoot for real. The valley was hard to find, but when we arrived, I was taken aback by its beauty. It resembled an alpine garden with flowers across the veld giving a meadow-like appearance, so out of place for my clichéd take on Africa.

The targets were set up at fifteen, ten and five metres, which doesn't sound far. However, when the adrenaline is pumping, they might as well have been at 150, one hundred and fifty metres. Until this point, we had been shooting with a .375, but today we progressed to a .458. My anticipation of the recoil was immense, and it certainly lived up to expectations.

I can't remember where my first three rounds landed. The rifle slamming into my shoulder and jamming my finger was a distraction. The sheer power of the weapon is frightening, and watching the destruction of the trees behind the targets was sobering. I'm still not at ease with a gun, but I think that means it has my respect.

The next drill was to hit all three targets in quick succession, starting at fifteen metres. My aim improved, with two bulls and an almost bull. Strangely, I performed better when moving quickly, without overthinking it. I suppose muscle memory really does work.

In the afternoon, it was dry drills once again and then into the riverbed for a run-through of the lion charge. When you first see the charge machine, you could be forgiven for laughing at the lack of realism. Still, I can assure you when you're on the receiving end, it's anything but funny.

In reality, a lion charges at eighty kilometres per hour, and there's a strong possibility that multiple lions would be approaching you. As if that weren't nerve-racking enough, one must wait until the lion is within ten metres, ideally five metres, to give it the opportunity to abort its charge. This means that if you are forced to shoot, you have only one shot during the charge; missing simply isn't an option.

The lion is represented by a life-size poster of the animal in full flight. This is set atop a sledge and attached to a pulley powered by the battery from the Landy. The sledge comes at 10m per second, less than half the speed of the real thing but when the drill happens, it's like nothing else exists. You do not know what you're shouting or doing, it's all a blur. Afterwards, you know you've made mistakes, but you don't know what.

There's plenty of time for practice between now and the actual lion charge, which is a good thing as my first attempt ended with me on my backside. Falling on your bum during the charge is not textbook. However, getting back up and continuing helps reclaim a morsel of credibility. Instructor Geoff reassured me that all was not lost; he had faced charges from two lions himself and lived to tell the tale, even after stumbling from the rifle's recoil.

Appropriately I fell to sleep listening to the roar of a lion across the riverbed.

12th December 2013

Back to Secret Valley for more drills. Twelve rounds in the morning with the .458 meant my shoulder was feeling tender. Still, I'm faring better than some whose shoulders are looking beyond sore given the level of purple.

First up, three shots at fifteen metres with no time restriction.

'Firing live, ear protection,' Bruce bellowed.

As I stood on the firing line with the rifle in my hand, I was wearing ear protectors. For everyone watching, however, the instruction was simply to cover their ears. It's important to cover both the ear canal and the surrounding area, as this provides better sound dampening than just plugging the ear canal with your fingers. On my second attempt, I surprised myself with the grouping; all three holes were connected.

Next, the pressure ramped up with the

introduction of a timer. We had to fire three rounds and hit all the targets in under fourteen seconds. If it took us longer we would lose points.

I was quick, firing all three rounds and chambering a fourth in under nine seconds. The ten-metre and five-metre shots were solid, but I was low on the crucial fifteen-metre one—an automatic fail in the real test. Such a failure would have sent my Trails Guide aspirations up in a cloud of spent gunpowder. Fortunately, this was just practice, not the real deal.

After the lion charge yesterday and this morning's timed exercise, it became clear you don't have the luxury to think. Everything happens on muscle memory, or at least you hope it does.

Confidence in the camp is low for the assessments tomorrow. It will be demanding with six exercises—one fail, and its thanks but no thanks. On the last course, only one in five passed. I'm desperate to pass, only if it's so I can give the lion charge, which comes at the end, a go again. I want to get it right this time, but at the very least, I don't want to fall on my backside.

13th December 2013

After a week of training, assessment day arrived. More might have been made of it being Friday the thirteenth if anyone had known what day of the week it was. We left for the range at six o'clock. After setting up, Bruce gave us a pep talk against the backdrop of the ever-present ascending trill of the woodland kingfisher.

I wasn't one of the first to go, nor did I have to wait long. When my turn arrived, most of my predecessors had failed, and only Pieter made it through to this afternoon's lion charge. It was like waiting to bat against an incredibly fast bowler, while all the batsmen ahead dropped like flies.

I surprised myself by doing well in the fifteen-metre accuracy exercise, taking ten seconds to score two bulls and a five. I sailed through the misfire drill before scraping through with the buffalo brain shot at twelve metres and eight metres.

The range session ended, and we headed back to camp for breakfast. The morning results: Pieter and me through to the charge while Ulrica fell at the final hurdle. I was gutted for her, but she took it in her stride.

After a full English and many cups of tea, we returned to the range. Sorting out the sledge and winch took an age which built the pressure in the stifling heat. The intensity of the sun was so strong I could feel it breaching the sun cream, sweat and dust to burn away layers of my skin.

The drill was more realistic now as we were no

longer in the riverbed but in the bush; it meant the lion would come out of a thicket along a dirt track.

Pieter took the opening slot and nailed it in an impressive display of shooting; he hit the lion right between the eyes. This display of quality marksmanship added to my self-imposed tension.

To pass the assessment, I would need to score a minimum of eighty out of 110, and the bullet must hit the brain. There are points for following procedure, shouting at the lion, and giving commands to your clients as well as keeping them informed and reassured.

With a nod to the controller, I approached the lion. As expected, it thundered out of the undergrowth right at me. I did a lot of shouting before dropping to one knee with the rifle automatically coming to my shoulder. Without warning, the metal sled tumbled over, kicking up dust which hung in the air, obscuring the scene.

My shouting must have been effective. It stopped the charge.

No time for a joke, I thought. I couldn't relax. There was a round in the chamber. I needed to control my breathing. I had to clear my mind and let the blood flow to my brain. I ensured the rifle was safe and declared it so.

The pressure built again as they set the lion once more.

This time the charge was complete. I fired my shot and executed the drill without any faults. But it still wasn't good enough—I shot the lion in the mouth. Even though it could have been a fatal shot, it's counted as a failure because it wasn't the brain.

Luckily, you get two attempts on this final exercise. With the pressure building to burst, the lion came once more, and once more, it cartwheeled. Could things get more intense?

Finally, the charge was complete; I got my shot off, almost as the lion ran into the riffle's muzzle, but I didn't know if it hit the brain cavity. I fired my second shot, a dummy round for safety reasons, and then moved my guests away. While delivering the coup de grâce, I saw I'd hit the target. Now all I had to do was not screw up with the last steps. I got through it despite jamming a round whilst making my rifle safe. That jam cost me ten points, leaving me with a score of one hundred.

Almost over.

Back at camp, it became a waiting game until the final test. This time, it was basic rifle handling. Under a time limit, we needed to load the rifle, aim, and then make safe—all while wearing a blindfold. It was the most straightforward test of the day, and I nearly messed it up.

After an hour of rifle cleaning, Pieter and I finally secured the all-important Advanced Rifle Handling certificate. The rest of the team will get a second chance tomorrow. Right now, it was time for a cold beer.

CHAPTER SEVEN

'Adopt the pace of nature: her secret is patience.'
Ralph Waldo Emerson, Transcendentalist.

North West Province & Western Cape
15th December 2013 to 7th January 2014

Having transferred up to Johannesburg, there were a small group of us staying at Emerald Guest House. It was an excellent way to acclimatise to going down from a group of fifteen to one as we all went our separate ways for Christmas.

Options for dinner and beer were limited. Six of us lived it up by going to the Keg and Aviator, the bar at the airport. I can't say I've ever had or will ever again have a night out at the airport without getting on a plane at the end.

The following morning, California Cliff and I went for a run. I can assure you that two shirtless white chaps running around the airport district of Johannesburg attracted considerable attention. Indeed, when a taxi driver arrived at the guest house, he recognised us and declared us mad.

The first port of call for my three-week break was Leopards Lodge at Hartebeespoort Dam. I'd previously stayed there for my great friend Marc and Cherith's wedding in 2010. It's a stunning location, a quarter of the way up a mountain overlooking the dam. The lodge was situated on a small farm with no dangerous game. This meant I could run daily through the bush whilst keeping an eye out for spoor and listening to bird calls. However, the mountainous setting made for rather torturous running.

Ten minutes before I arrived, I got news that Marc and Cherith welcomed their first child, Amelie. Given they got married here three years previously, I christened her by writing her name in the red African earth using stones.

After a week of uninterrupted me time I flew south to spend Christmas with my Aunt Paddy and Uncle Peter in the Western Cape. First in Betty's Bay and then at their farm near the small town of Villiersdorp. The farm has spectacular views and a great run along the irrigation canal.

The Dall family like a party which meant these runs were needed to compensate for a week of overindulgence. On each run, I carried a small index card on which I'd scribbled three to five scientific names of trees. As I pounded the path I'd glance down at the card before parroting the Latin to myself.

Peter and Paddy generously lent me their car for the third and final leg of my Christmas holidays. I headed to Cape Town International Airport to pick up my friend Amy, who had flown in from London.

We spent three days in Cape Town for the

penguins at Boulders and a trip up Table Mountain before heading along the Garden Route. The first call on our whistle-stop trip was Stellenbosch, where we joined a minibus tour of four vineyards. Neither of us wanted to be the designated driver. We were enthusiastic patrons and stocked up on wine and cheese. Simonsig and Boschendal emerged as clear winners in the vineyard stakes.

Three weeks away from the bush gave me time to think about what I want. I want to make a go of it out here; I want to become a guide; I want a life for myself in the bush.

CHAPTER EIGHT

The African buffalo is one of the great reasons why so many visitors never get into the wilds at all. He regards it as his duty to keep them out.' *Harry Syner, Author & Hunter.*

EcoTraining, Makuleke
8th January 2014

The whack on my head woke me. Or at least me whacking my head on the mini-bus window did as we hit a pothole. After wiping dribble from the windowpane, I became transfixed with the imperial baobabs as we sped along the R525 to the northernmost parts of the Republic of South Africa.

We were almost at Makuleke after an exhausting eight-hour slog, especially after a night of catching up, drinking Castles, and eating pizza. Everyone got stuck in. I'm not saying we're all suffering, but after the excitement of the night before, the bus was quiet.

Today we start the trails part of the course where we learn to lead groups of guests through dangerous game territory on walking safaris.

As we pulled up to Pafuri Gate, it struck me how desolate the place appeared. Barely a mature tree remained standing. Such a stark contrast to what we had driven through and what we could see through the fence line of the protected National Park. The apocalyptic scene resulted from some of the 781 inhabitants of Bende Mutale, chopping down the finest specimens for firewood.

This would be understandable if it were for subsistence— people must keep warm and cook. But there's a chance the wood was being sold on, perhaps even in Johannesburg. It was being poached, yet can I blame those doing it? Once again, they need to eat, and selling firewood provides a means to that end. What was clear was how vital National Parks are with the deforestation so starkly halting at the fence.

After a long journey, I felt the relief to stretch my legs, even if it was only walking to the SAN Parks offices to hand in my papers and passport. With time to kill—either we had arrived early, or our pickup was late—I flitted between the inside and outside of the gatehouse. Outside, I savoured the sun on my face while watching the weaver birds busying themselves in the acacia trees. One reason I love Africa so much is the climate. Still, it can be oppressive, so I frequently returned indoors to the shade of the thatched roof and the breeze of the ceiling fan.

As I circled the park buildings, a mixture of brown and yellow mopane leaves crunched under my feet. After the meadow-like appearance of Botswana's Secret Valley, this is the Africa I know, tinder box dry and ready to burn.

Our ride arrived, two battered four by fours, one towing an equally battered trailer. We loaded our bags and bumped our way through the bush towards camp. The breeze of our momentum chilled us, but we still needed protection from the sun. It was flaming down relentlessly. After a 30-minute journey along the private dirt roads, we arrived at camp. Bruce and his wife Dee greeted us. Dee was the Camp Manager, and apparently an efficient and formidable one. She ran a tight ship, and we would have to be shipshape.

I heaved Baby Elephant onto my back and followed one of the support staff along a wide path with rotting wood marking the edges. To be more precise, I followed a Back-up, this is a past student who has stayed on to gain the encounters, experience and hours required to qualify as a Trails Guide. For the privilege, they help around camp and walk as second rifle when the instructor takes the students out for walks.

The path narrowed to make way for a small wooden bridge crossing a dry ditch before opening to reveal the camp. To my left was the campfire and a thatched deck. Both were in the shadow of a giant nyala tree. To my right stood the kitchen building which, like the deck, was elevated on a raised platform. The concession had apparently suffered recurring flooding issues and been decimated the previous year.

Compared to our previous camps, this site offered pure luxury — the Savoy of the EcoTraining portfolio. Ten thatched, tented rooms stood proudly, each boasting its own wooden deck. Inside, proper beds awaited, along with en-suites for added comfort.

The greatest luxury, a wooden door framed within the canvas tent; no more bending over to enter my tent.

They gave Ben and me a tent to share at the far end of camp, number six. Our accommodation offered a fantastic view of the bush. Kruger Park was literally on my doorstep.

They gave us the customary safety briefing and camp rules. The number one rule being never ever, ever, ever should food be left out or kept in the tents. Failure to comply would result in instant dismissal, as it would undoubtedly lead to the baboons and vervet monkeys becoming a nuisance in camp. Currently, all primates, both human and non-human, live peacefully side by side.

We met our course instructors: Ben, whom we knew from before, and Alan McSmith who will stay with us until Sean returns. After welcoming us with chocolate muffins, they gave us downtime, so California Cliff and I lapped the 400-metre firebreak.

The downside was having to repeatedly run past the end of people's tents. Did they feel guilty watching me, or was I feeling guilty for disturbing their respite? Still, this route should be just a short-term fix. Once Bruce is happy with our situational awareness — that is, do we spot the elephant before we run into it — we'll graduate to the 1.2-kilometre outer firebreak.

9th January 2014

The welcome pack in my tent introduced Makuleke as one of the most spectacular concessions in South Africa. The 26,000 hectares is a real wilderness area that borders Zimbabwe to the north and Mozambique to the North East. It is also known as the Pafuri Triangle because of the Limpopo and Luvuvuh rivers coming together. The land at this confluence earned the name Crooks Corner due to the criminals who once lived there. It was an ideal hideout for those wanting to stay one step ahead of the law by jumping borders when they felt the heat of the law.

This place is the last frontier, totally unspoilt with no evidence of cattle farming. The flora and fauna are exceptional in this distinct ecological region — it has ninety-five per cent of Kruger's biodiversity in five per cent of its footprint. This is largely due to the birdlife, with between 350 and 400 species being recorded in the summer with the arrival of migrants. Beyond the wildlife, it's the space and solitude that Makuleke offers that sets it apart from the rest of the concessions. I believe I've come to Paradise.

Two walks in the day were a challenging introduction given the humidity, and even in the shade, it was a suffocating thirty degrees. It's the dehydration that takes the toll. My biggest lesson learned so far: drink more water, much more.

We stumbled upon several old settlements. Kneeling in the scrub, examining the various remnants of human occupation spanning thousands of years, was both humbling and fascinating. These were true artefacts, ranging from Stone Age scrapers to ancient pottery. But what about a butter knife, is that an artefact? The rich past of Pafuri would undoubtedly become a prominent fixture of our time in this place.

The Makuleke people would have lived in close proximity to dangerous wild animals. This was made clear by the spoor of two lions that we followed for two hours. Despite our efforts, we had no luck spotting them and continued until we stumbled across leopard tracks.

The dehydration wasn't due to the walking alone; it had a lot to do with Bruce. He put California Cliff and me through our paces. The exercises appeared simple—effortless, in fact—and we only had to complete three sets. Yet, after just seven and a half minutes of work, I found myself doubled over, desperately trying not to be sick.

This was my first introduction to Tabata, the high-intensity interval training developed by Professor Tabata from a study of Olympic speed skaters. I'm no Olympian, so for me, it felt like hell on earth.

I spent my recovery laying in the dirt watching a rock monitor raking the ground in search of food with its dragon-like talons. I felt on a par with this guy, reduced to a crawl myself after the workout.

Despite the workout I managed the afternoon walk across Lala Palm Plains to the springs before looping back to camp. The highlight was an approach on a massive male kudu to within fifteen metres. While his buddies bolted at first sight, he froze in place to avoid detection—a strategy I respected. If I looked as impressive, I'd do the same, standing tall with my chin out and horns spiralling proudly toward the sky.

On our way into camp along the outer firebreak, we found the tracks of a male leopard. I needed no further excuses to unpack the camera trap.

10th January 2014

We parked up at a disused quarry next to the tar road. This isn't some gaping, deep hole, more of a scraping with a large puddle in the centre. If the standard was the diamond mine at Kimberley, then this would be little more than a pothole. Still, like most things man-made, it wasn't pretty. From here we walked south down to the sandstone ridge where we picked up buffalo tracks to follow for 40 minutes before diverting back to our original destination, Masashiti Springs.

None of us saw it, the lone buffalo, half-submerged and caked in mud at the fringe of a wallow screened by scrubby bushes. And he didn't see us until the last moment when we were upon him. He took off, exploding from the water like a Polaris missile. Crashing through the bushes in the opposite direction, he was no slouch. Buffalos can run at thirty-five miles per hour — that's 15.6 metres per second. And at three-quarters of a ton, you don't want to get in the way.

Unsighted at the moment of take-off, Bruce and his Back-up swung their rifles to ready by opening their bolts. They thought he was coming straight at us. They made an incredible split-second decision between firing or holding. One day, I might find myself in a similar position.

This was an unforgettable lesson on the danger of dagga-boys— the grumpy old men of the bush. They're the older bulls that choose to withdraw from the herd and wander alone or in small groups of like-minded cantankerous gentleman.

They get their name from the Zulu word for mud, owing to their preference for wallowing to enjoy the spa-like benefits. Due to ageing buffaloes' deteriorating hair, they have little protection against the sun and parasites. So they cake themselves in mud to act as a sunblock, which also suffocates ticks and similar parasites. They then remove the dead parasites through a process of exfoliation, achieved by rubbing against termite mounds, trees or rocks.

As there's no longer safety in numbers afforded by the herd, these loners are skittish, always on high alert ready for fight or flight. This is what makes them dangerous to us as a walking safari. For hunters of old and their modern-day equivalents, they are considered incredibly dangerous given the wily mammal will often circle back on their pursuer. For a buffalo, attack is the best form of defence.

This was our first encounter as a group, so I recorded it in my dangerous game logbook. As part of my Trails Guide training, I'm required to log at least ten encounters, either as Lead or Backup.

Dangerous game includes elephant, buffalo, rhino, lion, leopard, and hippo—though for the latter, it would need to be on land. I must document every detail of the encounter. What was the wind direction relative to my position and the animal's? How strong was the wind—was it constant or gusting? Then there's the sun. Was it behind me, preventing the animal from seeing me approach? What were the terrain and vegetation like? Was there anything I could use for cover or to escape to? Just as important, was there an escape route for the animal, ensuring I didn't corner it? Did I manage to get in and out unnoticed by the animal? How enjoyable was the experience—had I taken too many risks, making my guests uncomfortable? How did the animal respond? And most importantly, what lesson did I take away from the encounter?

There are four types of encounter. The first is making a deliberate approach to view dangerous game on foot without them being aware of our presence throughout, even the retreat. This is the perfect encounter. Then there's a deliberate walk on to the game, but this time the animal notices us because of either guide or guest error, and sometimes due to changing factors such as wind direction. The third is unintended contact such as our fleeting encounter with the lone buffalo today. Finally, the deliberate avoidance of dangerous game, a good example, is coming across the spoor of a lioness and her cubs disappearing into the long grass. This is a dangerous situation and should be avoided.

Our second encounter of the day took place on the return leg of our walk. A herd of buffalo moved ahead of us. Bruce changed our route to avoid them, to pursue them would cause stress and could result in them standing their ground.

By the time we reached the watercourse, we'd been walking for several hours with the mercury topping out at thirty-four degrees. The trek was worth it. The stunning springs offered crystal-clear water. I submerged my hat in it, savouring its refreshing coolness as I put it back on.

Bruce often visited the springs and clearly loved the place. He told us to find some shade where we could rest, taking in the beauty of our surroundings. As the sun climbed higher, the welcome relief of the tree's shadow felt heavenly. I settled on a rock ledge overlooking the clearing—it was the closest I'd ever come to visiting Eden.

I lost all sense of paradise when Bruce led us to the clearing itself. He walked around the long grass, parting it in places with his walking stick. He was clearly searching. Had Bruce dropped something on his last visit here? Whatever it was, he'd just found it.

'Gather round', he said in a sombre tone.

'What's that?' he asked, prodding a long white skull that was blackening with dirt and decay.

'Giraffe', someone from the group confidently proffered.

But no, was his prompt reply. There weren't too many options left, so the unthinkable was suggested sheepishly.

'Rhino?'

'Correct. Poachers killed two white rhinos here in August - our last two on the concession. Look around, you should find the other one nearby. Hyenas have taken the rest of the carcass, so you won't see much more. Now, take a close look at the skulls'.

On taking Bruce's lead, I scrutinised the skull. I wasn't sure what I was supposed to be looking for, but it became clear when Bruce said,

'Panga'.

The marks across the nose were not natural. A machete had left these scars as poachers hacked off the horn, probably while the rhino was still alive.

We gathered ourselves and trudged back with heavy hearts.

Bruce cottoned on that California Cliff, and I enjoyed our fitness. Ahead of the lecture, he said we had something to look forward to. At least it couldn't have been worse than yesterday's Tabata. I was wrong.

Bruce handed each of us a pair of gardening gloves and led us to the inner firebreak, where a 120-kilogram log lay in the cracking mud. The task was to flip the log end to end around the 400-metre circular track. Working together, we thought we could handle it easily. We were badly mistaken. That was not how this worked. Instead, whilst one of us flipped the log, the partner raced around the track as fast as possible to avoid leaving the other person flipping alone too long. The heat and humidity felt relentless, and our legs, forearms and shoulders burned under the strain.

We finished in under thirty-five minutes, a respectable time. But the biggest challenge still lay ahead: stopping sweating before lunch. If this experience taught us anything, it's that lions and leopards are smarter than Cliff and me. They wisely choose to lie in the shade, avoiding the sun at its meridian.

13th January 2014

The morning drums didn't wake me when they beat out at four-thirty. I was already wide awake with the lactic acid from the self-selected fitness sessions preventing a restful night's sleep. That plus the resident bats squeaking as they traversed across the green mesh of the tent windows. Their mouse-like feet and hands on the end of their paper-thin wings scratched the surface as they jostled for the best roosting position.

While it was business as usual today, two walks and buffalo encounters, there was one significant change. We, the students, now acted as lead and a Back-up Guide. Whoever is the designated lead for the walk picks the game path to follow, interprets for the group, scans for game and plans the approach on sightings. The rifles we carry are not loaded, it's simply to become accustomed to carrying a weapon and doing so safely. Alan and a Back-up walked number three and at the rear to ensure if we made any mistakes, it didn't end in disaster.

For the morning walk, we parked at Jachacha Pan and set off in a northerly direction to take advantage of the high ground. This gave us our first encounter, a herd of twenty buffalo at a safe 300 metres with the wind in our favour. Such a gentle encounter did nothing to raise the blood pressure, unlike the excitement of yesterday's walk when a gigantic yellow and black snake burst from the long grass. At lightning pace, it shot between Will and me before disappearing down a hole. It, the snouted cobra, was huge, at least a metre and a half.

After a second encounter, we reached our destination: the Limpopo of Rudyard Kipling fame. Kipling's short story *The Elephant's Child* described the river as 'the great grey-green, greasy Limpopo'. I'm not convinced about the greasiness of the river, but the grey-green hue was apt, and its greatness undeniable. The river must have been 300-metres across at the point where we stood. We rested, gazing across the fast-moving channel. Here, the waters separated the Republic of South Africa and Zimbabwe, still under the iron fist of Robert Mugabe. Interestingly, on this journey of mine, someone I met and trusted told me of having the dictator in their sniper rifle's sights. It was not as sinister as it sounds - they had worked with the South African National Defence Force, providing protection detail during a state visit.

I always thought the encounters with dangerous game would be the highlight of each walk, but for me, it was quickly becoming the trees. Whether a majestic sycamore fig perched on a riverbank or the Middle Worldly baobab, they were fascinating and striking. On this occasion, it was the fever tree that entranced me with its spreading crown and distinctive yellow trunk covered in fine dust. The tree earned its name from early pioneers, who believed it caused fevers. In reality, the fever, was malaria, contracted from mosquitos breeding in the swampy habitat where these trees thrive.

Back at camp after the lecture, we played tape-ball cricket in the car park before one of Bruce's torture sessions. Today we got off lightly — a few sprints, fireman's lifts, and rock carries — so I finished with a three-kilometre run.

14th January 2014

As the lead for this morning's walk, my duties started last night. Once I'd wiped the tables clean from splatters of Bolognese, I pushed my chair back. The chair produced a suitable attention-grabbing scrape and thud, scrape and thud, scrape and thud on the slatted wooden floor. I stood tall with my hands grasped behind my back, which helped puff my chest out.

'Good evening, ladies and gentlemen. I trust everyone enjoyed the fine cuisine put on for us tonight—the best spag bol outside of Italy! My name is James, and I will be your guide tomorrow morning. My Back-up Duncan will go through what you need to bring on your walk. But first, can I check you have signed your indemnity forms and handed them to Dee.'

Now, this last part seemed pointless. Not because it was an exercise, but because if anything went wrong out there and I or someone from the lodge made a mistake, no indemnity would save us. We would be to blame and totally accountable. Saying that I'm not a solicitor, so don't hold me to it.

Anyhoo, back to the drill.

'If any of you have a medical condition or allergy that could affect your experience tomorrow, please see me at the bar. Now for the hard part, the drums will beat at four-thirty. On getting up you will find tea, coffee, and rusks available on the deck. We will then leave at five-fifteen prompt from the car park as we will be driving to our walk-off point.'

Duncan then ran through what the guests should bring. The list was exhaustive. They needed a hat, sunscreen and neutral coloured clothing. The right footwear was essential - walking boots or closed sandals. Each person required at least half a litre of water, binos and a camera. A reference book for their primary interest completed the list.

Then it was back to me.

'To finish, I'd like to find out if anyone has any particular interest, perhaps a species they'd like to see?'

My fellow students were kind. They wanted to see buffalo and impala, nice of them as we'd seen little else since arriving in Makuleke.

Today was the day I led a walk, but despite my excitement, it wasn't quick in coming. Ben and I were on duty, so we woke up at four to set up the morning tea and bang the drums. Before I could enjoy a cuppa and many rusks, I needed to sign out my rifle. I also had to collect the fake rounds for the bandolier that would sit as a slider on my belt.

I felt shattered before we even stepped foot out of camp. It would not get any more comfortable when the sun rose, and the humidity drain kicked in. I sat in the front row of the truck behind Bruce. I wanted to stay close to him; his knowledge and experience were invaluable, and I was determined to absorb every bit of it I could.

Clutching the cased rifle between my legs with the butt seated on the ground, I rehearsed my pre-walk briefing and steeling myself for what would be a long walk. I then started muttering to myself, *head up, don't switch off, ears open and miss nothing.* My trance-like preparations were interrupted as we lurched to a stuttering halt. This wasn't a stall, not that anyone would call Bruce on that. The vehicle had finally given up the ghost. All we could do was push it off the track to avoid blocking the road. There was the remote possibility that someone might want to get past.

Our destination had been Palm Springs on the Sand Veld. Instead, we set off to camp through the mopane woodland. I say woodland, though that might be stretching it a bit—it was more like scrubland. To make the walk more interesting, we diverted to Ndekazane Springs.

On approaching the springs, I gave a thick wild date palm bush a wide berth on the off chance there was something untoward behind it. As I rounded the thicket, I saw a herd of fifteen buffalo ruminating. I shot up my right arm, bent at the elbow with my fist clenched, the sign for freeze, immediate danger. The buffalo saw me and jumped to their feet, turned and ran. They pirouetted in unison like a flock of choreographed ballerinas.

The surprising light-footedness of these 700-kilogram beasts brought back a vivid memory of a drawing I'd seen of a tutu-wearing hippo. The last time I thought of that postcard was during my first shift as Visitor Experience Manager at ZSL London Zoo. I received a call over the radio. Though my memory is a bit rusty, I believe it played out something like this.

'Cassons to VEM'.

Being super eager to impress, I promptly replied

and listened nervously to the transmission.

'Somehow one of the pygmy hippos has got a buoyancy ring stuck around themselves. We're going to take it off now but wanted to let you know.'

Not knowing how to respond but keen to sound in the know I asked them if they would be going to tranquilise the hippo first.

'No need' came the response. 'We have a team of keepers here, we'll be fine.'

Oh, I thought, and left it at that.

Half an hour later, when I was at the Asian short-clawed otter enclosure, another call came through.

'Just to let you know, a keeper has been injured by the pygmy hippo and will get medical treatment. They're ok, and the ring is off the hippo. Out.'

I digress, let's return to the here and now, back to Africa. Having pirouetted like an ensemble from Swan Lake, the herd took a step towards us with their noses outstretched, resembling a snooty Chelsea girl. They didn't like what they saw, turned, and took flight. For me, it was an exhilarating encounter that quickened my heartbeat, but I hadn't considered my guests. I held the freeze seconds too long so only my Back-up, and I saw the buff. I should have brought the guests up straight away.

After the thrill of the buffalo, reality hit. The walk to camp through the mopane was a struggle as the sparsen vegetation offering no clear game trail to follow. The animals clearly meandered wherever they liked. My orientation was further hampered by the grey sky, which removed the sun from the way-finding equation. Without the hum of the generator, I might have embarrassed myself by leading the group straight past camp and over the horizon. Fortunately, it was running, and I nonchalantly took a hard right to emerge on the outer firebreak.

With the rifle cleaned and locked away, I removed my canvas gaiters, kicked off my heavy boots, and peeled out of my thick sweaty socks. I collapsed on my bed with a cuppa for five minutes of bliss before the breakfast drums. I was utterly drained.

Over breakfast, I caught up with Ben who, like me, was leading today. He had a buffalo encounter too. Still, the real excitement came when he nearly stepped on a puff adder, which subsequently reared up at him.

15th January 2014

Happy birthday to me and my birthday buddy back home. Today is my thirty-ninth birthday and that of Charlie, my best friend. Over the years, we've shared schools and parties, rugby and cricket tours, possibly even the odd girlfriend. Basically, we grew up together. It's been a great friendship and a painful one — mainly as we both play sport to win. Add to the mix that Charlie is built like the proverbial brick house. He has broken my jaw, removed a few of my teeth, knocked me unconscious and put me in the hospital with a suspected broken neck. What else are best friends for?

While I can't imagine there's a better place for me to spend my birthday, I do envy Charlie waking up in a pretty village in Northumberland with his wife and two boys. I can't help but think, will I ever get that, it's certainly something I want but at the moment it seems a millennium away.

Birthday day was a relaxed affair, like every day when Alan McSmith is in town. He creates what is best described as a spiritual environment for all animals in his company, human and non-human. Back in 2011, he was invited to Amsterdam to give a *TED* lecture, which he did in full khaki including sandals. He spoke on wilderness not being a place but a way of life. That wilderness experiences can happen anywhere in the world, whether it's standing in the rain or walking hand in hand through the forest. Wilderness is the golden thread that binds us together. I guess he was saying that we should allow ourselves to connect with nature at every opportunity.

The morning's walk lasted four hours, taking us through the Fever-Tree Forest, a destination fast becoming a favourite of mine. Our arrival was heralded by the thundering bahoo of a baboon.

It wasn't the mammals that stole the show on this walk but the birds, a crowned eagle and a bateleur. The latter is a stunning bird of prey with black plumage that contrasts with its red beak and feet. This adult plumage takes over seven years to develop. The bateleur has a distinctive short tail which reduces drag in flight helping it cover great distances, up to 400 kilometres per day in search of food. The sacrifice for less resistance is instability, which the bird compensates for by tipping from side to side. This is in fact why the bateleur is named such, it is derived from the old French word for tumbler or acrobat owing to the birds tightrope walking appearance. However, the best description for the bird lies in its scientific name *Terathopius*, meaning marvellous face and the species name, *ecauadatus*, meaning without tail.

17th January 2014

Last night, I spoke to Bruce about doing my work placement at Makuleke and Mashatu as a *Back-up Trails Guide*. If I got accepted, it would be somewhat of a coup in terms of my development. I'd be able to clock up the encounters and hours to qualify as a Lead Trails Guide quicker than if I'd gone straight to a lodge. This morning I followed up with Dee—fingers crossed I've set the wheels in motion. Now it's a case of there being a vacancy, passing my exams, and acing the practical.

I was lead for the afternoon walk, but we never reached our destination. Another group radioed to say they had found a zebra whose neck was deeply lacerated by a wire snare. The metal was still embedded in its flesh. Bruce turned the vehicle around. Once we arrived, we received permission from the state vet to put the animal out of its misery. Bruce went about the job quickly with one shot and no histrionics. We hauled the carcass onto the trailer to take it to the anthrax vulture project to act as bait.

Once we'd unloaded the zebra, we opened it up for the vultures. Up until now, my sheath knife had only been used to spread cream cheese on a cracker and chop a branch down. This was its true christening as I cut along the zebra's belly to let the entrails spill across the African dirt.

18th January 2014

The duty team slept in this morning, not something you want to do on Bruce and Dee's watch. Despite this, everybody got up, albeit for a slightly late departure.

As lead, I got to choose where we walked. Of course, I opted to follow up on a brace of rhinos we saw yesterday following the zebra incident. I hoped they hadn't moved too far overnight. When we arrived at our start point, some vervet monkeys were alarming. I gave a rapid brief before we headed in search of what I hoped would be a lion or leopard; the rhino were a distant memory.

Every step I took was done with care to minimise unnecessary noise. I regularly stopped to listen for clues, and with each flick of my wrist, I let the ash stuffed in a sock drift on the breeze to signal wind direction. I didn't want our scent to give us away.

By the time we'd reached the vervets, the alarming had died down. We carried on past them to check if the predator was still in the area. At one-point Ralph, our new instructor, steered me away from leading the party into thick bush. Not wanting to walk into a lion or a leopard, I heeded his warning and changed direction.

The excitement of walking through the long grass and wooded glades played tricks on me. I spotted the rump of an animal about a hundred metres away, and convinced myself it was a lion. I brought my Back-up and instructor forward but embarrassingly it turned out to be a bushpig. The only redeeming feature being the pig hadn't noticed us. I had used the wind well and led the group with minimal noise.

With no luck in finding the predator, we headed towards the pan. On the way we discovered fresh tracks of a female leopard - she almost certainly had triggered the alarm calls.

20th January 2014

I acted as back-up for Francois when he took the three *28-Day Safari Course* students for a walk. There was one slight change, which made quite a difference. My rifle was loaded with three .458 Lotts, and a further ten on my belt. I carried these rounds not to use in anger, but to help me acclimatise to carrying a loaded weapon through the bush. Psychologically this was big, knowing that the rifle could go bang is considerably different from carrying one that goes click.

We met up with the rest of the group for coffee at the Land Cruiser; they had a pleasant walk but like us, no encounters. On leaving, we'd driven five minutes down the road when Pieter announced he'd left his rifle propped up against a tree. This, we quickly learned, was the most heinous of crimes. He must now keep an old rifle shaft on his person for the foreseeable future.

While taking a breather on this afternoon's walk, I was sure, but not 100% sure, I'd heard lions. I quietened everybody down, but the sound didn't come again. I dismissed it as nothing. As we walked to the vehicle, we heard them as clear as a bell and they sounded close, probably within a kilometre. The sun was almost down so we couldn't go after them.

22nd January 2014

A day off today, so we slept in until six-thirty. We could have slept longer if California Cliff and I had not suggested staging the inaugural *Makuleke Half Marathon.* It drew a decent turnout: five people completed the half marathon, two ran the ten-kilometre course, and several others ran a few laps for fun.

Our organisation of the event appeared professional, with the start being signalled by the primer of a cartridge being struck. Then, Big Cliff acted as race adjudicator and recorded individuals as they completed each lap.

I slightly overestimated the length of the firebreak, which meant the total distance was 19.11 kilometres, not a full half. I realised this halfway by looking at the GPS watch I'd borrowed from Bruce. I tried telling people as we passed on the course that we needed to extend it by a lap or two. This didn't go down well, and for my safety, I didn't pursue it. Cliff won with a time of one hour thirty-seven minutes; I couldn't keep his pace all the way around and crossed the finish line a few minutes later.

24th January 2014

The heat and humidity made our five-hour morning walk gruelling. Not even halfway through at seven o'clock, it was pushing thirty degrees. As an Englishman, I never imagined I'd be actively seeking shade. Now, with five months' experience under the African sun, I sought it at every opportunity. The only relief came during breaks, with the shelter of a tree offering brief respite. But the moment we resumed, it felt like someone opened the door of a fan-assisted oven mid-Sunday roast.

Today's lecture was a sobering affair. First, it concentrated on crime scene management–what do you do if you come across a rhino that has been shot and its horn hacked off. Then it focused on incident management. This time, what do you do if you shoot an animal in self-defence? Every now and again there are moments that remind me that nasty stuff can happen, and I mustn't fall into the trap of thinking that it will never happen to me.

25th January 2014

I've done the most walking so far — ninety hours in total — but I'll lose my pole position whilst I skip a few walks to revise for Tuesday's exam. I've been far too complacent about the theory, concentrating instead on the practical. I'm panicking now, as I need to achieve seventy-five per cent in both the rifle ballistics and Trails Guide exams.

After lunch, seven of us along with Bruce and Back-up Jomi were dropped at Masashiti Quarry to walk to the Luvuvuh River to camp for the night. It was a bit of a route march to get there before nightfall.

We set up camp in the fine sand under a spreading nyala tree on the banks of the river. The setting was stunning, made even more magical when a couple of eles sauntered down to bathe in the darkness.

We shared guard duty through the night, an hour each. By the time my shift arrived, I barely slept, feeling cold without a sleeping bag and waking up to insects crawling over me. Mine was the final shift, though I had no idea what time it was, as we'd surrendered our watches at base camp to fully embrace the wilderness experience.

A small fire crackled, where I spent most of my duty drying my shoes and socks from an earlier downpour. I've learnt there's nothing worse than wet feet when you're walking. I could have speeded up the drying process by throwing the tin of gunpowder on the fire. This propellant was our best form of defence against any unwanted visitors during the night. The flash created would have frightened any animal into next week.

Towards the end of my shift, I started the little gas burner to boil water for the morning brew to combat the chill. I wandered down to the Luvuvuh to wash the mugs out; it was peaceful down by the river. It reminded me of the crisp mornings in the UK when I holidayed at Strangford Loch or on the Norfolk

Broads. However, I couldn't allow myself to daydream. It was critical I concentrated on the water so not to miss a lurking croc that could grab me in a scene reminiscent of Crocodile Dundee. I didn't want to die, and I didn't want Bruce to be my Mick Dundee.

It took longer to break camp than it took to set up. This was because we didn't want to leave a trace. This meant throwing the ash and any half-burnt sticks into the river, so they'd be spread far and wide. We returned any unused firewood to where we found it. We left feeling good about what we'd left behind—nothing, not even footprints, as we'd swept those away, too.

29th January 2014

The morning was dedicated to assessments, starting with field observations—tracks, signs, birds, insects, and plants. The test consisted of seventy-five questions, including scientific names for plants and weird names for various things scattered throughout the bush. I was particularly proud of correctly identifying and naming an ootheca, the cocoon of a praying mantis. This was followed by a bird slide and sound test. The results came immediately, and I was pleased with my performance. After breakfast, we tackled the final two exams: navigation and a scenario test for *Viewing Potentially Dangerous Animals*.

30th January 2014

Today was hot, swelteringly hot. From a navigation perspective, the clear sky helped me orientate using the sun. Now, at the end of the day, I am completely drained and feeling the effects as I write this. In the excitement of the pre-walk preparations, I had left my hat in the Landy. Since this was my assessment walk, I did not want to use the spare in my bag in case a guest needed it. In hindsight, that was a bit stupid.

I led the walk to Palm Springs on the Sand Veld, with Ben acting as Back-up. My group consisted of four people, including Dee and two armed individuals, Bruce and Korbus. The walk proceeded smoothly despite the disappointment of no encounters. I blotted my copybook when I needed to backtrack after taking the group over a ridge into the thick bush. There was no way I would go any further, especially with the assessor's wife among my clients.

I'll be eternally grateful to Ben for pointing me in the right direction of the Landy when I was about to march the group the opposite way as our walk was ending. Navigation is clearly not a strength of mine.

Ben led the walk in the afternoon, and I was his back-up. We headed to the Sand Veld again but walked into an unfamiliar area. The trail progressed with perfection until near the end, when Bruce, who was at the back of the line, decided to stop walking whilst the rest of us continued. This happened twice. The first time, we were tipped off, and the second time, we hadn't got far, maybe fifteen feet, before we noticed. Still, it was quite a balls-up; I should have noticed.

I'm not sure if this constitutes a fail, I guess we'll find out tomorrow when we have our debrief. We received our theory results this evening; I got a perfect pass in both sections, so my qualification hangs on tomorrow's meeting.

Now and then, I feel a pang of homesickness; this evening was one of those moments, and it hit hard. Was it a genuine desire to go home and get on with my life, or was it just sunstroke and anxiety over the test results?

31st January 2014

Getting up this morning was tough—everyone was dog tired. The course is demanding, especially if you throw yourself into it and add on the daily fitness sessions. The morning walk was blistering hot, and I was still feeling the effects of yesterday's sun.

After breakfast, I joined Bruce on the deck of his tent for my assessment meeting. I wasn't sure which way it was going to go, and I started off the session with a critique of both my *Lead* and *Back-up*. Bruce thought I was being harsh on myself and gave me encouragement. However, he held no punches with his constructive feedback. He mainly focused on the importance of keeping my head up when walking–which I admit, is fundamental—and on my positioning at breaks amongst other things, including…

'James, I enjoyed the overview of basalt that you

gave. It was excellent. Unfortunately, the rock in front of you was sandstone.'

The meeting was thirty minutes; the conclusion was I'd done well with my *Lead* and gave me a competitive score. Likewise, for the *Back-up,* but it came with caveats. Critically, he passed me as competent. I am now a qualified *FGASA* Back-up. But the best part, Bruce offered me a placement as Second Rifle at Makuleke and Mashatu.

1st February 2014

Heavy rain from the middle of the night through to lunch kept us camp bound with no walks. This allowed me to talk to Dee about my placement. When everyone else leaves on Tuesday, I'm going to stay on for the next three weeks before taking leave to meet Mum and Dad, as well as my brother and sister-in-law in Cape Town.

Walking trails is what I've wanted to do from the start of this journey. Alan, early in the Trail's course, said that from a safari point of view,

'Driving is like watching the movie, but walking is like reading the book'.

He's spot on with this analogy: when you're walking there's no distracting engine noise, no smell of diesel or earth shuddering vibrations. Instead, your senses come alive and prosper. On walks you see and hear the full life of the bush and notice tiny things, the things that make the bush tick, the termites and dung beetles that if lost would bring the entire ecosystem crashing down. On a walking safari, you can absorb and be absorbed.

The rain cancelled our fitness session, but Bruce set us the challenge of doing 500 push-ups in a day which Cliff, Jomi and I managed within two-and-a-half hours. There really wasn't much else to do. Back home, I would have wasted those hours slouched on the sofa watching trash tele.

2nd February 2014

Today marked the first time I opted to drive over walking. I wanted to support Ulrica in her *FGASA* assessment drive, and it proved to be the right decision. Firstly, because she passed, and secondly, because thirty minutes in, we witnessed an incredible sighting. We were watching a woodland kingfisher when Annalise spotted a female leopard lying up in the long grass below the magnificent blue and white bird.

The female leopard watched us for a while, her tail flicking before she charged. This reaction stemmed from our spotting her despite her camouflage and now looking directly at her. A golden rule when bumping a leopard on foot is to avoid eye contact. Once the cat realises they have been seen, it is fight-or-flight.

3rd February 2014

We scored a sleep in with the rain coming down hard. I occupied myself with light duties to introduce myself to the role of Back-up. My task was simple: strip and clean two rifles. I was happy with the job I did — until I discovered a part of the second rifle left on the table. This is ok when you're building IKEA furniture but not when you're reassembling a rifle.

Cliff and I carried on with our preparations for fines night, the *charges* needed to be edgy but not offensive, after all, we weren't on a rugby tour. Cliff is a comedy genius, so this wasn't a problem. The rest of the day was taken up with some road repairs and then a final fitness session with the regulars.

Fines night was a success; everyone took their punishment in good spirit. Even those that thought it disgusting to drink from a dirty old boot still stepped up and took their medicine.

4th February 2014

Some sore heads this morning, mine included. Despite this, the entire camp was up and sat around the deck chatting with relative animation over steaming cups of tea and coffee.

My first duty of placement was to take the group to the gate to meet their transport back to the city. Saying goodbye to everyone was tough—I've made some great friends throughout the course. But the fear of missing out was the hardest pill to swallow, they'll be going to the airport's Keg and Aviator tonight, and I'll be left here.

Driving back to camp, I felt alone and down. Lots of crazy thoughts going through my mind. But I realised this is what I wanted; I'm driving a Land Cruiser through the African bush. It's just me, no instructors, this is my life for the next six months, possibly longer.

I caught up with Wien who was driving the Landy ahead of me. I pulled up behind his stationary vehicle to watch a hyena having a satisfying roll in a muddy puddle. We drove on, passing half a dozen zebra. Scenes like these took my mind off being left behind.

Walking back into camp, once again it hit me. It was all but deserted. There was nobody on the deck studying or playing cards, nobody around the fire pit having a smoke, and no laughter coming from the usual tents. I felt homesick, and if someone offered me a flight back home, I'd jump at it.

If I did head home now, I'd be unrecognisable. Gone is the paunch. Instead, I have a lean body with a flat stomach. There is no six-pack. That will never happen, mainly because I like six-packs of beer more than I like sit-ups. The cricketer's tan is still there, but my arms and face now glow with a deeper chestnut sheen.

Back-up Jomi showed me the ropes for my new role. First, it was restocking the drinks fridge. This took longer than usual given the hammering it got last night. Then a tutorial on how to operate the generator, including what not to do that would cause the camp's lifeblood to seize up and fail. The worst chore was left to last, emptying the fat trap.

The fat trap in one form or another has been around since Victorian times. It is a piece of plumbing which prevents grease and solids from entering the water disposal system. In our version, there was a plastic bucket which I had to reach down to and pull free. The contents were buried on the edge of camp, along with the campfire ash.

After breakfast, we packed away two dome tents, and I moved into my new quarters. It's going to be strange having a new roomie, well two new roomies. I'm going to get on well with Jomi and Wien, but I have shared with Ben pretty much one hundred per cent of my time over the course, so it won't be the same.

We welcomed the new guests to camp with afternoon tea before they went out on a game drive. As soon as I heard the roar of the vehicle as it drove off, I instantly regretted not going with them. I'd opted to stay in camp to write some emails to send on the rubbish run in the morning. Staying back gave me the opportunity to chat with Dee about anything and everything which lifted my spirits. Regardless of all my time out here, today was the hardest for missing home. I guess I'd lost my surrogate family of the last five months.

CHAPTER NINE

The magic thing about home is that it feels good to leave, and it feels even better to come back.' *Wendy Wunder, Children's Author.*

EcoTraining, Makuleke
6th February 2014

It was weird doing duty without my sidekick, Ben, but with only four guests, it wasn't onerous. When they left on their game drive, we, the Back-ups, drove to Lala Palm floodplain and spent three hours pulling out the invasive *Datura.* Wearing gloves to protect me from the thorns, the plant was relatively easy to pull. With large white trumpet-shaped flowers, this was an attractive plant. We needed to remove as many as we could before the pods burst and the river flooded, dispersing the seed even further.

One of *Datura's* pseudonyms is moonflower; this refers to the fact that it blooms at night with the flowers opening in the early evening. It's other names, and it has many, include devil's trumpets, hell's bells, and deadly nightshade, all of which refer to its sinister side. The seeds and flowers are poisonous, and the plant has been used over millennia for a variety of reasons. The Aztecs used it for divination and medical purposes including local anaesthetic. They fully understood its potency and the potential side effect of madness. The Native Americans used it for its hallucinogenic properties in ceremonies. That particular use has caused several deaths in contemporary times with people ingesting it to get high.

After lunch, we set off for a walk—my first as a qualified Back-up. I felt a mix of nerves and excitement. The feedback from my assessment was fresh in my mind, providing me with plenty to work on. Jomi took the lead with Bruce in the party too. The walk to the pan was two hours with no encounters. A gentle introduction.

While taking a break, I placed a round upside down in the muzzle of my rifle. This was a ploy to stop dust from getting in the barrel. This seemed sensible, it's what everybody does. The only difference is that most, if not all, remember they've done it. We were crossing the floodplain when I realised I was one round short. My mind surged into overdrive.

'This is not good, not good at all. What do I do? It could have dropped anywhere; I'll never find it. Do I keep quiet? I need to stay quiet; I'll keep quiet. Bruce will flip. I'll keep quiet. I can't keep quiet, that's irresponsible, I can't leave the round of a large calibre rifle lying around the bush. No, I can't keep quiet, anyhow. All the ammunition is signed out, and must be signed back in. I need to confess, the longer I leave it, the further away we'll be.'

Here it goes. 'Bruce, I've…'

Luckily, I found it straight away when we returned to our rest spot. But that didn't stop Bruce presenting me with a dummy round on a piece of paracord at dinner. I must now wear this around my neck.

The journey back was the highlight. I operated the spotlight with the reward of being splattered by countless insects attracted to the equivalent of ten million candles. The peppering was worth it, though—first, we spotted a pair of black-backed jackals, and then, a leopard.

We spent ten minutes with the cat who approached the vehicle. This was interesting, given my legs dangled from the tracker seat. We followed her along the road, watching her spray bushes as she went. The drive back was complete with a genet lounging in the fork of a dead tree beside the road.

8th February 2014

It started raining at nine o'clock last night and didn't let up until lunchtime, delivering over a hundred millimetres. The camp was flooded with many fast-flowing channels cutting through it. The drainage line transformed into a raging torrent; you could easily see how people get washed away in these situations. We walked out of camp and up to Middle Road, which was completely submerged. We threaded our way around to the floodplain which lived up to its name. Rather than heading back, we spent the next hour pulling *Datura.* The phrase 'shutting the stable door after the horse had bolted' came to mind.

Aside from my goal of qualifying as a Lead Trails Guide, another reason I wanted to stay on at Makuleke rather than start afresh somewhere else was to be settled and established ahead of my family's visit. First up would be the arrival of my brother Johnny and his wife, Emma. I can't wait to show off the reserve, which I'm becoming proud and protective of. Their visit is giving me an extra incentive to study. I'll hopefully surprise them with my knowledge, but regardless of how much I know or don't know, they'll be bowled over by what they'll see here.

Being from a close family leaves me conflicted about my stay in Africa. On one hand, I see this as the gap year that it is. On the other hand, I want to be paid to walk trails for a year or two. After which, I can head home to the UK with experience and credibility. Both of which should stand me in good stead when looking for a senior management position in a zoo or safari park. Whatever happens, I can't see myself being away from home for too long. Still, I shouldn't be stressing about this now, there's plenty of time until decisions must be made. Alan McSmith shared the following quote with us earlier in the year, which is now making sense. I've tried to find the source with no success:

'If you are depressed, you are living in the past. If you are anxious, you are living in the future. If you are at peace, you are living in the present.'

10th February 2014

I experienced my first encounter as an official Back-up this morning; it was like my first on the Trails' course a month ago. We were walking to Masashiti Springs following fresh buffalo tracks. We didn't realise how fresh; a sudden crash and the thunder of hooves caught us off guard. Bruce dropped his stick and went to make his rifle ready; I followed suit and swung my rifle towards my right shoulder with my palm open, prepared to work the bolt. All was fine as the buffalo bolted away from us. Further down the trail, we bumped him again before we decided to take a wide berth. If we'd pushed him, he was likely to get the hump and turn on us.

We'd almost reached the vehicle when one guest, Marianne, announced she'd left her glasses at Masashiti Lookout. The rest of the trail carried on, and I returned to see if I could find them. This was a dream come true —walking through the African bush alone with just a rifle for company. The experience would've been even better if I'd found the glasses. But there was no chance of that; I couldn't even find the ledge we'd been sitting on. After forty-five minutes, I returned with the bad news, admitting that I wasn't entirely sure I'd been searching in the right spot.

We returned in the afternoon and found Marianne's glasses. After the walk, Bruce and Dee continued on to Wilderness Safaris, leaving me to take the guests back to camp. This was the first time I'd been alone with paying guests in a game vehicle.

My positive disposition and friendly nature

masked any lack of confidence about my ability. Being a nice guy goes a long way. The web of life was now my job to interpret and share with my audience.

As we drove back, I spotted a Swainson's spurfowl. I turned off the engine, said a few words, and we watched it. I don't know if those in the vehicle realised, they had become the recipients for my first piece of official guiding. I realised guiding isn't about standing up and presenting, it's about letting nature do the talking. I'm here to add more if people want it.

While I'm doing what I love, I started questioning what I'm doing here. I guess I was missing family and friends. I'm a long way from home with little telecoms to keep in touch. Today feels like another one of those homesick days.

12th February 2014

A full-on day of Back-up duties, first up I walked second rifle for Bruce with the EcoQuest students to Hutwini Gorge. With summer here, the mornings are cooler, so I donned my fleece as I prepped for the walk. Preparations meant setting up the teas and coffees, finalising my kit, signing out a rifle and then getting the Landy ready. For the latter, I got all mechanical and got my spanner out to change the battery. Back home I'd have paid someone to do this for me.

It got hot quickly, and despite walking through thick mopane, there was little shade. We were on the trail of a breeding herd of elephants for a while but never caught up with them. We headed to Hutwini

Lookout for a break. As we approached our spot, we heard the faintest sound: a hoof clicking on a rock. Then came a crash as a buffalo broke cover, charging through the trees.

Like a few days ago, my rifle instinctively swung to my shouldering side. However, with a clear view of the buffalo, it quickly became apparent that we had startled him more than he had startled us. He turned to give us a cautious once-over, but that was all he intended to do.

Straight after breakfast, I headed out in the Landy with Jomi and a full trailer to run some errands. This included dropping chef Olivia and housekeeper Alisha at the doctors. Then it was a mad dash to make it to the dump before it closed. A mad dash is the correct phrase, the vehicle used for the rubbish run is a Landy that's designed for game viewing. There are no seat belts, no door, no roof and no windscreen. When I wasn't weaving in and out of cows, goats, donkeys, and potholes, I was steering with one hand while holding my hat in place with the other.

Everyone I passed seemed super friendly, including the children who ran alongside, shouting and wanting to know our names. It's like the Africa you see in Disney movies.

The rubbish run is as it sounds. All the wet waste and recycling is hauled onto the Landy and trailer along with empty petrol and diesel jerry cans. There is, however, a silver lining, and that's a mobile signal strong enough to download and send emails.

Our destination for this trip is a coal mine, I

mean this literally. On arrival, Jomi hopped out to open the gates before we drove straight into the jet-black landscape, which was the mine complex. From a Health & Safety point of view this wouldn't happen back home. It seemed bizarre that we could do it here.

Solomon, a chirpy chappie at the mine, greeted us and helped us with the unloading. I presumed this was his real name, not one he'd adopted because he worked at a mine. I knew of the book King Solomon's Mines, but I didn't realise how influential it was. Apparently, it's the first English adventure novel set in Africa. It is believed to be the forerunner in the lost world literary genre.

He must have thought me stupid not to minimise the distance we had to carry waste by not backing the trailer up to the rubbish bays. This was not stupidity but a lack of skill on my behalf as I'm still to learn how to reverse with a trailer on. But what I am perfecting is the switcheroo handshake pump. Here the hand is rotated and switched vertically between two positions, either side of the thumb with a gentle fist pump at the end thrown in for good measure.

After the mucky job of unloading and sorting the rubbish, it was onto the One-Stop shop to pick up the mail and grab the odds and ends that Dee requested. While the shop staff filled the jerry cans, we did some personal shopping, downloaded emails, made phone calls, and indulged in ice cream. The trip took four hours, during which I committed the error of not putting any sun cream on my knees. Ouch.

14th February 2014

It was my turn to back-up the morning walk, an excellent start to any day. We drove to the Sand Veld to walk Palm Springs. Right from the beginning, it was clear there were elephants about. This followed through with a sighting of two bulls at thirty metres. The visibility wasn't excellent, but that didn't matter. It was my first elephant on foot as a qualified Back-up. The encounter was smooth with the wind in our favour and several escape routes. Still, most importantly, the elephants seemed unaware of our presence.

As we made our way back to the vehicle, we passed through a clearing where Bruce was charged by an elephant cow last year. He talked us through the incident, and it was clear how dangerous these animals can be. The event showed how vital the role of the Back-up is. On this occasion, they saved Bruce's life by driving the elephant off him. It was a stark reminder that this is no game.

We spent the time between the morning and afternoon activity slashing the long grass around camp. I enjoyed this task despite the work leaving my hand red-raw between the thumb and index finger. After a shower to freshen up, Dee asked me to take the afternoon game drive. This was special; it was my first time taking out clients for a dedicated game drive. This time, it wasn't a case of driving them from A to B and stopping for some animals in between. No, this is what they paid hard-earned cash for and given up the one thing they can't get more of, time, the most precious commodity on earth.

Marianne wanted to see elephants; well, she wanted to see elephants at less than five metres, so quite a tall order. We headed to the Sand Veld and saw some fresh signs, and then Manfred spotted what we were after. A small breeding herd eighty metres away and heading into the mopane. Marianne didn't get her five-metre worth, but we got ele, so the job was half done.

After sundowners, we ventured to the far end of the concession, and that's when things took an embarrassingly wrong turn. Both figuratively and literally. I got hopelessly lost. Rather than bearing left, I turned right and ended up at Crooks Corner. A nagging feeling told me I was off course, but I convinced myself it would all come together. It didn't. As the frog calls intensified and a narrow track led me deeper into the Fever Tree Forest, I knew I was properly lost. In the fading light, I executed a seven-point turn and retraced our path back the way we came.

In Africa, dusk comes fast, and there is no escaping the night that quickly follows. Before long, complete darkness surrounded us. I had no real sense of where camp lay, but I kept driving anyway.

I eventually bit the bullet and stopped to explain the situation to my vehicle chock-a with clients. My predicament didn't surprise them; Manfred, a regular at Makuleke, had figured out I was lost ages ago. I couldn't have asked for a better group to get lost with—they were good-humoured and eager to help.

While Manfred knew how hopelessly lost I'd

become, he couldn't guide me back to camp, and I wasn't getting us there without some outside help. There was only one option left: I had to radio camp—and hope Bruce wasn't the one who picked up.

'EcoTraining, EcoTraining James for EcoTraining Camp

Immediately came a response, 'Go ahead for EcoTraining Bruce'

'Oh well', I thought — 'he was going to know about this anyway, and he's the best person to get me and my guests back safe and sound.'

'Hello Bruce, James here, everything is ok, but I appear to be temporarily disorientated…'

Once we'd established my location, getting back was straightforward. It was merely a case of turning around again, and heading back along the same road, but this time keeping right.

The worst thing about using the radio to sort things out is that everyone on the concession hears it. Even if I said, 'go up one' to take the conversation onto the next channel for privacy, it would have made no difference. Everyone would go up one themselves to find out what was going on. In the bush, the radio was the equivalent of an awful soap opera with nothing else for competition.

The drive wasn't a complete write off as I stopped for two-spotted hyena which we watched for a quarter of an hour as they sniffed around the Landy. We also parked in the middle of a breeding herd of buffalo and saw another hyena before finally making it back to camp.

While the guests were in high spirits on arriving

back at camp, I can't say the same for Olivia and Alisha. They felt rightly miffed at me. My moment of exploration meant we didn't sit down to eat until nine o'clock, which ate into their personal time.

Despite everything that happened, we ended up having a fun evening. Dee was supportive, sharing stories of her own misadventures getting lost on the concession, and a few Castle Lites helped lighten the mood.

Guiding is all about creating memories. In that sense, my first drive was a success—it's a journey none of us will forget.

16th February 2014

As soon as we stepped off the vehicle at Masashiti Quarry, we promptly noticed fresh elephant and buffalo tracks. After fifty paces we realised how new the ele tracks were. A bull suddenly charged out from the trees, giving us a fright. He held himself high, making it clear who was boss from the opposite side of a large puddle. At twenty metres away, he was quite a sight, and for a moment, time stood still as my heart pounded.

The ele made another lunge as if to come through the water at us. Bruce dropped his stick to be ready with his rifle. I took a deep breath to compose myself.

Luckily, the elephant reconsidered; however, he veered around the water to investigate what we were. In response, we moved in the opposite direction, keeping as much of the water between us as possible.

In the end, he strode one way and we in a different direction as we carried on our walk.

The rest of the trail, all five hours of it, was as eventful with a further six encounters, all buffalo. This left us shattered, it's totally draining being on constant alert. I suppose it's like driving fast along a motorway; you must keep concentrating, or you could end up having a nasty accident.

Once we delivered the guests back to camp, I drove to Pafuri Gate to pick Jomi up before taking the afternoon game drive. I intended to make this one more successful than my last one. It was, but it certainly wasn't without its challenges.

The Landy's battery failed halfway through, leaving us unable to switch off the engine and without headlights. We navigated back using a torch for light—though this beam would vanish from the road each time Jomi got distracted by movement in the bushes. It was a long, exhausting drive back, but it delivered some fantastic sightings: spotted hyena, buffalo, and a black-backed jackal.

Nearing home, the lack of light seemed to hone Jomi's senses.

'Can you smell the popcorn?' He said. 'There should be a leopard nearby.'

As we rounded the corner, there he was—a big male, strolling down the middle of the road, his back to us. He paused, casting a glance over his shoulder, eyes glowing in the torch's beam. My feet stayed planted on the brake and clutch. Stalling wasn't an option—we had no doors, no windscreen, no roof, and no lights. One slip, and we'd lose all power. And if things went south, Jomi, perched on the tracker's seat just metres away, would likely be his prey.

The leopard carried on his chosen course, switching from one side of the road to the other to get maximum coverage as he sprayed the bushes with his scent. The olfactory marking was the buttery popcorn clue that Jomi had noticed. Our leopard did this for another fifty metres before disappearing off-road and into his night.

19th February 2014

My trip to the rubbish dump was made enjoyable with an enormous bull elephant standing by the road ten minutes from camp. He seemed moody but soon settled back to feeding, much to my relief, as my reversing a trailer wouldn't happen. It was probably the same elephant that had been outside our tent last night. This was my new normal— sleeping in a tent, elephants browsing over my head, leopards patrolling the perimeter and hyena cackling on the floodplain.

Sitting in the Landy watching the elephant feed on the mopane — I couldn't help but think, 'what was my old normal? Do I want to go back to it? And what would make me go back?'

My old normal was London, a city forever synonymous with noise, crowds, anxiety, loneliness, stress, and frustration. No, I didn't want to return—at least not to that London-style existence. But there was one thing that could draw me back to that kind of life: being close to family.

The afternoon game drive was successful. At the Luvuvuh bridge, we saw one of the concession's specials, a Pel's fishing owl. I'm still not there yet with my birds to understand why people get so excited by them. However, I radioed it in with the confidence of somebody who knew exactly what they were looking at. For me, the real special—as always—was the leopard sighting that capped off the day as nightfall approached.

CHAPTER TEN

'Sometimes you will never know the value of the moment until it becomes a memory.' *Dr Seuss, Children's Author.*

Western Cape
21st February to 4th March 2014

For two days, my cousins looked after me in Johannesburg before I flew to Cape Town, where Mum and Dad picked me up from the airport. The reunions continued at my aunt and uncle's farm in Villiersdorp when brother Johnny and his wife Emma came by for a braai before continuing their belated honeymoon.

After five nights at the farm, it was on to Cape Town for the next leg of leave, but only after a quick visit to the barbers, doctors and dentist with the latter threatening a root canal.

Entertainment in the city included corporate hospitality at the rugby for a *Super 15s* match. The Stormers won by one point in a last-minute thriller. This was followed the next day with hospitality for the cricket Test Match between South Africa and Australia. We squeezed in a family visit to Hidden Valley vineyard for a spot of wine tasting. On the last afternoon, we ate afternoon tea at the Mount Nelson Hotel with some family friends.

My entire week's leave was terrific. Lovely spending so much time with family and friends. We went to some great restaurants and spent time at the Kelvin Grove private members' club. It was a far cry from life in the bush, and given my decadent living, fitness took a back seat.

This opulent lifestyle ended when Johnny, Emma, and I tried to find our guest house after flying up to Joburg. This entailed driving through the airport suburbs looking for our accommodation in the pouring rain. We weaved our way through sketchy areas complete with prostitutes. Even when we reached the right address, the surroundings didn't improve.

EcoTraining Makuleke
4th March 2014

We set off early from the guest house for our seven-hour drive to Makuleke. The weather was rotten, with rain pelting down, making our departure tentative. Along the way, we jotted down meticulous notes of way markers and service stations to help Mum and Dad make the same journey a week later.

As we got near to Kruger's Pafuri gate, I was clearly getting excited. Excited about returning to the bush, but most of all about showing it off to Johnny and Emma for the next four days.

We made excellent time and unloaded before Wien arrived. Thankfully, the weather shifted, now 30 degrees and humid. It was a pleasure to climb into the Landy and have the wind cooling us down as we drove to camp. On the way we saw an ele, which was a relief—I'd been worried Johnny and Emma might not get to see one during their visit.

We were given a warm welcome at camp, and after lunch, I took them out on an exclusive drive. Guiding them was a fantastic thing for me to do. I felt proud to be showing them around my back garden. I'm confident they enjoyed it, especially with the thrill of seeing plenty of buffalo and a massive bull elephant.

5th March 2014

Johnny, Emma, and I went for a drive in the morning while the rest walked. The sunrise was breathtaking, with the mist hanging above the ground like something out of a movie set. Emma, much to my brother's concern, was quick to conclude that I'd never leave this place. If the African bush came with family and friends, she'd be right, but it doesn't. But there is one thing for sure; I'll find it hard to live in a big city like London again.

After seeing the only ostrich in the area last night, we saw the only two giraffes on the concession this morning. There were lots more buffalo on our drive, as well as the little things that fascinated Johnny and Emma. They said they were realising there was more to a safari than chasing cats, which was music to my ears, although I'm not sure I believed them.

After lunch I was on official rifle-toting back-up duty, meaning Johnny and Emma saw me doing what I loved. For the walk Emma tested her new GPS and heart rate monitor. Each time we entered the long grass, her pulse shot up, reinforcing why it has the name, adrenaline grass. There was plenty of game to spot despite having no close encounters. With Bruce as Lead giving them his full attention, Emma and Johnny learned a lot.

I loved walking with my bro. The only downside being I didn't get the chance to talk like we would have done on a drive. They both enjoyed themselves and are eager to go again tomorrow—likely influenced by the sundowners under the big baobab, Mr. BB, which is always something special.

7th March 2014

Johnny and Emma's stay ended this morning. They were upgrading, leaving Makuleke to stay in a luxury safari lodge in southern Kruger. They joined me at five-fifteen for the food run so they'd get an early start for their long journey.

We were delayed having stopped to watch a hyena for a while and then a big breeding herd of buffalo. Once there, I loaded the trailer while Emma and Johnny packed the car and prepared to leave. We said our goodbyes, and they followed me as far as they could before I turned off to camp, but not before one last farewell. Then they were off, heading east along Pafuri Main into the morning sun.

8th March 2014

We earned our breakfast — well, lunch really — after a mammoth six-hour walk this morning. It proved hard going up and down ridges, through thick bush on such a humid day with the thermometer hitting thirty-two. The idea of walking so long was to get encounters, but all we managed was a lone buffalo bull.

Because we were back late, there was no afternoon activity. Instead, we endured a Brutal Bruce fitness session and then drove to the Outpost for the rugby.

The latest warring of my inner mind is that if I stay longer in Africa, perhaps another year, it will look stronger on my CV. The counterargument is that a gap year is a common occurrence, and one year out of business should not put me far behind. Who knows what the right answer is? I don't think I do, and I know if I asked family back home, they would be on the side of returning sooner rather than later.

9th March 2014

After breakfast, I had a perfect excuse to miss fitness; I was meeting Mum and Dad at Masisi. While waiting, five local children joined me, clearly enjoying themselves as they sat in and climbed all over the Land Rover.

My parents appeared remarkably fresh after their long journey. That was until they stepped out of their air-conditioned car. At this point, they found the heat and humidity a shock.

Back at camp, I'd settled my folks into their tent and shared the obligatory cup of tea before taking the Landy for a trundle. We didn't spot any big game, but driving Mum and Dad around was amazing nonetheless. They seemed relaxed and content with my four-by-four skills—quite a contrast from the roads of Yorkshire, where I last drove them.

10th March 2014

The weather was miserable this morning, and at one point, I thought the rain might force us to stop. Fortunately, we managed to carry on with what turned out to be only a brief shower. We certainly fared better than those who visited the shooting range twenty k to the west at the far end of the concession. The torrential rain they received meant they aborted after two shooters.

Luck was on our side during the afternoon drive. We saw plenty of zebra, kudu, and jackal, along with buffalo, impala, nyala, and a lively troop of baboons, who quickly became favourites. The rarest sighting was a trio of ground hornbills at Rhino Boma, just as we headed to the bridge for sundowners.

As we made our way back to camp, we heard a leopard calling. I became excited and suggested we take a detour to see if we could see it. Mum wasn't keen to be charging around the African bush at night looking for a big cat. I think she was more worried about me getting lost than anything else. Dad, however, got caught up in the moment. On one occasion his standard calm exterior gave way to boyish excitement when the spotlight caught the eyes of an animal on the road ahead. I loved seeing this side of him and wished for a leopard instead of an impala — it would have really made his day.

11th March 2014

This morning's mission was to find elephants, but luck wasn't on our side. We broke up the drive with a cup of tea at Mutale Weir. Mum and Dad reassured me that they weren't here for the big game—they'd come to see me, to understand my world and better picture it when they returned home. I needed little more encouragement to carry on boring them with everything I'd learned so far. With tea in hand, I went about interpreting the tell-tale signs of the animals that had trodden the sand the night before. If I wasn't pointing out a track, I was picking up herbivore poo and opening it up to show its consistency. I acted like an overexcited toddler. If anyone could appreciate this enthusiasm, it was my parents—they'd seen it all before, some thirty-five years ago.

Tomorrow morning's drive is the last chance to show Mum and Dad ele and leopard. For today they'll have to settle for the only ostrich on the concession and a member of Kruger's Big Six birds, the saddle billed stork.

It's been amazing having my folks here; it's great they know where I am, what I'm doing and how much I'm enjoying it. Dad told me he gets why I've done what I've done. That was reassuring. No matter how old or independent you are, you always want the approval of your parents.

I would be satisfied and contented if my year in Africa finished today. The moments I spent guiding my family made this experience the most wonderful I could have imagined.

13th March 2014

Mum and Dad left camp just in time. After the flood warnings yesterday, the heavens opened in the early hours of the morning. I was secretly hoping the rain wouldn't stop as I was drained and did not fancy a couple of long, hot walks. But the sheer power of rain in Africa can never be a convenience. We had ninety mils, turning the drainage lines into raging torrents through camp once more.

I maximised the downtime through self-study, ploughing through countless species and noting fascinating facts about each that would surprise my guests. The plan for the afternoon was to walk, but that didn't materialise. Instead, the three of us Back-ups stayed in camp to carry out light maintenance and general chores. While we dirtied our hands, the students embarked on a birding drive which yielded a decent leopard sighting, twenty-four hours too late for my folks.

15th March 2014

Jomi and Wien both walked this morning. This left me in camp to go about basic duties. Instead, I ended up entertaining two of the four children staying in camp. The other two, still toddlers, usually stuck close to their mum. The ones with me seemed about seven or eight, but they knew their stuff. We checked out the skulls and bones on the study deck, then browsed the library before walking the fire break to see what we could spot. I enjoyed myself. This is what guiding is about, inspiring the next generation to love and protect wildlife.

I walked in the afternoon but not with the Trails group. Instead, I took one of the freelance instructors, Brendan, out to show him the area. Given my navigational issues, I'm not sure I was the best person for the job. Still, I wasn't going to turn down the opportunity to walk.

Before setting off, we took a moment to discuss what to do if a situation unfolded. He said,

'Should something happen. I only have two commands. The first is 'WARNING' for you to fire a warning shot and the second is 'KILL'. I never fire a warning shot so if I fire it is open season'.

The reason for the First Rifle or Lead Guide never firing a warning shot is because they would not have time to reload should the animal not heed the warning. If a warning shot was to be fired, it would be by the Second Rifle aka the Back-up.

This was a stark reminder to me that this is not the proverbial walk in the park. I need to concentrate.

That evening, Bruce's voice crackled over the radio at ten o'clock, waking us up. He and Dee had gotten bogged down on a rough stretch of road while returning from the lodge. They were in a Land Cruiser so needed the Landy to pull them out. Built for these conditions, the Land Rover tackled the task effortlessly, and we had them unstuck and back home in no time.

16th March 2014

No walking today. Instead, we spent the day fixing roads. The work felt hard under the sun but rewarding, and after five hours we returned to camp, proud of what we'd achieved. As a bonus, a spotted hyena appeared from the scrub to watch our efforts.

After breakfast, Dee and I drove to the rest camp at Punda Maria to fill up the jerry cans with petrol and diesel. It was refreshing to see another part of the Kruger, as well as a few elephant bulls along the way. Knowing we wouldn't be back in time for lunch, I did my usual on reaching civilisation. I gorged myself on chocolate and crisps.

Once back at camp, I put a solid couple of hours into my studies before joining Bruce and Dee on their deck. One drink turned into a few, and then many more over dinner. During the meal, Jack and Michelle shared their experience of a remarkable kill they'd witnessed. From their deck they watched a two-metre-long black mamba raiding a squirrel's nest. It was a bad day for the squirrel, though it managed to escape with its life—at least for a moment. Fixated on the mamba from a safe distance, it shook its tail in alarm, oblivious to the genet behind it. In an instant, the small cat-like predator pounced, pretty much two generations of squirrel wiped out in a blink of an eye. The wild is a dangerous place. I wish the genet had gone for the mamba and then something took the genet. It would have made the nursery rhyme, 'I Know an Old Lady Who Swallowed a Fly', appear very tame indeed.

18th March 2014

Jomi and I dropped the students at the quarry to walk to the first campsite of their two-night wilderness sleep out.

This left the two of us with no duties, so we headed to Rhino Boma to walk for encounters. It was the first time we'd been allowed to go solo. No one accompanied us to prevent poor decisions. The responsibility lay with us, and we were accountable for our actions, which could quickly end in tragedy.

I've never been so conscious of escape routes. With each step forward I mentally noted every termite mound, big tree and rocky ridge that could offer protection should it be needed.

Of all the escape routes possible, the tree choice wasn't my most favoured as the trees tended to be full of thorns. In my mind, the towering mounds built by fungus-growing termites, which reach two to three metres in height, provide excellent refuge — and there are so many of them. Made with a mixture of soil, saliva, and termite faeces the substance dries as hard as concrete and is strong enough to be used as a rubbing post by elephants.

Jomi led, and I backed up. We began our walk by climbing the hill to scan the plain and locate the buffalo. There were two herds in the area. We snuck up on the first before picking up the second on our return to the truck. Two more for the tally.

20th March 2014

The baboons woke me this morning, along with a large herd of impala that had taken over camp. That all changed the moment I went to put the kettle on—my bipedal presence sent them scattering in all directions.

Today was all work and no play. First up, a trip to the rubbish dump, which took longer than usual due to San Pad Road being out of commission.

At the dump, I had to do some running repairs as the alternator wasn't charging the battery. Once finished, and with a push start from Solomon and his colleagues, I was on my way.

The worst part of the rubbish run isn't the rubbish itself but the empty gas cylinders that we must take in and swap for full ones. These weigh a ton, about one-hundred-kilograms each, and hauling them, single-handed, on and off the Landy isn't enjoyable.

22nd March 2014

My cousin Alison and her husband Graham, visiting from Johannesburg, arrived yesterday. It is great to have more family here, although it did prompt Bruce to ask who was next to arrive.

With no walk this morning due to the Trails group's final *ARH* tests, I took Alison and Graham on what turned out to be an epic drive. Sean from Head Office joined us, adding a bit of pressure. However, he proved to be the perfect guest, and any anxiety I felt soon dissipated.

Regardless of my guiding skills, this was a drive that nobody would forget. As we drove west down Pafuri Main, just short of the San Pad turn off, Alison exclaimed,

'Cat'.

And crikey, there was a cat, a huge male leopard.

We followed him for fifteen minutes down the road while he scent marked his territory. He was relaxed, probably knowing nobody would mess with him, including us. He reinforced this by turning his head a few times to check us out over his vast shoulders. This type of attention made my heart race, and only after he disappeared into the drainage line did the pounding in my chest subside.

23rd March 2014

This morning, we walked, an exclusive walk with Bruce, Alison, Graham and myself and one which I led.

With so much water in Nwambe pan and Reed Buck Vlei, the walk was short. This suited Alison and Graham, as they had a long journey to Joburg ahead of them. No heart-pounding encounters this time, but they weren't necessary—walking in Kruger is magical, no matter what you don't see.

On finishing the walk, I set up the coffee station, tablecloth, and all, on the Landy's pull up table. While having our well-earned cuppa, Bruce discovered a baby tree squirrel in the back of the vehicle. It must have fallen from the thatch of the carport at camp. Bruce popped it into his hat, and we took it home. Once back, we left the hat and squirrel in the front seat of the Landy. Surprisingly, the mother returned, picked it up by the scruff of its neck, and took it back to its nest.

24th March 2014

Rhodes arrived in camp with private clients, a father and daughter from Canada. He needed a Back-up, and I was it. The plan was to spend the entire morning pan hopping, so we took a bush breakfast to avoid rushing back to camp.

Once finished, I returned to my tent, shaving after my shower. At that moment, Alisi arrived with my laundry and said,

'James, if you get a chance, can you look for that snake?'

'Which snake?' was my reply, standing there in my towel. To which her answer came,

'The black one that lives under that bed.'

I took a quick look under the beds but found nothing. I must remind the boys to check their sleeping bags tonight.

25th March 2014

Today there was no chance for breakfast or lunch. Instead, I grabbed food where I could. It turned into a busy day, starting with a drive to Punda Maria for fuel.

Once back to camp and unloaded, it was then a dash to the bridge to meet a transfer service to swap the cook and housekeeper over for relief staff. As I pulled into camp daydreaming about a cuppa and a muffin, I met Steve.

Steve Faulconbridge is the Trails Guide who will be running the Pafuri camp where I'll be backing-up. He was after someone to show him the area, so I spent the next fifteen minutes packing my backpack and finding him a rifle and ammo. Any excuse for a walk.

27th March 2014

The rubbish run proved backbreaking. With everyone out walking, I found myself alone at camp, which meant hauling the wet waste onto the trailer by myself. To fully grasp the nature of the beast, wet waste is all the food scraps and juices from camp, gathered into a single wheelie bin.

I couldn't manage the lift unaided, so I improvised steps with the spare tyres. I dragged the deadweight up tyre by tyre before launching the bin over the edge of the trailer gate and onto my foot—cue a massive sense of humour failure on my part.

I took some cans of coke on the bin run for Solomon and his guys as a thank you for helping me out last week.

Coca-Cola goes down well but not as well as old milk crates, people really can't get enough of those. The ladies selling firewood on the side of the road at Masisi looked disappointed when I said they were promised elsewhere; the recipient, Solomon was thrilled.

The round trip is the best part of five hours, I literally baked in the heat for the entire journey, there's no hiding place in an open-top Landy. Given the lack of doors even your feet get cooked.

Once back at camp, it was time to unload the gas, firewood and clean the bins before grabbing breakfast and a well-earned shower, albeit a cold one.

This job isn't nine to five, it's five to nine, it would be an earlier start, but the days are shortening. Luckily, we can't walk in the dark.

That afternoon I backed up the final assessment walk of the week; it was Michelle's turn. She and Jack, an Aussie couple, have been doing the course as a taster. They've learnt so much and gone about everything with professionalism and enthusiasm. I hope they find the outdoor career they're looking for when they go back to Australia next week.

28th March 2014

Over the coming months, I'm working on and off as a freelance Back-up rifle for one of Africa's leading safari companies, Wilderness Safaris. They have a seasonal camp in Makuleke. I'm not sure when my first trail is, but it's going to be soon. Steve and I paid a visit to the campsite this morning to see how it was progressing. The kitchen was set up, and a few of the tents were up as well.

The primary reason for our trip was to plan some walks. This turned out to be great fun; it brought a creative element to the job as we were scoping out experiences we could show our guests.

We did some serious bush bashing with Steve virtually running up cliff faces as he planned the routes. This mountain goat approach to our discovery session left me shattered. After cleaning and securely locking away my rifle, I treated myself to a twenty-minute power nap.

I'm freelancing tomorrow too, this time at the Outpost, which is a five-star lodge in Makuleke. They have a big wedding, so have hired a guide and a vehicle from EcoTraining. I'm the guide, and I washed the Landy. We're pushing the boat out and using the Land Rover with doors. I'm not sure whether I'm driving wedding guests from A to B or acting as their guide.

The Outpost, Makuleke
29th March 2014

Because they were so busy with the wedding, it meant there was no room for me to stay over. Instead, I had a genuine commute to work, in all about an hour and a quarter from camp to camp. A much longer journey than usual as one road is still out of action, but no complaints from me. It beats any of my commutes back in the UK for scenery and congestion.

The day's work wasn't taxing, with a seven-to-seven shift. Upon arrival, I attended the staff meeting, which began with a hymn and a prayer. Then they put me to work—first task, driving to the wedding venue to set out the tables and chairs.

The instructions from my boss for the day, Sarah, left margin for error.

'Please can you set the tables up in the Fever-Tree Forest. I've put a stick in a pile of elephant dung to mark the spot' she said.

Luckily, I followed the guys who visited the site the day before. We found it without a problem.

With the guests, it wasn't a case of providing them with a guided experience. It was driving them to and from the wedding venue. Since leaving them alone in the middle of the bush wasn't an option, we kept a discreet presence nearby, ready to step in if a seven-ton wedding crasher decided to make an appearance.

The bush ceremony continued until sundown. This meant driving back after nightfall. All was fine until — *thud, duff duff duff duff.*

Puncture.

As luck would have it, we were out of Ambush Alley and on the tar road, Pafuri Main.

Changing a tyre with the aid of a high lift jack and all the practice I've had is straight-forward. What was not was keeping ten guests in one safe spot. They were in high spirits despite the momentary stop. The day's steady flow of booze left everyone both emboldened and in urgent need of a wee. With no facilities around, they kept wandering off, ignoring my repeated warnings to stay near the vehicle. There could have been anything in those bushes. Often, I see buffalo along the verges, and I've regularly seen leopard on this stretch of road. Once the tyre was replaced and all ten guests accounted for, we got back on our way.

On the final approach to The Outpost, we literally ate dust from the Landy in front. To give them space and us relief, I killed the engine, switched off the lights and suggested we enjoy the moment. This worked a treat, mainly because there was no moon so the stars popped in the night sky, but I couldn't have scripted the finale, a shooting star which got a collective, *wow*.

With my day at the Outpost over, I dashed back to camp to take part in the Trails group festivities of Fines Night. The drive on a moonless night heightened my senses as I was aware an elephant has the same skin tone as both the tar road and the night sky. If I'd ploughed into an elephant, only one of us would have been walking away — and it wouldn't have been me.

While I played chauffeur, a lot happened. Jack and Michelle got engaged at Langer Gorge, and Dee was flat out in bed with malaria.

EcoTraining, Makuleke
30th March 2014

The Trails group were leaving camp today, so I was back on wake-up duty. While getting the teas and coffee ready in the kitchen, I found myself in a comical tug-of-war with a rat over a bag of bread—luckily, I won.

After dropping the students at Pafuri Gate, we enjoyed a relaxed breakfast before a few of us headed to Mr. BBs to collect my camera trap.

It was a frustrating walk as I failed to find the location after getting disorientated in the ridges. I thought it was going to be quick and straightforward.

This was a low point in my guiding and something that comes up time and time again, my poor sense of direction. Knowing where you are is essential when you're leading guests into the wilds of Africa. Episodes like this eat at my confidence

After a day of introspection and a period of flip-flopping between options, I finally decided not to stay in Africa—I would go home. No single event pushed me over the edge, not even getting lost again. I suppose I'd come to realise how important family is to me. I want what my parents have; they genuinely seem happy.

We all learn from our parents, and as Prince Charles once said,

'I learned the way a monkey learns - by watching its parents.'

I'm wrestling with a business idea that would see me having the best of both worlds, a life in Africa, in the bush I love and one in England with the family I love. The Afrikaans have a phrase for this, Soutie or Sout Piel. This means salt penis. It stems from some Brits having one leg in the UK and one in South Africa, leaving the penis hanging in the saltwater. The concept sounds great. Making it a reality will require hard work, money, and some luck. I have about five months of cash for living expenses back home. After that if I'm not well on the road for the Soutie life, then it's midlife crisis over and time to find a job in a zoo and set myself up to enjoy village living. Ultimately, I want somewhere to call home.

1st April 2014

Another early morning workout with Bruce was on the agenda today. It included the bench press, which is never fun, especially when looking closer at what is living on the underside. We found a sac spider, a violin spider and a brown button spider, three of the most venomous spiders in the world. Knowing they were there encouraged me belt out the reps in no time.

Hoedspruit
2nd to 6th April 2014

Dee surfaced from her malaria induced absence and announced that if I wanted to take leave, I could do so. It would be with immediate effect, and it wouldn't be for long, four nights only. So, I was off, but without a plan.

Jomi lent me his car, a white Nissan 1400 Champion — 'The Champ', as it was known. Its most defining characteristic was its size — like a Tonka toy, it was tiny. When you're sat close to the ground and pull up next to an elephant, you feel small. As small as a mouse. But it works and works well despite the odd quirk. When I park, I must disconnect the battery, so it doesn't drain, this also acts as an immobiliser.

With 'The Champ' I drove through the park, taking photographs as I went. First up a clan of hyena, then a bull elephant, then another one and another one. Plenty of bull elephants. Before long, I wasn't stopping for them unless they blocked the road.

I stayed the night in the park, this wasn't cheap. I noticed the expense more now than before as my last pay cheque was in rand and not pounds.

Kruger is a divine place, it's incredible that anybody can jump in their car and go on their own safari. But it felt restrictive, not being able to get out and walk where I wanted. This was especially true on the first morning when I set out early. I could see the sunlight on the sycamore figs nestled along the river's edge. They looked inviting, and I was desperate to explore their surroundings.

I made it to Hoedspruit by lunchtime, and before anything else, I went to Sleepers for a pizza, beer and the internet. I took the opportunity to contact Ben, who is working at a lodge up the road. We met that evening back at Sleepers, it's a bit of a dive but my kind of dive. It was a full-on evening, which resulted in my first hangover for a month.

The next day I drove to Tshukudu Lodge, where Ben works and had booked me a complimentary room for the night. During my stay, I joined the morning bush walk that he led. This wasn't like an EcoTraining excursion — it was informal. In fact, a hand-reared cheetah joined us halfway round.

I Skyped home and explained my plan to set up a travel business, splitting my time between the UK and leading walking safaris in Africa. As always, they supported me, though I could imagine them thinking, 'James is off on one of his dreams again.' They were probably right, and even during my brief break, I got sidetracked when Blackbrook Zoo came up for sale. Naturally, I asked the agent about the price. When they got back to me, it wasn't the cost that deterred me—it was the fact that the current owners planned to keep the house in the middle of the zoo. How could anyone run a business with the previous owners living right on site?

I'm based in South Africa's most northern camp, so it can take an age to return from leave. I left my guest house, Hoed and Berg, early and drove into the park via the Orpen Gate. This was the right choice as I saw a pack of twenty African hunting dogs, the first I'd seen in the wild. Despite numerous distractions along the way, I arrived back at Makuleke right on time to meet Bruce and the students at the main gate.

Driving back along Middle Road, we rounded a

corner to see a lioness and three one-year-old cubs lying in the sand. It was surreal seeing them, my first sighting of a lion on the concession.

CHAPTER ELEVEN

Time is free, but it's priceless. You can't own it, but you can use it. You can't keep it, but you can spend it. Once you've lost it, you can never get it back.' *Harvey MacKay, Businessman and Author.*

Trails Camp, Makuleke
7th April 2014

Jomi has been backing up at Pafuri Trails for the last four days, and I'm now to take his place. I'm excited, but anxious.

He limped into camp, shattered from his experience. While he dropped his kit in our tent, I put the kettle on, ready to quiz him over a quick cuppa. Short on time, we managed only a brief catch-up. I had to peck at my tea in tiny slurps, careful not to burn my lips on the enamel mug, trying to get some down before heading off.

If my three nights were half as full of encounters as Jomi's, I was going to be in for a breath-taking introduction to trails guiding. He even scored a leopard on foot!

I met Steve at the staff village. He'd been freshening up at the main camp manager's house. Not that a main camp still existed—it had been washed away in the once-in-a-hundred-year floods last January, and they were still waiting on the insurance.

I was handed a freshly ironed, off-white Wilderness Safaris shirt. It looked smart, and I felt like the real deal. I loaded my backpack and rifle into the Land Cruiser before meeting our clients at the bridge.

My first view of the completed camp was at the same time as the guests, and it couldn't have been better. It was stunning, with two staff members waiting for us with wet cloths and a welcome drink.

The fly-camp is set amongst super-sized sycamore figs and majestic mahoganies on the banks of the Luvuvuh river.

The tents are two-person domes with an en-suite chemical toilet. This isn't an attempt at luxury, it's so guests do not wander the unfenced campsite at night. If one of our charges were to become a chew ball for a leopard, they'd be unlikely to tip well.

After briefings and afternoon tea, we drove to Mangala. We took a stroll up the kopje for the view over the Luvuvhu. Despite being a short walk, it was testing; this allowed Steve to assess what type of trails the group would be keen on.

As sundowners rounded off our drive, we returned to camp with the aid of our headlights. Once again, the camp team, Flora and Ellen, welcomed us, having lit the camp with paraffin lamps and set the dinner table beneath the central sycamore fig.

Steve and I served pre-dinner drinks, which guests enjoyed in the lounge chairs before sitting down for a three-course meal. I've been entertained in some fantastic places over the years from dinner on Nelson's HMS Victory to a State Banquet at Edinburgh Castle and even a champagne reception at Buckingham Palace. But this was something else. The scores of paraffin lights twinkling around camp cast their light on the architectural trees making this the most magical place on earth.

After dinner, our guests retired to bed with a reminder not to leave their tents during the night. If anything unusual happened, they had a compressed air horn to blow. I'm not sure what we'd need to do after that—a 120-decibel blast from one of those would send even the bravest of the hairy and scary running for the hills!

I slept with a loaded rifle beside me — something that unsettled me. Growing up, I religiously removed any kind of weapon from my room when going to sleep. I didn't want to have a crazy nightmare that ended with me bludgeoning my family to death with a cricket bat or hammer. I was now turning in with a loaded rifle within touching distance, here's hoping for sweet dreams.

At the last minute, I ran into a hitch with my zip, leaving the tent unable to close. To be safe, I stacked a few milk crates in front of the door as an alert in case anything tried to come in. Realistically, though, by the time the clattering crates woke me, a hyena would probably be dragging me out, or a leopard would already have its jaws clamped around my skull.

9th April 2014

Even though I lay snug under a fluffy duvet, I slept poorly, constantly waking to check my alarm.

At five o'clock, it was uniform on, plus fleece and windbreaker for warmth. Despite my head torch, the most crucial part of my kit was the handheld torch, which allowed me to scan my surroundings as I navigated the dark, lightless camp.

After setting up the coffee station, I walked from tent to tent with a bucket of hot water, which I poured into the canvas basin standing outside each tent porch. With this, I uttered a gentle but cheery, 'good morning', and waited for a grunt that could be classed as acknowledgement. Once everyone was up and caffeinated, we set off on our trail.

The lack of sleep left me bushed, but I found a cunning technique to rest my eyes. I scanned for birds in the trees using my binoculars. Instead of finding anything, I would discretely close my eyes in the hope my clients wouldn't notice a snoozing safari guide behind the binos.

10th April 2014

Between trails, I spent twenty-four hours back at EcoTraining. When I arrived, I met Jomi, who boasted about his seven trail encounters compared to my zero. I didn't take it to heart; it was just bad luck. It wasn't as if I missed anything—I was simply unlucky.

At this point, Bruce joined us in the car park and told us to stop joking around as a five-ton bull elephant was standing behind us. Sure enough, said elephant had come through the bushes from the firebreak. He gave a flap of his ears before turning his attention to eating. Maybe I wasn't unlucky, perhaps I'd walked past all the game?

11th April 2014

After breakfast, I returned to Trails Camp. Steve and I met the new guests on Luvuvuh Bridge. There were six blokes, all here to celebrate a fortieth birthday.

Once again, I set up my hyena crates, as the zip still hadn't been repaired. Before settling in for the night, I spent some time de-frogging. I don't mind sharing with the occasional frog, but where there are frogs, snakes are usually close behind.

It's my turn to be forty next year. I've no idea where I'll be, what I'll be doing or who I'll be with. Have I made the right decision to give everything up and come to Africa? These chaps are successful in their careers, married and raising families. Where did I go wrong, or have I got it right with all that to come? I think so, or at least I hope so.

12th April 2014

I haven't known Steve long, but I know he is keen to test people in the bush. One way he does this is to walk people hard. So, if the group wanted a tough walk, they would get one.

We headed to Masashiti Springs before coming

back across the ridges. With its constant climbs and descents, the challenging terrain exhausted the city slickers. So, instead of walking in the afternoon, we went on a booze cruise to Lanner Gorge.

As per protocol, we used the radio to announce our route back. On doing so we were told the road was closed. Cara then followed up to query,

'Did you not get the email? The road has been closed until further notice.'

Of course, we didn't get the email. We don't have running water, phone signal or a generator, never mind the internet.

On our diverted route, we were hit by the strong smell of an elephant in musth. The next thing we knew, he charged out of the mopane trumpeting at us. The engine whined as Steve hit the accelerator, speeding us away.

The testosterone levels of a bull in musth can be sixty times greater than at any other time. This brings on overtly aggressive behaviour, a dangerous situation we found ourselves in as the bull relentlessly pursued us.

The guys buzzed about this Jurassic Park scene, though we had no wing mirror view to complete it. Looking over our shoulders into the murky darkness, we could only see the faint red glow of our taillights illuminating dust in our wake.

Over dinner, each person in the group took it in turn to make a speech, with the birthday boy responding to everyone individually. I found it somewhat cheesy, forced and distinctly new-age. At one point, I thought they would hold hands and say how much they loved one another.

The cost of this walking safari for these forty something bankers would have been pocket money. Saying that, I felt a great responsibility to meet and exceed their expectations. A safari is an enormous investment, whether that's time or money. Even the richest must sacrifice a considerable resource, their time.

Even though I was cynical about the self-congratulatory eulogies, the evening had a profound effect on me. I need to work harder at my friendships as I'm terrible at keeping in touch. I expect people to be there when I need them. My defence is that if they're loyal friends, they will be, as I will be for them.

13th April 2014

One reason birthday boy Sean chose our trail was the wilderness aspect. He liked it that there was no reception to distract people by turning them into phone zombies. But zombie-like behaviour surfaced during this morning's game drive. Someone announced they had a signal. Our guests were then transfixed by their screens. The only indicator of life was the manic tapping of fingers and the groan when the signal disappeared as quickly as it came.

In the afternoon, we inched our way through the dense riverine forest along the Limpopo. There was a boatload of buffalo poop and trampled vegetation. You didn't need to be an expert tracker to work out that a buffalo herd had been here last night, if not this morning.

We moved cautiously, mindful of the possibility of a dagga-boy appearing unexpectedly. Aside from a kudu bolting from a bush, there were no scares. But the experience put everyone on edge, everyone including Steve and me. I quietly chuckled to myself when one of the party announced,

'I'm not convinced I wouldn't run. If we had a full-on encounter, I don't think I could stop myself legging it.'

I loved his honesty in such an environment, which until now had been full of almost as much testosterone as our musth elephant.

Over dinner I was positive I heard rhino calling. I've only seen a couple since being at Makuleke but none on foot. Now that would be a fantastic sighting and one over Jomi. Not that there's a competition, but I am losing.

14th April 2014

After breakfast, we said goodbye to Sean and his party. Steve and I then set about cleaning our rifles before I headed back to EcoTraining. My timing was impeccable—I scored a second breakfast.

That afternoon, I found out that a rhino was killed, taken down by a .375 round. Well, a poacher was the real culprit. I couldn't help but take it personally. I'd only been on the concession for four months, but it felt like my concession. How dare someone trespass and murder one of my rhinos.

The timing made sense. Not being allowed to take our preferred route back from Lanner, we would have driven through the crime scene. And the rhino I heard last night; it must have been crying out for its companion.

EcoTraining, Makuleke
15th April 2014

New Back-up Hein and I stayed in camp to do a few chores. For our efforts, we were rewarded with a breeding herd of elephants surrounding the camp. I sat on the deck to draft emails while watching the wildlife go by. This included a young calf in full trumpet chasing a baboon, impala coming through camp, a martial eagle flying level with the tree canopy and the baboons using the roof as a trampoline.

17th April 2014

I woke to an elephant feeding right outside my tent. Despite this noisy neighbour, I dozed off again before my four-forty alarm sounded. Momentarily forgetting elephants roamed the camp, I stumbled around in a drowsy state. Luckily for me — and for whoever would've had to scrape me off the ground — they had moved on.

Hein didn't know the route to the rubbish dump so rather than go out walking I did both the rubbish and the food run. I took the 'Landagreenie', the one with no lights, which meant I used the spotlight to navigate the roads. This, apart from the bitter cold on my extended hand, was fine until the spot stopped working a quarter of the way to the gate.

Now, without any lights, driving became difficult in the dead of night, with a blanket of low clouds obscuring the moon. I did have my head torch, but it was perpetually dim. Note to self: don't buy cheap batteries.

On my way again, I spotted three hyenas, one of which was a little too inquisitive. This would've been an ideal time to be in a Land Rover with doors. Still, I didn't need to stop for them, but why wouldn't I? The food delivery could wait. It wasn't as if I were picking up a pizza that would go cold.

Tomorrow is Good Friday, so everything was shutting down, including the rubbish dump. Solomon and his crew must have taken off early. There was no way I could head back with all this rubbish, so I convinced a security guard to come down and open the gates for me.

On my way back, I lost the trailer on the newly re-opened San Pad. Not that I realised my error until another kilometre down the road. The trailer popped off the tow bar due to the weight of the firewood in the wheelie bins at the back. A weight too great for me to simply hook the trailer back on. I'd lost my sense of humour by now, that is what having to unload and reload a trailer in the middle of the bush does to you.

Once back at camp, I hoped to take it easy, but there was still more to be done. I'd been on the go for eleven hours now. Missing breakfast and lunch for two days in a row didn't help my mood. I'm also feeling run down—it's the first time I've had mouth ulcers since leaving the London job. Tomorrow, it's back to Trails Camp for six nights, and I doubt that's going to provide the rest I need.

CHAPTER TWELVE

'In those moments, your heartbeat becomes the loudest sound in Africa.' *Robert Ruark, Author and Hunter.*

Trails Camp, Makuleke
18th April 2014

It felt cold last night, or at least I thought so. I wore my base layer and slept in a sleeping bag under a duvet. I also felt what seemed like a hangover, though the confusing part was that I'd only put away three Castle Lites.

I felt worse as the day wore on, a thumping headache, a stiff neck, swollen glands, and hot flushes. I then discovered a spider-like bite that was black in the centre. The consensus is, I've tick-bite fever.

It's clear how I got the illness. The name gives it away somewhat. Somewhere there will have been an animal, probably a buffalo or impala with a bacterial infection. The disease carrying animal was bitten by a hungry tick. After three to four days, the blood swollen tick would have dropped off.

Having dropped off, the tick would have prepared for its next life stage. On reaching that point, it would climb a blade of grass and hang out until a new beast walked along, in this case, me.

It will then have launched itself at my leg, clung on and climbed up to a dark and secluded place. On this occasion, the back of my leg but usually the groin or an armpit. On biting me, the pathogen transferred to my blood in the tick's saliva. I now have the virus. Perhaps I wouldn't have been such a welcoming host if my legs weren't so hairy.

When I arrived at Trails Camp, I found Steve full of fever too.

After picking up our guests, we bumped a breeding herd of elephants on Ambush Alley some thirty metres from camp. To test us, the mamma gave the front of the Cruiser a nudge with her tusks. Welcome to Pafuri.

To my relief, dinner didn't run too late. I sat there bundled up like an onion, wearing every layer I could find, while everyone else lounged in just a T-shirt.

I don't want to be sick; I can't be sick as there's no back up for a Back-up. But critically, I don't want to ruin my record of not missing a day's work because of illness since early 2004.

19th April 2014

An elephant bull wandered through camp last night. He fed his way down the access road, past my tent and out via the bucket showers, sucking them dry.

Hutwini Gorge was a real struggle this morning. I felt so weak I could barely keep my head up. The stiffness in my neck forced me to turn my whole body just to check on the guests behind me. By the end of the walk, I truly understood the phrase 'being brought to your knees.'

I haven't felt this bad since returning from a school rugby tour of South Africa in 1992. What I assumed was an atrocious hangover led to a week-long hospital stay. I was subjected to low-degree isolation and test after test, with my blood samples sent to the London School of Hygiene and Tropical Medicine. They never discovered what was wrong with me, but my South African aunt remained convinced it was tick-bite fever — I think she may have been right.

20th April 2014

I was feeling stronger after a peaceful night's sleep. But that was short-lived. When we started walking, my thumping headache returned.

We came across a hornbill without a tail, a peculiar thing to see. As we discussed it, we must have woken a sleeping buffalo in the wallow behind us. The bull jumped up from where he'd been lying, eyeballed us and bolted, thankfully in the opposite direction.

This grabbed my attention and reminded me not to switch off, no matter how tired and ill I was.

We continued the walk through a thicket of lala palms. Partway through, Steve gave the instruction to remain still. He cautiously moved ahead to scout the area while I stayed with the guests. Suddenly, a rustling sound came from the bush beside us. Things just got interesting.

However, the guests ignored instructions, too caught up in their curiosity, craning their necks to see what was going on. Our retreat was far from textbook. If the proverbial had hit the fan, my only choice would've been to shoot some guests so I could face down whatever danger was coming our way. It reminded me of what Alan had told me during our Trails course.

'The bush is the safest place in the world. That is until you hear the voice of a human.'

21st April 2014

Once we said our goodbyes, it was up to the manager's house for a shower, shave, and power nap. We headed to the pick-up point to do it all over again. Our charges for this trail comprised two individuals — a pair of honeymooners from Cape Town. Or, to create a collective noun for newlyweds, 'a smugness of honeymooners'.

Collective nouns in the English language originated from France, becoming a hunting tradition in the late Middle Ages to name groups of animals with artistic flair. The first English book on the subject was *The Book of St. Albans*, first published in 1486 and reprinted many times throughout the sixteenth century. My personal favourites are 'an exaltation of larks' and 'an implausibility of wildebeest.'

We took our welcome fruit punch to the lounge

to enjoy the shade of the sycamore fig. It was now time for Steve to give the all-important safety briefing.

'As we drove into camp, you'll have noticed we didn't pass through any gates. The camp is unfenced. This means wild animals can come and go as they please... er, like these elephants, in fact.'

As if stage-managed, a breeding herd of elephants paraded through camp. Enough said.

After a brilliant start to the trail, the afternoon's activity didn't disappoint. A frisky bull elephant provoked a female into an ear-piercing trumpet. This caused Mrs Honeymooner, Naomi, to jump across the Cruiser and almost out the other side.

Once we left the vehicle and started walking, it was encounter after encounter with elephants and buffalo, forcing us to proceed with extreme caution. When it was finally safe to talk, Naomi spoke up.

'My senses have never been more alive than they are right now. I hear absolutely everything, and my heart is thumping.'

'The Groom has his work cut out to top this level of excitement when they retire to their Honeymoon tent tonight,' I thought.

We headed to a pan in the wooded glade next to the airfield. The guests sat on a log, and we positioned ourselves for a 360-degree view of the area. Then we waited.

There's one thing for sure, if you stake out a waterhole, you'll see some buffalo. They eat such a large quantity of coarse material they need to drink regularly, up to twice a day managing as much as thirty-four litres in six minutes.

After twenty-five minutes the buffalo appeared cautiously at the water's edge. They drank but stopped after looking in our direction. Their sixth sense was telling them something was amiss. They were only thirty-five metres away, but with the wind in our favour they did not know who or what was watching them.

Fingers crossed; I'll get some rest on this trail. I imagine our smugness will want to go to bed early each night.

22nd April 2014

We walked through Hutwini Gorge before coming back on ourselves, albeit vertically, to reach the top of the heads. We took thirty minutes sitting in the sun looking out over the floodplain and hills beyond.

There's been plenty of talk about meditation, and Steve is an advocate. I don't understand how it works. To me, it feels like a cock-and-bull excuse for a snooze. Still, I was happy to find a comfy spot and switch off. Since I was on duty, I couldn't fall asleep, but it wasn't easy. I had to work hard to stay awake, with the constant risk of whiplash as my head rolled back and forth like a nodding dog.

As we made our way down, the painkillers wore off. This meant I could feel the blinding headache behind my right eye again. This combined with hunger and a desperate need for a cuppa was putting me in a grump.

After more painkillers, I recovered enough for

the afternoon walk, not that I had the option to stay in camp feeling sorry for myself. The reward was a walk in the fever tree forest, which was stunning in the early evening light.

We headed northeast, both of us exploring unfamiliar territory, so it was a delight when we discovered a pan littered with brilliant white-water lilies.

We returned to the vehicle along a donga, a dry gully lined with jackal berries and sycamore figs. It was here that we spotted a young warthog waddling towards us. The wind was on our side, giving him little chance of seeing us, with his nose glued to the path ahead. We crouched down to enjoy the sighting as he went about his business.

Back at the Cruiser, we watched the sun go down until the forest was all but black. As we finished, two silhouettes lumbered towards us. The sound of breaking trees confirmed our eyes were not playing tricks —elephants had joined us for sundowners.

Steve and I worked well together; his wealth of experience and specialist knowledge of medicinal plants never failed to fascinate. He led the trails and drives with his conventional interpretation of animal behaviour and plant use. In cricket commentary terms, he was the anchor. I was the special guest, contributing bizarre facts, anecdotes, and jokes delivered with dramatic pauses before the punchline. We complemented each other, and the banter between us and the guests was enjoyable—or at least I thought so.

After years of dreaming about becoming a safari

guide and months of training, I was finally doing it. Despite picking up some dodgy African disease from the local fauna, it was going well.

24th April 2014

The fever is subsiding, and I felt strong when I got up this morning. This showed in my demeanour; I was getting back to my chirpy self, the part of me I've rediscovered since taking this year out.

The luck of the newlyweds continues. First up, a herd of buffalo—their eleventh encounter. The previous trail only had three. We approached the herd downwind, using some *Crotons* for cover. As we reached the end, the view opened up, revealing we'd split the herd — another fifty-plus 'buff' stood to our north. Slowly, we picked our way through and emerged on the other side.

This positioned us perfectly for the primary aim of the morning—to find a leopard, and we knew a female was in the area. The location was prime leopard territory, with plenty of game, thick bush, denning sites, and the smell of death in the air. As Steve brought our little party to a standstill, I whispered,

'This is looking a little thick.'

He turned, gave me a wink, and then addressed our honeymooners.

'We know there's a leopard in the area. It's a female, and we think she has cubs. There's a good chance we may bump her. To recap on the rules, always stay behind the rifle. Walk in single file. Keep completely silent. Do whatever James and I tell you to, and finally, whatever you do, don't run.'

I thought he was raising expectations but so be it. It looked perfect for leopard, and I was desperate for such an encounter. Remembering the fiasco of the last trail when the group got split into two, I added,

'If I ask you to back off, then you should do so immediately, don't hang around looking, and stay behind the rifle.'

Between us, I think we managed to put the fear of God into them. We weren't exaggerating or overhyping the situation—we were simply following the rules by the book.

Within five minutes of the briefing, we walked up a gentle incline. As we reached the crest, a female leopard jumped up from behind a fallen umbrella thorn. She crouched on the trunk, looking straight at us. The view was perfect, for what seemed an age. In reality it was only seconds before she left as silently as she'd appeared.

Steve gave the order to retreat. We did so, and at some pace, at one point I told the 'smugness' to slow down, fearing they would break into a trot. Once we'd reached a safe distance, we could breathe again and most importantly exchange grins. I'd remained calm through the encounter, which delighted me. It wasn't until we weaved our way out through the buffalo that I went weak at the knees.

At the vehicle, we opted for our coffee break so we could celebrate and compare stories. Today was my vindication. After forgetting the coffee plunger yesterday, it was Steve's turn to do so today. As well as the plunger, he'd forgotten the whole hot box. We weren't far from Trails, so we bumbled our way back and regrouped there.

With the trail complete, I headed back to EcoTraining. I was desperate to get there. I wanted to say those three special words, leopard on foot.

CHAPTER THIRTEEN

'Stay curious, keep learning and keep growing. Don't let anyone tell you you can't do something.' *Unknown source*

EcoTraining, Makuleke
26th April 2014

The 'Landagreenie' will soon be retired from the Makuleke fleet. For many, it's a sombre day, but not for me. I'm not a fan. This Land Rover doesn't stop when you want it to, and the breaks squeal when pulling into a sighting. The only thing I will miss is driving around the mighty Kruger in a vehicle that has no doors.

As I drove back from the gate in the new Landy with two new students, we met a bull elephant in musth. He swaggered down the road in a similar vein to a punch-drunk Geordie in Newcastle's Big Market.

I pulled over to the side and killed the engine. It was showtime. The bull walked right up to the vehicle with no hint of malice in his pinprick brown eyes. He clearly didn't have the energy or inclination for a fight.

His trunk rested over a tusk, and he paid us little attention.

The only way the encounter could have been better was if we were in the unprotected 'Landagreenie'. With no roof and no doors, we could have really appreciated his size. Turns out I am going to miss that rotten old vehicle. The new Landy, 'Tambookie', comes with a roof, windows, and brakes. Great for the city but rubbish for the bush.

27th April 2014

Bruce and Dee left for their three-month trip across Australia this morning. I'll be gone by the time they return, but I'm confident I'll see them again. They've left Jomi in charge as Camp Manager, and as American lawyer and orator Robert G. Ingersoll supposedly said of Lincoln in the 1890s,

'If you want to test a man's character, give him power.'

Jomi, you'll be all right.

After dropping the Trails group at Makwadzi, Jomi and I left the vehicle at the bottom of San Pad for them. Keys in the ignition and at the ready. It's what everyone does in the bush. If you fancy a Land Rover or Land Cruiser, go for a walk in Makuleke. I'm sure you'd find one to your liking. Some even come with doors.

I led the two of us back through the Fever Tree Forest. The bush was thick, but we wove our way through—well, up to a point. I veered right of a pan instead of left, which took us away from the fever trees and into the mopane. I thought, or rather hoped, it would open up again, but it didn't. With the light fading, I pulled the emergency cord. The contingency plan was to hotfoot it back to camp along Middle Road.

Walking along the road, we ducked into the bush for cover several times. Once when the Trails group drove past, and then again for the wildlife vets. We weren't going to fail—we wanted to get back under our own steam—and we managed it just as the last light was snuffed out below the horizon.

29th April 2014

Because different groups were out this morning, Jomi and I had just one rifle between us. With his lead assessment coming up soon, it was only right to let him take the rifle. I, therefore, opted for the camera instead of a weapon.

Our mission was to see if the Fever Tree Forest was accessible from camp, given all the recent rain. Exploratory walks are my favourite—no set route and no telling what you might encounter. I suppose this was a mild version of what Victorian explorers like Livingstone must have experienced.

We edged our way slowly through the tall *Sporobolus* grass on the floodplain. We frequently stopped to listen for tell-tale sounds of buffalo. There were buff about somewhere—at least that's what the spoor told us. The tension was palpable, and I found myself inadvertently holding my camera in a rifle-ready position.

We emerged from the long grass into a clearing. As soon as we did, Jomi raised his hand, signalling for us to stop. A herd of fifty buffalo stood ahead. The moment they caught our scent, they bolted. We veered west of our original route to give them space, and soon, we entered the Fever Tree Forest.

The dew was fresh on the grass, which was soothing to my scratched shins. They've taken a hammering from three months of walking, not in the bush but more often than not, through it.

Jomi proceeded tentatively as he carefully unhooked the webs which the golden orb spider spun through the night. He'd then reattached them to another branch so we could make our way along the path. Wherever possible he would avoid breaking a spider's web, as the arachnid would have spent so much energy spinning it.

As we walked, hundreds, if not thousands, of butterflies surrounded us. These added to the forest's magical quality. The butterflies were broad-bordered grass yellows and brown-veined whites. The forest opened into a clearing, where a stately sycamore fig stood at the far end. Alongside was a pan, lined with golden-trunked fever trees that gleamed in the morning light.

The forest was alive—not just with butterflies but with frogs hopping across the leaf litter, a snake slithering through the grass, and a baboon sounding its familiar bahoo alarm. Birds filled the air with voice: the grey-backed camaroptera bleating, the crescendoing song of the white-browed robin-chat, the wailing of the trumpeter hornbill, the drumming of the bearded woodpecker, and finally, the lilac-breasted roller, whose call resembles two chimpanzees taking off in a helicopter.

As much as we wanted to linger in this enchanted forest, we needed to complete our task of finding a safe route for the students that afternoon. The only path available wasn't suitable for a larger group. It wasn't a route we would normally take, but time was pressing. Our path involved getting our feet wet, which didn't bother Jomi—he was wearing sandals.

30th April 2014

The third night in a row of not sleeping properly. I woke up at half two and I don't think I drifted off again. Not sure what is causing these sleepless nights, it's certainly not anxiety.

There were lots to keep me entertained as I lay in bed. The animals seemed to be having a field day out there. The hyenas were close to camp, their whoops echoing as loudly as a police siren, yet far less jarring. Well, that's what I thought, the eles thought otherwise and gave a trumpet as if to tell them to pipe down. The hyenas didn't listen and carried on calling. This seemed to incite one ele into an almighty trumpet. This time it worked, and I didn't hear the hyena again until dawn was breaking.

The camp is peaceful when everyone else is out on trail. I wasn't scheduled to walk, so I took the chance to lie in bed, waiting for the Landy to start up.

As it pulled away, I jumped out of bed and headed to the study deck for a cuppa and some breakfast. The camp was practically all mine.

The animals appreciated the quiet as well. Around fifty impalas milled about. Jomi enjoys an empty camp too, and it wasn't long before he joined me. He was after the same thing, so there was no need for small talk.

With a soft glow, the sun rose to my left as the baboons descended from the enormous nyala tree that shades camp. That's when the peace was shattered—there's always some domestic squabble, with one baboon beating up another or worse. I felt like I should have called the cops.

As I started my third cuppa, a small baboon was chased by a larger one, who in turn was pursued by an even bigger one. The clock ticked over to seven o'clock, and I decided it was time to crack on with some work.

I made my last preparations for my friends arriving today, Chubby and Claire. My remaining task was to check the eaves of their tent for snakes. Their tent, number three, has a history of black mambas taking residence. Not that I'd tell them this.

Their journey from London to camp was twenty-four hours. Understandably, they arrived exhausted. The seven-hour drive on no sleep must have been a killer. After a short game drive aka a booze cruise, it was a few beers around the fire while people shared animal stories. Chubbs, Claire, welcome to my office.

1st May 2014

Just before the drums signalled wake-up, a leopard called close to camp. The best part was that both Chubby and Claire heard it too. I want them to truly grasp how wild and wonderful Makuleke is.

Our morning walk took us to Nwambe Pan on the Salvadora Plains, named for the abundance of narrow-leafed mustard bushes, *Salvadora australis*. It was the perfect introduction to trails for Chubby and Claire. The area felt quintessentially African, with its iconic scenery and an abundance of plains game on display.

Because the students are walking as Lead and Back-up, I carry out my official duties at the back of the line. Now and then Chubby and Claire would rotate to the rear, allowing us to snatch a quick word.

We had one encounter—a small splinter herd of buffalo that had come to the pan for water. They didn't see us, but we were caught in the open, forcing us to crouch down. This proved difficult for Chubbs, whose long professional cricket career had led to multiple knee operations. He eventually gave up and sat on his backside.

In the afternoon I took them to Luvuvuh West for sundowners at Second Lookout. This is a stunning place, made even greater by two hippos, countless white-cheeked bee-eaters hawking over the river, and a herd of elephant coming down for water as the light faded.

We were in the 'Landagreenie' again, which meant no lights. However, tonight I had a plan. I

Sellotaped my torch to the bull bars.

2nd May 2014

Our ride dropped us ahead of our planned walk-off point as fallen trees blocked the approach to Deku. Actually, felled trees, the elephants have taken a liking to pushing over corkwoods.

Deku was one of the larger former settlements on the concession. It once housed a community of Makuleke people, a tribal group from the region, before they were forcibly removed. In 1969, the military and National Parks Board evicted 3,000 residents from their ancestral land. This was done to expand Kruger but also for strategic military reasons. Allegedly, African National Congress rebels hid in villages like Deku or used the area to cross in and out of South Africa.

There wasn't much to show for the village's former life apart from some foundations, fallen mopane uprights, metal implements, glass bottles, wire, and some pottery.

The next landmark on our walk was Hutwini. As we walked into the gorge, rock hyrax perched high on the cliff face monitored our progress. Chubby was understandably dubious when I explained that fossil evidence suggested the hyrax, despite being fifty centimetres in length and 3.5 kilograms in weight, is closely related to the elephant. The similarities they share include a protracted gestation period, tusk-like incisors and their foot structure.

We worked our way to the top and looked out

over the alluvial floodplain of the Luvuvuh where instructor Harry gave a talk on the basic geology and a brief history of the area. The key feature was Thulamela, visible from where we stood. This stone-walled palace, dating back to 1460–1650, sat across the river atop a sandstone kopje dotted with baobabs.

Further into our walk we picked up signs of elephant —a breeding herd was somewhere ahead of us. After checking many piles of dung along the way, I eventually found a warm poo. It must have been deposited less than one hour before.

We eventually bumped them. There were four on the top of a hill amongst the purple pod cluster leaf. I barely saw them, and unfortunately, Chubby and Claire only got the African salute as the elephant's grey bulk of a backside disappeared into the trees.

They or the rest of the herd must have got wind of us causing one to trumpet a call which reverberated off the cliffs behind us.

On arrival at Masashiti Springs, I directed the group to the rhino skulls from the poaching incident. People must see the realities of Africa.

My view is that by sharing the full picture, no matter how horrific, you may inspire somebody to act. You don't know who is on your trail. There could be a high-powered executive, a politician, a journalist, or someone with bags of energy who could make a difference.

After the seven-hour walk this morning, we took it easy in the afternoon with a sedate bumble in the Landy. Leisurely it was, but uneventful it wasn't. First, we encountered an elephant breeding herd on San

Pad. I'd inadvertently split a juvenile bull from the matriarch, who was some way behind. He was getting all uppity but never showed real aggression. Once I realised what had happened, I backed up, and the large female crossed the road, bringing calm to the situation.

We left the herd as they disappeared into the mopane, only to run into a big bull in musth as we joined Pafuri Main.

We saw him some way off, which meant we could pull off the road. This gave him all the space in the world. As he came towards us, I thought I'd talk to him. This seemed to go well until he was almost past us. At this point, his demeanour changed for the worse.

I can't remember the exact sequence of events. I think he first charged at us, which made me raise my voice. That took the wind out of his sails. He then milled around for a bit before coming up with a new plan. He pushed over a knob thorn. Impressive, but he wasn't done. Next, he moved on to a mopane tree, this time aiming it directly at us. That nearly finished off poor Claire, who was eager to move on. However, I was concerned that if we drove off, we'd give him the upper hand, leading him to chase the vehicle. Fortunately, an opportunity to leave presented itself when a car passed by. With this distraction, I pulled away slowly to avoid provoking him.

3rd May 2014

Harry gave me the lead for Chubby and Claire's last walk at Makuleke. As we strode off towards the enchanted Fever Tree Forest, I imagined my friends from the North must have found the experience surreal. There they were, deep in the African outback, following me along elephant tracks—me, armed with a rifle and just eight months of experience.

As the walk progressed, the temperature rose. This is what the butterflies were waiting for, perfect conditions for flight. I had the best position, walking at the front through colourful *Lepidoptera* confetti.

We stopped for a break at Racket-Tailed clearing, named after one of the signature birds of the concession. A flock of white-crested helmet shrikes were feeding, and the location lived up to its name. Four racket-tailed rollers doing what they do best, rolling in an aerial display.

After dropping Chubby and Claire at the gate, Duncan and I cleared up the mess that the musth bull wreaked last night in his testosterone-fuelled display. The mopane was easy to sort, but knob thorn is never fun. The best solution I found was to soften it up with multiple swings of the panga before pushing it off the road with the Landy.

4th May 2014

Harry and I walked the Sand Veld this morning. As a pair, we had license to explore and push the boundaries. Without guests, we could ignore the rulebook.

I'm curious to know how old Harry is. He's retired from his corporate job, allowing him to do what he loves: tramping around the bush and lecturing on the subject. Regardless of age, he bounces from rock to rock. I think he could even outdo a startled klipspringer in a head-to-head race. And this is no mean feat, as klipspringers are truly remarkable rock climbers, earning their Afrikaans name, which translates as 'rock jumper'.

Having slipped and scrambled our way down the side of the sandstone rock face, we found ourselves in a donga where perhaps no one had ever walked before. It was hard work with most of it spent lowering ourselves from boulder to boulder. It was worthwhile when we reached the banks of the Luvuvuh to discover the spoor of a Cape clawless otter.

Under Harry's precise guidance, I found the rock art site. It was humbling to know that Bushmen lived here until 500 years ago. I took some time alone, giving myself the chance to take in the paintings. Sitting by the ledge, I found the old tools laid out for others to see. The spearheads and scrapers were unmistakable, their craftsmanship still evident after all this time.

I painted a picture in my mind of what it must have been like all those years ago. My inspiration came from Jean Auel's *The Clan of the Cave Bear*. The story follows Ayla, a five-year-old Cro-Magnon girl orphaned by an earthquake and adopted by a Neanderthal clan. Despite struggling to fit in due to her different appearance and abilities, she learns their ways and what she must do to survive.

I could have stayed all day, but we needed to move on. I will be back, perhaps for a sleep out.

En route to the vehicle, I took a shortcut between two kopjes, where we heard what I thought was an elephant feeding. I suggested we climb over the rocks for a closer look.

As I reached the top, there was nothing. But as I moved forward, a leopard leapt from a tree. It hit the ground with a thud and was gone in an instant. I climbed back down to Harry and said,

'I know we shouldn't have a closer look, but there are only two of us.'

He turned and lambasted me, or at least that's what I thought he was doing when he replied,

'James, never ever pass on an opportunity like this, of course, we're going to investigate.'

The noise I couldn't place in hindsight became obvious—it was the crunching of bones. The leopard, a small female, had dragged a large impala up the tree. We could see the claw marks on the trunk, and above us, the antelope dangled face down.

CHAPTER FOURTEEN

'Africa is a cruel teacher. She shows you your place in the scheme of things, and it's usually at the bottom of the food chain.' *Peter Hathaway Capstick, Author and Hunter.*

Trails Camp, Makuleke
16th May 2014

The seven-strong group for the next three nights arrived this afternoon. They seem decent and have brought luck with them too. On our first short walk, we encountered four elephant bulls at Rhino Boma.

The drive back to camp was the highlight. First, we parked amongst a herd of buffalo that were crossing Pafuri Main. Rhodes rolled in, killing the engine and lights. We sat there listening to the grunts and mumbles as they milled around us.

We drove back over the old landing strip; I swept the immediate area with the searchlight, back and forth, high and low in a defined arc so as not to miss anything. This bore fruit, a thick-tailed bushbaby who was happy to sit in the spotlight for some time.

As we approached camp, guest John, mentioned he'd seen a hyena turn off the road. Sure enough, something had veered off the road, walking down the sandy track toward camp. But it wasn't a hyena—it was a large, scent-marking tom leopard.

I'm not sure if I was overreacting—probably was—but nonetheless, I called Eva and Flora frantically on the radio to warn them. I pictured them waiting for us at the end of the road with hot towels and big smiles. Their warm welcome would instead greet a hungry leopard rather than a Land Cruiser full of safari-goers.

He left the track before reaching camp and laid up in the scrub. On turning off the engine, we could hear Flora and Eva chatting. Not just us, the leopard as well. His ears pricked up, and he cocked his head towards them. It wasn't long before he got bored with eavesdropping and disappeared into the night.

I've come a long way over the last eight months. I now feel at ease in these unfenced camps. However, I was apprehensive when I wandered up the same track ten minutes later to do my own scent marking. I scanned left to right, right to left and then left to right again, praying I wouldn't catch a set of emerald eyes in the beam of my torch.

As I turned in, I lay in bed, still captivated by all the activity under the gibbous moon. Elephants trumpeted in the distance, while the impala rut echoed across the night. Baboons and vervets erupted into chaos as a leopard prowled through their territory. Zebra and hyena joined the chorus, all set against the steady symphony of crickets—a fitting soundtrack to yet another magical night in the Motherland.

18th May 2014

It wasn't long after the start of our walk when Rhodes raised his right hand to give the universal signal for stop. As he did so, twenty elephants stampeded across our path, their massive bodies thundering through the landscape.

They were fifty metres in front of us and were clearly agitated by something. It certainly wasn't us, as we'd been silent, and the wind was in our favour.

Afterwards, we'd narrowed it down to one of, or a combination of, three things.

1) The wind throughout the night may have unsettled them as the wind severely inhibits elephants' most valuable senses, hearing, and smell.

2) Duncan had driven along Middle Road. He may have inadvertently spooked them.

And 3) We later saw a lone bull elephant trailing them. He may have been a bit of a sex pest.

We hastily retreated and watched from what we thought was a safe distance. Well, that is, until an adolescent bull appeared from around the corner of a bush. This caused another immediate but quicker retreat to higher ground. It was the bull sneaking up on us that made it a proper heart-thumping encounter.

Once we'd stabilised our vitals, the sighting was ours to enjoy. Despite the opportunity for further encounters, we deemed it unwise to walk through the coverless fever tree forest with the breeding herd heading that way.

Even if we'd gone west, our scent would have carried to the eles and added to their stress. Instead, we got back into the Cruiser and walked from the bottom of San Pad to Makwadzi.

This wasn't plain sailing, though it should have been. Rhodes was leading us through a pass surrounded by relatively thick bush. As per standard practice, I was walking behind Rhodes as second rifle. It was at this moment that I let out what I can only describe as a stomach-rumble burp. The instant it escaped, I apologised. Unfortunately, Rhodes didn't hear me and sprang into action, moving forward to investigate what might have caused the 'growl'.

By the time he returned, it was too late to admit it was my breakfast. The guests were speculating about what it may have been, perhaps a buffalo or a leopard–no one had a clue it was me.

Driving to our afternoon walk-off point, no one was paying attention to what was happening in the bush. They were engrossed in conversation. That is, except for a lady named Nicola, who suddenly shouted,

'Stop, there's a leopard in the baobab.'

Rhodes wasted no time in backing up. There it was, bold as you like, lounging in the radiant afternoon sun, draped along a branch as if posing for a National Geographic photoshoot.

As we manoeuvred into position for a better view of the big cat, I got a tad over-excited. I suggested to Rhodes that we should walk him, to which he replied that he'd been thinking the same. Despite Rhodes' similar inclination, I carried on making my case.

'We should walk him, it's not as if he's going anywhere and we're not getting a decent view from the road. How about walking from the airstrip access road, it's only 750 metres away? We should walk him; we must walk him.'

It wasn't long before we'd disembarked the vehicle and set off on foot. The wind was in our favour, but the crunch of leaves under our boots was not. Our approach consisted of two phases—the first gave us a decent view at one hundred metres, but it wasn't photo good. We pressed on, aiming for the adjacent baobab, just forty metres from the leopard. From there, we could see the killer cat clearly, but it wasn't long before he raised his head and spotted us. This was make or break. We needed to remain statue-still and monk-silent.

Not helping matters was a tickle in the back of my throat that wouldn't go away. I took off my hat and coughed into it to muffle the sound. Up until then, I hadn't realised just how big the leopard was. Suddenly, he leapt to his feet, bounded along the thick-set limb of the massive baobab, and launched himself, spread-eagled, out of the tree like a base-jumping Garfield. The jump must have been twenty feet, if not higher. He hit the bushes with a thud and vanished.

We carried on to the baobab to see the tree for ourselves. It was enormous. Neither Rhodes nor I thought he would jump like that. There was a chance he'd catch onto our presence, but I felt at worst he'd shin down the tree and be off. We took a thorough nose around the area. Rhodes found some drag marks which we followed to find an impala carcass.

24th May 2014

A near-perfect start to the morning, leopard tracks coming in and out of camp past my tent. Why had I not set up the camera trap?

The morning was stunning. The fish eagles called out their usual seagull-like cry, a sound that has become synonymous with my time at Pafuri Trails. It was cold again, cold enough to take my breath away. The chilly air brought a thick mist that clung to the ground, with only the giant sycamore figs rising above the fog.

The trick on these mornings is to act like a reptile by finding a bit of sun poking through the tree cover. Then, if time allows, stand there and enjoy the warmth on your skin and the energy it brings.

This morning's walk at Nwambe Pan proved exceptional. We spotted a kori bustard before we arrived and heard the southern ground hornbill. Two of the Kruger's Big Six birds ticked off. On the walk, we encountered three elephants. One, a bull, bore the scars of a previous snare wound on his trunk. I clearly saw the damage and heard him breathing through the hole in the side of his trunk.

This made him wary. He approached within thirty metres of us as we sat on the sandy floor. I was hoping he'd come closer, maybe twenty, even fifteen metres. But this was as far as he was willing to go.

Each time he considered coming closer, he'd catch our scent and back off.

It was the last encounter that was the climax. We were having a break at the western end of Nwambe Pan. I'd been to the *lavatree*, followed by Rhodes. Two of the guests, Oscar and Alice, asked if they could go too.

'Of course,' I said, 'simply go the way we came in, it's all clear.'

The next we knew the two of them popped up from around the corner frantically, trying to catch our attention.

It turned out they weren't alone. An elephant was coming down to the water. In fact, two more bulls followed him. Luckily, the elephants chose the south side of the pan rather than ours, probably because they'd bumped Oscar and Alice.

We walked Hutwini Gorge in the afternoon. It's a long walk for that time of day, but it's fantastic to see it bathed in the evening light. The walk back was interesting—no Big Five encounters but walking as the sun dipped below the horizon was exhilarating. In the low light, I spotted a herd of what I thought were buffalo, but they turned out to be 'rockalos' and one or two 'logadiles'—not crocodiles.

It alarmed the baboons to see us walking at this hour. To escape our presence and reach the safety of the cliff face, they stood upright and 'waded' through one of the pans—forearms held high, clearly detesting the experience. The poor guys would have been soaked through when they roosted.

A nyala bull and ewe also found it strange we were out and about. They couldn't work out whether to scarper or to stay rooted to the spot. This time clearly didn't belong to us. Instead, it belonged to the leopard and lion, hyena, and jackal. If you're not a predator, this is the start of a long night.

Rupert, the camp's resident buffalo bull, grazed in the long grass behind us as we sat around the campfire. He's not a quiet eater, but his masticating broke any awkward silences in the conversation. At such an interlude, we would look at the night sky or stare into the fire while listening to the munching Rupert. The soft, haunting *hoo hoo* of a wood owl, the yelps of hyena, and a leopard announcing its territory helped fill those lulls in chatter.

CHAPTER FIFTEEN

'Every 15 minutes, an elephant is killed by poachers. At this rate, African forest elephants could be extinct within 10 years.' *International Fund for Animal Welfare (IFAW), 2013*

The Outpost, Makuleke
29th May 2014

I'm guiding at The Outpost for a few days. This comes with the trappings of five-star lodge life. Most notably, the food, which I salivate for as soon as I think of it.

Our guests didn't arrive until lunchtime, which meant I could have a lie-in. Well, by safari standards, it was a lie-in, as the morning meeting started at seven o'clock. The pinnacle of my morning was opening my bedroom door to find a magnificent baobab right in front of me, set against the sandstone ridge. Given the darkness when I arrived last night, I hadn't noticed it before—such a magnificent tree.

The meeting, held in the bar, introduced me to a lot of staff. Trying to remember their names, along with the nineteen guests, will take a lot of work. Who am I kidding? It's going to be impossible. I'm terrible with names and often avoid using them rather than risk getting them wrong. This all stems from a day when I was doing a photoshoot with two England cricketers up in Durham. One was Stephen 'Harmy' Harmison, whom I knew well and was on nickname terms with. The second player was Andrew Flintoff, better known as 'Freddie Flintoff'. Since I didn't know him personally, I felt calling him Freddie was inappropriate. So instead, I mistakenly called him Paul, thinking that was his name. I didn't understand why they looked at me with bewilderment. I only realised my mistake when I explained to a colleague that the photocall with 'Harmy' and Paul went well, and they, too, looked at me with the same bewildered eyes.

The primary task of the day was to ensure we had enough booze for the guests. Whatever happens, we can't run dry—that was the gist of the briefing. Each of us packed two large cool boxes onto our brand-new Land Rovers and set off for the airfield at Tshikondeni.

The guests arrived at one-thirty in two smallish planes. We served them plated sandwiches at the airfield and the customary safari G&T before taking them on to the concession. After visiting Banyini and Makwadzi, we called it a day and took the guests to the lodge, where dinner awaited. I was officially off the clock, so I grabbed a couple of Heinekens and some snacks from the bar before heading back to my quarters to continue reading *The Ivory Trail.*

The book, first published in 1954, was written by T.P. Bulpin, one of South Africa's most popular travel writers. It's a true story set in Pafuri, though it does have the slight issue for me of glorifying big game hunting. *The Ivory Trail* recounts the adventures of S.C. 'Bvekenya' Barnard's hunting expeditions, based here in Makuleke, operating out of Crook's Corner. The location allowed him to evade the police by hopping across various international boundaries for sanctuary, with his destination depending on which state was after him. He lived as an outlaw for twenty years.

Bulpin was able to tell Bvekenya's story as an ivory poacher, blackbirder and conservationist following a meeting with Barnard himself. Like me you might not know what Blackbirding is, it's got nothing to do with ornithology or pie-making. It's a form of slavery. It involves the coercing of people through deception, sometimes by getting them drunk, and/or kidnapping them to work as unpaid or poorly paid labourers in countries far from their native home.

Tonight's reading was brought to life by the distant trumpeting of elephants, their calls echoing across the veld to my digs. I hope it wasn't a sign of poaching. In May this year, the first elephant to be poached in Kruger in a decade was found in the Pafuri region. The elephant had been shot and its tusks hacked off. The rangers on the scene identified footprints of four people leading towards Mozambique. This may be the first for some time, but I doubt it will be the last. Growing human populations are becoming desperate to survive, and demand for ivory is fuelled by greed and ignorance.

EcoTraining, Makuleke
3rd June 2014

I stood down from backing-up for the day so Mercenary Steve and Jomi could walk together one last time. My fellow walkers included Jomi's parents, visiting from Dublin. It ended up being a decent walk; we were dropped at Banyini and walked to camp. It took us seven hours to cover the sixteen kilometres.

We kicked up dust as we moved through the scorched earth. Friendly hawkers—small flying insects—swooped in to snatch up the bugs we stirred from lower down the invertebrate food chain.

As we closed in on the Limpopo, there was spoor from the opposite end of the food chain. Humans. The footprints, probably immigrants crossing in from Zimbabwe, were following the same path where we found lion prints. Immigration is a risky business.

The day was getting hotter and hotter, so any shade the ana and apple leaf trees provided was welcome. While we struggled in the sun, the African darters, aquatic diving birds, were revelling in it with their wings outspread as they air-dried.

Makwadzi Pan was lined with splendid apple leaf trees, their leaves hung heavy with dehydration. They looked as I felt. I was thrilled when Jomi said we'd stop for breakfast, but that joy quickly faded when he pulled out a tin of corned beef and some rice crackers.

After this hearty meal, I gratefully left the watch duties to those in charge, found the welcome shade of a large tree and had a snooze.

The forest down by the Limpopo was as

incredible as ever, with enormous stands of fever trees surrounding us as we followed an elephant path. An impressive collection of animals littered the trail, including vervets, baboons, impala and nyala moving aside as we passed through.

In the majesty of the forest, I forgot how heavy my boots were feeling. We'd been walking some time—I'd sucked dry the three litres of water in my CamelBak and was now onto my reserve. As we crossed the floodplain to camp, we spotted lion scat. I would love a lion encounter, if only to find out how I would handle it.

The birding was excellent, Jomi's speciality. I'm struggling in this respect. However, I enjoyed close sightings of several fish eagles, a bateleur, tawny eagles and plenty of storks - yellow billed, woolly-necked, saddle-billed and black.

The wildlife experience hardly ever ends when you return to camp. As I stepped onto my deck, a spotted bush snake, basking in the sun, slithered off through Duncan's gym shorts and onto the roof of our tent. It's worth noting Duncan wasn't wearing his shorts at the time.

Margaux and I stayed back in the afternoon to set up for the graduation dinner. I cooked the pork and beef joints on the Weber. Because I was braaiing, it felt only right I drank some beer. After the formal elements of graduation, we retired to the deck for Fines Night; I presided over the affair with my boot being used as the Fines' vessel.

CHAPTER SIXTEEN

The art of life is a constant readjustment to our surroundings.' *Kakuzo Okakaura, Philosopher.*

EcoTraining, Makuleke
6th June 2014

Running was hampered by the many Castles the night before. Although I did muster extra energy during the run when a black and yellow snake forced me into a full 360-degree mid-air turn to avoid it.

After lunch, I bashed out a quick email to my brother.

From: James Bailey
Date: 6 June 2014 12:54:12 GMT+02:00
To: Jonathan Bailey
Subject: Hope your travels are going well

Hi Johns,

We're home alone at the moment, just us Back-ups in camp, that's Jomi, Hein, Duncan (although he's gone to Trails Camp this morning), a new guy Max and an old Back-up Mike. The last of the instructors left yesterday, so we've no programme to follow. Only a few jobs needed to be done, and we broke the back of the main one already, painting the floors of each bathroom. This was a challenge, as I drank way too much last night. I felt distinctly ropey this morning.

I'd taken Elisa and Olivia to the clinic. That was a long and hot journey, especially as I had to wait outside for a while in only a little shade. Got back and the guys had packed a big cool box. We were heading to Pafuri River Lodge to meet up with Sarah and Cara. We took 'Tambookie', the new Landy, and headed off. Plenty of beers on the way there despite the newly invented drinking game - General Game Drinking Game, being a disaster, as we saw no game. Should you ever want to play it, the rules are - Impala, kudu etc = one finger, nyala = two fingers (as they're cool) and any Big Five = seeing off your drink.

The Park gate closed at five-thirty, so we didn't have long, but we were able to negotiate an extension. I don't think it was bribery. We asked Jacob what time the gate closed, he said five-thirty, 'what if we're late and bring you some drinks?' So that was our extension sorted. On speaking to Sarah, it transpired the gates close at ten o'clock for residents.

Good crack in the River Lodge with too many beers to count. No wonder I felt so rubbish today. We got back at half-nine to find nobody at the gate. One guy was walking around outside who said he worked there, and he'd get the gates opened for us. He did so by climbing over the main fence and disappearing off to the staff village. It worked. One guy appeared in his pyjamas. We mentioned Jacob and handed over some cokes and beers and wished him a good night. I'm not sure if we'd bribed our way into a National Park, but we did live there.

We pulled off Pafuri Main and parked up on the Outpost Home run dirt road and had ourselves a little party. Sarah had a stereo in her car, so that provided the music, I think there may have been dancing, I can't remember. I was now feeling tired, so I had a snooze on the back seat of the Landy. This small party in the middle of the wilderness reminded me of you in the BVIs—much the type of thing you guys get up to, but with Land Rovers instead of boats.

Duncan was off the booze so drove us home with no drama. He and Max did the food run this morning. So glad it was them and not me—I would have struggled to get up at five o'clock after going to bed at half past one.

Hopefully, we're walking this afternoon. I'm certainly not keen on drinking. Tomorrow we're heading out on a sleep out. I've been banging on about wanting to sleep at the rock painting site. The guys have finally given in and agreed. Should be quite a spiritual thing to do.

I hope your business trip is going well.

Lots of love,

James

This afternoon Max and I walked the Fever Tree Forest from camp. We strolled for two or three hours with no purpose beyond enjoyment. The experience was rewarding as I shouldered full responsibility as the senior Back-up on the walk.

The walk was chilled. I followed the elephant paths in the approximate direction of where I wanted to go. I'd adjust at the next fork in the game trail if they deviated too much. After reaching Racket-Tailed Clearing, we took a break before heading north to explore the forest. Here, there were massive stands of wild date palms surrounded by the dusty substrate, making for excellent spoor.

As we crossed the floodplain, I mentally calculated the walking hours since my last encounter. As I reached ten in my head, we rounded a cluster of lala palms, and the clock reset to zero. Two buffalo heads stared straight at us.

This encounter was tricky. The wind was slightly in our favour, but it occasionally swirled, allowing the buffalo to catch our scent and vanish into the long grass. We glimpsed them now and again, but we couldn't be too sure where they'd gone. We were losing daylight, and this was our only way back to camp. I gave them some space, but not too much as I wanted them not to settle but to keep moving. This was a bit of a gamble; they could quickly become annoyed and circle back on us. It's this behaviour that makes buffalo so dangerous and feared.

We made it back to camp, an excellent way to bring up my 200th hour as a qualified Back-up. Once the rifle was clean and in the safe, I toasted the milestone with a beer and settled around the fire for burger night.

The Rock Paintings, Makuleke
7th June 2014

After a ten-kilometre run and a spot of lunch, we headed to the Sand Veld for a sleep out. A month ago, I'd visited the cave paintings and promised myself I'd make it back there to spend the night. I wanted to experience the Bushman's home for myself. I'm grateful for the opportunity, the only challenge being for me to find our way there. Not an easy prospect given my appalling sense of direction.

We parked at the junction of Lanner Drive and Caracal Link. Then it was a case of following the arrow on the GPS to our destination. But nothing is ever that simple, especially as the technology isn't sophisticated enough to show the various gorges along the way.

Fortunately, I remembered we needed to cross a gorge. Unfortunately, I didn't know about the several others in the area. So, when I spotted one, I led us down, through, and up—only to discover we traversed the wrong gorge. The silver lining and there's always a silver lining if you look hard enough, revealed itself in the stunning beauty of this new gorge. We might have ventured into places where no man walked before—or at least no man who could navigate.

Regardless of the detour, we got to the cave paintings in excellent time. Setting up camp was not onerous. It was a case of picking where you wanted to sleep, then laying out your bedroll and sleeping bag. I slept under the overhang of the cave so I could look up at the rock paintings.

We collected wood for a small safety fire. The only purpose was to warn off dangerous game that became too curious. It didn't take long to collect firewood as there were plenty of fallen Lebombo ironwood and silver cluster leaf to choose from.

In the spirit of our location, we made fire by friction using a corkwood baseplate and drill. With five of us taking it in turns to power the drill, it didn't take long before we'd created an ember. Using a clump of grass, we moved the glowing ash from the drill site to the fireplace, before using dehydrated elephant dung to really get the fire going.

With the fire taken care of, we sat up on the ridge to enjoy the view in the last of the light. It was pin-drop quiet other than a brown-hooded kingfisher, a natal spur-fowl and the distant roar of the Luvuvuh River.

Dinner was cooked over a gas stove, then after a cuppa, it was to bed. We'd worked out shifts. The first started at nine o'clock for an hour and three quarters. When I retired to my cave for the night, I left my rifle with the watch. What a spot I chose to sleep—more accurately, what a remarkable place the bushmen selected all those years ago.

As I looked up from my bed, I could see both the cliff face and the night sky, which reminded me of an extract from Bulpin's Ivory Trail. His poetic description of the African night sky, with stars peeking through darkness like holes in an old blanket, perfectly matched the view above me.

I've been on a few of these sleep outs now. I've learnt that once you accept you will not have a perfect night's sleep, you end up sleeping well, all things considered.

Hein woke me for my shift. It was quarter past two, and my priority was to get the kettle going for a tea and a rusk. The night was quiet, apart from the wild—the soft murmur of the bush alive with insects, a hyena giggling occasionally, and a leopard *sawing* hoarsely in the distance. There was the odd shuffle from somebody trying to get comfortable on the cold sandy floor, some snores, and some wild animal sounds I couldn't quite place. At four o'clock, Jomi took over.

The music and the presence of the rock art swept across me as I woke from my sleep in a wave of primeval emotion. The music was coming from Jomi, who was bringing the final watch of the night to a close. The deep blue of night gradually gave way to a palette of soft pinks and gentle oranges. It took me a moment to grasp what was happening—it felt like I was waking up on a movie set. The tune he was playing was from *The Lord of the Rings.* Perfect for our surroundings. This was the first time I'd ever heard something other than 'London's Burning' on the recorder, and it was utterly mesmerising.

I didn't jump out of bed; I was enjoying my temporary home too much. Luckily, I didn't have to, as Jomi appeared with tea and rusks for us all. I lay in my sleeping bag with my woolly hat pulled down, and my neckerchief pulled up. Here I lay watching the sun illuminate first the large leaf rock fig and then the paintings themselves.

The dawn chorus is not spectacular on the Sand Veld. I guess the habitat isn't the best. What I heard as I refused to emerge from the warmth of my sleeping bag were: Swainson spurfowl, white-bellied sunbird, the ubiquitous cape turtle dove, kurrichane thrush, which was a Jomi ID, rather than mine, dark-capped bulbul, crested francolin and grey-headed parrots.

Breaking camp meant leaving the site exactly as we found it. The fireplace had disappeared entirely. We'd mixed the ashes with wet sand and dispersed it over a wide area, we scattered any unused firewood and wiped away our footprints. The next group to come this way must not know we were ever here, that's the way of wilderness guiding.

I led back, a more direct route than before. Jomi took over when back at the vehicle and drove us to camp. As we drove down Caracal Link, he asked if any of us had our phones. Excellent, I thought, there must be phone signal here. Nope, he wanted to use the bird call app to try to call in an Arnott's chat. We had no luck, but as we were waiting and listening, we heard a leopard call.

Hearing the leopard seemed like a perfect way to finish, but it wasn't how our overnight trail ended. The conclusion left a sour taste. Close to camp, we spotted vultures on a kill. We jumped off the vehicle and ventured into the acacia veld to investigate. There, we found an impala ram strangled by a snare. It must have struggled for quite some time. The ram was skinny, and the bush the trap was tied to lay broken off beside him.

EcoTraining, Makuleke
10th June 2014

While on my pre-lunch run I discovered fresh leopard tracks and scat on the driveway. It's always exciting to see leopard spoor, especially when it's so close to camp. This chap must have walked the outer firebreak–aka our running track, into the car park and then out via the drive. When I'm back in the UK, I doubt I'll do what I did next - fetch my camera to take photos of the animal's poop.

We, the Back-ups and EcoTraining's roving maintenance guy, Robert, spent the afternoon bush clearing. This ended up with a visit to the bridge for a few sundowners. Some of Makuleke's Big Five inhabitants played their part with four elephants taking water in the Luvuvuh and three buffalo crossing as the sun sank.

After dark, we headed back to camp with talk of spotting a leopard. Jomi was especially keen, as he'd been stuck in camp and hadn’t seen one of these elusive cats in two months.

There was plenty of chatter on the way back—nothing like a couple or so Castles to get everyone talking—but we quickly fell silent when the radio crackled to life. It was Sarah, saying she had a leopard on Mangeba. We were on Mangeba! This was looking promising. Then we caught sight of her lights, she was around the corner from us.

We followed Sarah's vehicle, which was following a female leopard. She was relaxed, scent marking as she went. I should point out that I'm referring to the leopard, not Sarah. We watched her for ten minutes during which we got excited when she crouched, waited, then sprung forward into the bush only to return empty pawed.

11th June 2014

I don't know why I go into town; it ends up a frustrating experience. But I never learn and today I jumped at the opportunity of a trip to the bustling metropolis of Louis Trichardt.

A typical rural Afrikaans town in which you'd be hard-pressed to find anyone between sixteen and sixty not top to toe in hunting camouflage.

I once, naively, suggested I could spend my leave there. My plan was to get a lift from Pafuri Gate with the grocer on the day he brought in our food. This suggestion was met with, first, open-mouthed bewilderment, then laughter, and then a serious,

'No James, you shouldn't do that. They don't like

outsiders there.'

The reason for my visit was to send off my dangerous game logbooks to *FGASA* for approval ahead of my *Trails Guide* practical assessment. This was relatively painless by South African standards, but still frustrating. My teller didn't want to be there and barely raised a smile, despite my many one-liners. She didn't even crack a smile at any of the many text messages she received, but these were clearly more important than serving me.

Then there was the usual pointless toing and froing. I explained I needed an envelope, and I'd like to send my package recorded delivery. She sent me away to fill out a form. On my return, I was sent away to address the envelope. Back at the window, she stuck the first form over the address I'd written on the envelope.

It's sent now; my fingers are crossed that it gets there. However, I love the Post Office's apparent business model worldwide. If you want to improve the chances of your package being delivered, you must pay extra.

Jomi had his own battle. It wasn't much of a fight to be fair. He visited Home Affairs to sort out his visa, only to be told they couldn't help foreigners—his teller pointed to a sign saying so. Despite our admin frustrations, Louis Trichardt seemed welcoming enough. I'd be happy to return.

CHAPTER SEVENTEEN

'Our doubts are traitors, and make us lose the good we oft might win, by fearing to attempt.' *William Shakespear, Playwright.*

EcoTraining, Makuleke
12th June 2014

The day started with a sedate drive to the bridge. I was doing various drops for a conservation society as their driver for the day. They're staying with us for three nights while they conduct a census in the area.

We spent a fair bit of time sitting around as we waited for their armed escort to turn up. This allowed us to enjoy the sunrise, which revealed a thick mist hugging the Luvuvuh as it snaked in from the west under the bridge. To keep us entertained, we watched the guinea fowl and baboons coming down from their roosts to start their day of foraging.

The highlight from our observation point was the raptors, first the presidential African fish eagle that stood proudly in a tall jackal-berry. Then the long-crested eagle, a real tick for the birders. Quite a funky bird rivalling the crested barbet and the African hoopoe for the savannah's punk rocker title.

I drove one team east, including three armed men to their starting point. I was now free to head back to camp. During my drive, I listened to a great deal of chatter on the radio. There'd been an elephant carcass found by the *ARH* students on their way to the range. Luckily, not poaching, the likely cause of death was mooted as anthrax.

Once back in camp, I completed my chores before hitting the running track. Running first thing is more enjoyable than in the heat of the day. Not because of the temperature but because there are more animals about, the impala, vervets and baboons that live in camp are still hanging around. There were also ele tracks around the firebreak from last night. My alertness stepped up a level as the lack of heat would not be keeping the dangerous animals tucked away in the shade at such a time.

It wasn't long before I headed out in my taxi. I had the survey team to pick up from Mangala, which meant driving down Luvuvuh West, also known as Ambush Alley. It felt great to be driving there again—it's been a while since I worked Pafuri Trails. The bush was alive with activity, including a Verreaux's eagle and that familiar sweet popcorn scent of leopard nearby. I did run into some traffic: an elephant bull feeding with no intention of moving. I wasn't in any hurry, so I pulled a can of Diet Coke from my rucksack and enjoyed the show.

After picking up the survey team, I started the drive back. I'd only gone fifty metres when a six-foot-long *Croton* branch shot through a hole in the floor of the Landy. This was a shock, even more so for Alex sitting in the passenger seat.

Once we'd removed this obstacle, we carried on along Ambush Alley. Here we ran into a breeding herd of elephants. I worked my way past an adolescent bull who put on a show of bravado but soon became relaxed and resumed feeding.

I chose not to continue forward as the rest of the breeding herd had monopolised the road. I moved the Landy as far as I could, so I didn't separate the young bull from the herd. With no need to rush, we sat back, watched, and took photographs.

After five minutes, one of my armed passengers insisted we withdraw, claiming that one elephant posed a threat. This took me by surprise as, in my opinion, the cow in question was calmly feeding behind a *Croton* bush. The adolescent bull, who had initially trumpeted at us was also feeding, his tail flicking away flies—a clear sign of an elephant at ease. A distressed elephant would have its tail outstretched horizontally.

Alex, my passenger who had narrowly avoided being impaled earlier, translated the man's command to me from Shangaan to English. The ranked soldier then repeated his request moments later. I felt I should yield to his experience, despite the request going against my better judgement. I knew starting the engine would antagonise the elephants and turn an okay experience into a stressful one.

On starting the engine, the cow reacted to the sound and emerged from behind the *Croton*. I'd barely had time to assess the situation, never mind the time to talk the elephant down before the chap on the back of the vehicle chambered his semi-automatic rifle.

Then, this is the part I could not believe. He pulled the trigger. A warning shot from his R1 rifle screamed over the elephant's head. This exacerbated the situation. The elephant that had been feeding was now moving toward us. Sitting next to me, Alex shouted it down—and it worked. I was still too stunned by the whole chambering and shot to do more than look around in bewilderment.

The thunderous clap of the matriarch's ears as she shook her head brought my focus back. The cloud of dust released from her body by the vigour of her shaking hung in a menacing haze around her.

I reversed up the road at breakneck speed with my ears ringing and the smell of spent propellant filling my nostrils. We got to a safe distance and waited for the elephants to make their way to the river, which they did after ten minutes. Was I wrong? Was the soldier right? Like every story, there are three sides to it—mine, his, and the truth.

Back at camp, I learned that Jomi and Robert experienced a far more peaceful elephant encounter. While they worked on a vehicle, an old bull casually wandered past them, moving through the car park and into camp.

Late in the afternoon we took a cool box down to Sand Pit. Here we sat on the sandbank, looking out over the Limpopo. The place is awe-inspiring and always prompts one thing—silence. Nobody ever gives instruction; people automatically stop speaking. This moment of enchantment lasted twenty minutes. The voluntary silence was only broken by the occasional,

'Can you pass me a beer please?'

As the sun sank, it set the sky ablaze, a scene fit for a postcard. Our contribution to the moment was corny but worth it—we played Toto's *Africa* on the iPhone. Right on cue, within the first round of drumbeats, five elephants emerged from their hiding spot. They stepped out from among the tall sycamore figs and jackal-berries and waded across the river. Just as quickly as they appeared, they vanished again, this time into the tribal lands of Zimbabwe.

14th June 2014

I've been kept awake these last couple of nights thinking of what could have happened during the incident on Ambush Alley. Self-doubt wasn't just creeping in; it was kicking down the door, and I was in danger of letting it in and losing my nerve.

I accompanied the students to the shooting range for their final day of Advanced Rifle Handling. Those that were still to go looked tense, psyching themselves out of it. I recognised the symptoms - I had nearly done the same in December.

The range is on the Park's western boundary overlooking the Limpopo. The camp is called Mabiligwe, an old training base for the South African Recces, their version of the SAS. It is now used by the concession's Anti-Poaching Unit. We explored the old quarters and parade ground.

During my time at Makuleke, I've heard one man's name many times, Jack Greef. He, until six years ago, ran the Anti-Poaching Unit here. From what I understand, he was a no-nonsense guy running a disciplined team with zero tolerance for poaching. The base must have been like a second home for him. In his former life, he was a member of the Recces, where he became one of the most decorated soldiers in the South African Defence Force.

Walking around the partly operational ranger station, it was clear that conservation had been militarised. I easily imagined what it would have been like under Jack's command. In the laundry room, a row of stainless-steel sinks stood opposite two permanently fixed ironing boards, giving the impression of a place where the rangers were always immaculately turned out.

If there ever was such a thing as an animal graveyard, this was it. We walked around the largest building on the site, the mess hall, which was lined with skulls and bones. The collection was incredibly varied—crocodile, elephant, buffalo, hippo, kudu, leopard, hyena. You name it; they were here to be seen.

Some skulls were accompanied by a neatly placed bullet hole, indicating a perfect brain shot. Whether this had been a case of self-defence, poaching, or euthanasia was impossible to determine. It wasn't just a boneyard; it also resembled the den of a scrap metal merchant, filled with thousands upon thousands of snares. We were informed that what we saw was nothing compared to what had been collected under Jack's watch—a staggering 27,000 snares.

Inside the mess hall, a bar sat at one end, a remnant of the Recce days. The cafeteria was now completely empty, save for confiscated spears and fish traps, while animal bones decorated the windowsills, with old wire snares calcified into them. The last room I visited must have been the heart of Jack's operation. Nothing remained here except a dusty desk and a scattering of maps on the wall, one of which resembled a pincushion more than a map. I assumed each prick represented a poaching incident.

Throughout my training and work in Kruger, there's been a lot of bravado over the shooting of poachers, with very few speaking out against it. For me, the thought of using lethal force is a morally questionable practice.

I should point out that South Africa has no official shoot-to-kill government policy. Still, the use of lethal force is allowed in some circumstances. However, there may be a more aggressive stance taken on some private game reserves, and last year, Botswana introduced the controversial policy to combat rhino and elephant poaching.

There's no doubt that rangers need to protect themselves from poachers. Still, the rules of engagement should be akin to those used by a peacekeeping force. When threatened, the ranger's retaliation should be proportional. It should only use the least force necessary to neutralise the threat, and only after issuing a clear warning. This is easy for me to say as I've never been in a conflict. I imagine there are arguments that such an approach could put the rangers in danger. My counter would be that rangers should be well-trained and well-equipped to handle the situation.

Without the militarisation of conservation, it would be impossible to combat poaching effectively. But a heavy-handed approach to anti-poaching can lead to the alienation of communities who may start to view all conservation initiatives as threats rather than a positive force in their lives.

NGOs should focus on the root causes of poaching. Often, poachers come from poor communities with limited opportunities to earn an income. If they are killed, their families may lose their only source of income, driving them further into poverty and potentially into a life of crime.

Conservation efforts must be carried out in a way that respects human rights and the needs of communities. A more humane and measured approach will help build stronger relationships with local communities and foster a greater sense of trust and cooperation. Conservation should be about hearts and minds; people must understand and get on board for a sustainable solution.

The 'Shot Fired' situation is eating away at me. Knowing things can happen that are beyond my locus of control is denting my confidence and affecting my happiness. Whilst I know it was vehicle-based, I wanted to nip it in the bud. I woke Max up from his afternoon nap and persuaded him to go for a walk. We took the rifles and headed into the floodplain. This was just what I needed. We even had a buffalo encounter to exorcise the demons.

I can't get across how important confidence is. If I lack it, lack commitment, and don't listen to gut instinct, there is a chance I will be killed out here. Even worse than death, I could survive, but one of my guests who have placed their life in my hands could pay the ultimate price for my self-doubt.

CHAPTER EIGHTEEN

'Nature's great masterpiece, an elephant – the only harmless great thing.' *John Donne, Poet.*

EcoTraining, Makuleke
16th June 2014

When Alan is in town, there's sure to be one or two incredible elephant encounters. Today was my day to experience such an occurrence. Alan and I took the students across the floodplain and through the Fever Tree Forest. The first encounter happened at 300 metres, the second at fifty, the final at fifteen.

We saw a breeding herd making their way to the pan. We took this opportunity to position ourselves to watch them come down for their morning refreshment. While we were waiting, an ele bull approached to drink. He was in the early stages of musth with a slight swagger.

He was unaware of us as we sat comfortably on the ridge overlooking the pan. He didn't stay long before wandering off aimlessly, almost completing a figure of eight before disappearing to the east. I could have returned to camp content, ready to chat excitedly about this 50-metre encounter over tea and lemony creams, but this was only the beginning.

The breeding herd wasn't playing ball, so we carried on from Hlangaluwe Pan towards Mangeba for our pick-up. Here we came across our musthy bull again. He was coming back towards us. This is where Alan worked his magic, but before he waved his wand, aka his tracking stick, he gave us a couple of options.

'We could, in fact, we should retreat to the ridge, or we can stay here for what could be an invaluable learning experience.'

We chose the second option, remaining motionless and standing firm. The gentle giant carried on towards us, swaying slightly under the influence. Alan moved across the group. This made the elephant aware we were there. Surprising the elephant any closer would not have been advisable.

He kept coming, but now he could see us, he held his head up high. There was no anger, just curiosity. On more than one occasions, he swung his head towards us.

As he passed, I looked into his eyes. They were barely open—he was half asleep. He couldn't be bothered with the eight people frozen on the veld just fifteen metres from him. My heart thumped from start to finish, so much so that the elephant was undoubtedly aware.

19th June 2014

I woke up to a feeling of jealousy. On the way back from The Outpost last night Max and Jomi saw a lioness on Middle Road. So this morning, one group headed out with Alan to track the lions. It turns out there were four of them. Despite being hot on their tracks for three hours, they had no luck.

Henry and I took a group to walk the floodplain. From an encounter point of view, it was productive, one elephant bull, a small herd of buffalo, and a kin group of elephants.

Once back at camp, we shuffled vehicles. Jomi had left The Beige at the gate when he went to Home Affairs. Max and I picked this up using 'Tambookie' on what was a long and arduous journey. This new Landy was playing up as she kept losing power. The old-school Land Rover with its mechanical resilience doesn't short-circuit and fail like its modern-day cousins with their complex electronic systems.

On one of our power cuts, Steve from the Trails Camp stopped by to say hi. It was his day off, so he'd gone to get phone signal at the Outpost turn-off on Pafuri Main. He quickly told us about his encounter with three rhinos on his last trail.

This afternoon Alan was keen to continue tracking lions, so we picked up where the guys left off this morning. We were following the spoor of four lions: one lioness, and three cubs through thick bush consisting of scrubby lala palms, sandpaper raisin and elephant's ear.

This was Big Five territory with lots of tracks and signs of buffalo, lion, and elephant. Leopard prints were conspicuous by their absence. Perhaps the area was too intimidating, even for them.

I learnt so much from watching Alan at work. In thick bush, Alan often whispered he would not follow the current course. Instead, he'd gesture with his wand, directing us to circle around. After we circled the thicket, he'd cut the spoor again hot on the trail.

It became apparent we weren't the only ones tracking this pride of four. The spoor revealed a male lion who, I imagine, had sex and murder in mind. Whether there would be murder, I'm not sure. The three cubs, judging by the paw prints, had grown over a year old. Rather than committing infanticide, he might settle for driving them from his new territory.

After an hour we lost the tracks. Alan thought we could have found them again if we swept the area, but time was not on our side. Instead, we cut our losses and headed back to the vehicle.

20th June 2014

Walking the floodplain from camp has been productive of late, certainly for encounters. However, this morning they weren't coming, so I was resigning myself to it being nothing more than a picturesque walk through the Fever Tree Forest.

As we left the forest, Alan directed the student lead, Jeremy, to the small basalt ridge. The elevated position gave him height to scan the floodplain to the south and the riverine thicket to the north. As the student crossed the crest, it looked like he was performing a hand puppet show. Jeremy was trying to figure out which signal to use, raising his hand to stop, freeze, and stop again. In the end, he hissed through his teeth.

'Lion!'

I must have misheard him; I was certain he whispered 'lion.' Instead of freezing, I rushed up from the back of the line with my rifle. I wasn't aiming for a Kevin Costner *Bodyguard* moment; I just wanted to see it myself.

We can all make mistakes, and forgiveness comes after a few days of ribbing. I've mistaken a bush pig for a lion, and I watched Ben mistake an eland for one. I didn't feel hopeful this time, either. But sure enough—two lionesses lounged atop a rounded termite mound, bathed in the amber glow of the morning sun. They lay 120 metres away; wind blew in our favour, thick cover concealed us, and they remained completely unaware of our presence.

Alan told us to sit down. Unfortunately, Nico didn’t react quickly enough and was left standing. We watched for ten minutes, enjoying the sighting. They weren't sleeping but rather resting drowsily, heads up and soaking in the sun. The lioness on top of the mound was young, about a year old, her age revealed by the remnants of her youthful spots on her tawny coat.

Nico grew uncomfortable in his squat and became restless. Alan directed him to sit on a rock. Unfortunately, the yearling noticed his movement. She lowered her head with her ears forward as she tried to figure us out. She had seen enough and took off, kicking up a puff of dust as her claws gripped the hardened dirt. The mother paused for five seconds to check us out, then followed. As they moved east, we heard Natal spurfowl, then zebra, marking the lions' passage with alarm calls.

Alan put the sighting down to,

'We had it coming. Nature is funny in that way, you get out what you put in, it's like paying an honesty bill.'

Based on the tracks we'd spotted over the past few days and the various sightings; we identified seven individuals within the concession.

22nd June 2014

I walked with the college group. They gained plenty from it, not just skills and knowledge, but self-discovery. I guess their age encouraged this growth. Most insights emerged from discussing the incredible nature of elephants. Alan and I also experienced a moment of enlightenment when one student described their college lecturer as,

'He's really old, he must be over forty.'

If I didn't feel old before, I did now.

Nicole, the student lead, saved us from a tricky situation when she spotted some oxpeckers fly up from the tall *Sporobolus* grass 150 metres in front of our position. After five minutes of dissecting the area with our binoculars, we made out some buffalo. There was no way through. Instead, we backtracked and arranged a new pick up.

On our way, we happened upon across a dusty clearing surrounded by the tall grass waving in the gentle breeze. In the centre was a lone buffalo skull which we gathered round; such a find is always an opportunity for the curious. Alan used it for an impromptu lesson on anthrax, and I used it for a joke,

'And that's why we don't drink the tap water at camp.' I said.

Everyone bought it hook, line and sinker, going white with terror, believing they'd been drinking water laced with anthrax since they arrived in camp.

The afternoon walk started off with an impala ewe dead in a snare. She can't have died more than 24 hours ago. As always, we took down the coordinates and emailed them to the section ranger when we got back. Another group did the same last week when they found a dead nyala. The result was a positive; the rangers set up an ambush which yielded an arrest.

23rd June 2014

After we left camp, Duncan called over the radio to say he'd heard a lion roaring. We changed our plans, pulled the vehicle off the road, and walked toward the sound. It wasn't long before the roaring stopped. Now, it became a matter of spotting either the spoor or the lion.

We found his tracks and dutifully followed them, only to end up circling back on ourselves. He led us on a merry chase, doubling back and overlaying our footprints with his. Two students suspected he might be at the snared impala from the day before, so we headed in that direction. While we didn't spot him, their intuition proved correct.

The carcass was nearly devoured. The stomach had been removed with surgical precision. Almost the entire body was gone, save for the forequarters, and half the face had been taken in a single bite. An eerie imprint in the fine sand told the story—a lion's tail alongside the sweeping marks left by its tuft.

As we tried to decide which were the most recent tracks, we were rudely interrupted by a breeding herd of elephants. This took us off guard, and the problem was compounded when one bull elephant approached from the east while another appeared from the south.

We were busted, caught in the open with no cover and nowhere to go. We did what had to be done, put our faith in Alan and follow his orders to the letter. The first came immediately.

'Sit down.'

The first elephant advanced within twenty metres, checked us out, but decided against coming closer. It was the second one that got our pulses racing. The bull approached just ten metres from where we sat, the adolescent's trunk twisting upwards as he tried to make sense of our scent. We sat frozen in the sand, contemplating what could be our last moments on earth. The sheer size of the elephant towering over us left no doubt where our respect belonged. Even the Cape turtle dove paused its constant refrain—only for the alarm calls of a squirrel to take over, sensing the gravity of the unfolding situation.

To minimise noise, Alan gritted his teeth and whispered his next command.

'Stand your ground.'

We were still sitting in the sand, but we got what he meant.

This bull was up for a game of chase. He kicked at the floor in a game elephants play with impala and warthog. The idea is the *victim* takes fright at the cloud of dust and runs, at which point the elephant would chase. We didn't—we sat fast. We would not play ball.

Once it was over and we'd reached safety, we excitedly discussed what had just happened. Everyone acknowledged that Alan's calm energy and steady demeanour guided both us and the male elephants through the experience unharmed.

CHAPTER NINETEEN

'In the African wilderness, you learn what it means to be both predator and prey in the same instant.' *Ernest Hemingway, Novelist.*

Hoedspruit
24th June to 2nd July 2014

Rather than heading off to new places and doing amazing things for my last week of leave, I instead laid up in Hoedspruit. I checked into my favourite guest house and worked hard at doing nothing. Camp life is full-on with little time to yourself, so it was just what the doctor ordered.

It felt like a waste, but I needed it. I buried myself in some reading, did some study, and watched an inordinate amount of TV—far too much. My leave coincided with the Wimbledon Tennis Championships, so I caught some of that on the telly. The tournament means a lot to me, not because I'm a huge tennis fan, but because Southfields, where it's held, is where I live in London. I felt homesick for it; it's always a thrill when the biggest tennis show on earth comes to that sleepy London village.

There's a tiny pizza restaurant in Southfields, so small that to triple capacity they put a small lean-to tent on the side. The hospitality is excellent, and the pizza is out of this world. The tomato base they use should be illegal—it's irresistible. I was longing for the good times I've had there and the taste of their heavily mushroomed pepperoni pizzas. So often I have sat there watching the tennis-goers heading to and from The All England Lawn Tennis Club. Fascinating people-watching.

Despite my TV marathon, I got out for a run each day. Running up and down the roads isn't much fun for my knees, but the road names made it worthwhile. I personally would love to live on Giraffe Street or perhaps Duiker, but not Ferret Street.

Running around town brings with it many interesting sights. My run takes me past the ProTrack offices, one of the anti-poaching operators. They have a display on their front lawn, showing how many rhinos have been poached in South Africa in that year. A small white cross signifies each animal killed. There are too many to count, so they're forced to write out the number in black and white. Tragically it stands at 430 so far this year. In a few days this will be 433 given the current rate.

I didn't encounter many other runners, but one chap stood out. I was running up the main street when I spotted a man jogging towards me. He wore shorts, a t-shirt, a floppy hat, and a rucksack—nothing unusual. What was strange, though, was that he was cradling a big, mean-looking machine gun. He didn't seem military, so I wasn't sure what to make of him. However, no one was chasing him. We exchanged greetings and went our separate ways.

In between drifting from coffee shop to book shop to coffee shop, with the occasional stop at a pub, I had time to think. This is never ideal, and my conclusion was depressing. My year of living the dream as a safari guide was nearly over. Should you even chase your dreams in the first place? I was beginning to think not because to dream means you'll eventually wake up—they aren't sustainable.

One pub visit was to catch up with Ben. In the gloomy ambiance of Sleeper's, Ben shared with me the heart-wrenching news about Obelix, the colossal six-tonne bull elephant I encountered on my last visit to Tshukudu Lodge.

'Obelix wasn't just an elephant; he was a living legend,' Ben reminisced. 'Despite occasional grumpiness, he was a loveable rogue which made him a favourite to all who crossed his path' he continued.

Ben put the thirty-five-year-old elephant's grumpiness down to musth, and as the sole elephant on the reserve, Obelix's mischievous antics — from uprooting trees to chasing vehicles — suggested his frustration.

The tragic turn of events unfolded when Obelix's adventurous spirit, drawn by the scent of female elephants in the neighbouring Balule reserve, led him through a fence and across train tracks. A fatal collision with a mining train broke his spine, ending the gentle giant's life. If any solace can be found, it's in the fact that the accident occurred on Obelix's return across the tracks. There's a small chance he got lucky, and his legacy may live on through his progeny.

Ben was deeply affected by the incident, his voice heavy with grief as he said, 'It wasn't just the loss of an elephant; it was like saying goodbye to a family member.' However, what left the biggest impression on Ben wasn't the brutal way they lost Obelix but the clean-up that followed. Ben had to get hands-on as a ranger and deal with the remains. Due to the sheer size of the task, a chainsaw was needed to get it done.

The Outpost, Makuleke
4th July 2014

This morning's food run went off like clockwork. To maximize my time in bed, I had loaded the trailer the night before with crates and freezer boxes. All that was left was to grab a handful of rusks for sustenance, pull the Landy out, and hitch up the trailer.

Collecting the food went without incident if you ignore the broken jar of Bolognese sauce that bumped around the trailer. However, it turned out that further items hadn't made it safely back to camp either. We discovered packets of pasta and a jar of gherkins as we drove to The Outpost for a freelance guiding gig. I suspect I'll be facing several charges come fines night. My only saving grace was that the gherkin jar remained intact.

Jomi and I reached The Outpost by ten-thirty, leaving plenty of time to prepare, rest, run and read before heading out. My guests for the trail were a young family from Natal—a dad, mum, and two boys, aged seventeen and twelve. Any nerves I might have felt quickly faded when I met them. They had no specific interests—they were simply happy for me to do with them as I pleased.

With the vehicle prepped—full of diesel, blankets, a spotlight, reference books, snacks, and a cooler box—I was ready and waiting. As the guests settled into the vehicle, I stood in the doorway, leaning against the steering wheel. When I shifted my weight onto my right hip, I accidentally pressed a lever that shot soapy water into my eye. Not the most auspicious start!

Though they claimed no special interests, they asked about big cats, wondering about their chances of spotting lion or leopard.

'More chance of seeing leopard than lion here,' I said as a matter of fact.

'I've been in Makuleke since January, and I've only seen a lion on two occasions. I don't want to raise expectations. We'll try our hardest to find leopard though.'

We saw surprisingly few animals—perhaps because I had soap in my eye. Still, every game drive has special moments, and I was determined to find ours. Taking the long route back from Makwadzi along Middle Road to Mangeba, I aimed to maximise our chances of spotting a leopard. Every so often, I switched off the engine to listen for telltale signs of predators, like impalas barking or baboons sounding alarm calls. But luck wasn't on our side.

While we listened quietly, breaking branches revealed elephants ahead. I'd hoped for such an encounter. A bachelor herd would let us make the most of the sighting. But a breeding herd would force us to drive on, as the risk at night wouldn't justify staying.

We lucked out, a pair of bulls. I positioned myself adjacent to them before turning the engine, lights, and radio off so we could exercise our senses. As we sat under the cover of darkness, one bull, a big chap with tusks to match, came out of the bush. We stayed incredibly still listening to him walk, his stomach rumble and his buddy munching on lala palms. He stood there watching us for a while before going behind the vehicle. He must have passed mere metres from our bumper.

I focused on his behaviour during the encounter, watching his body language closely. Since I arrived, I've learned a bit about elephants, which wasn't difficult, considering I knew nothing before. From what I did know, he seemed relaxed. Still, that didn't stop my heart from being in my mouth, nor a film of sweat from forming on my forehead, despite the chilly night.

Leaving the elephant encounter behind, we closed in on the lodge. As we neared, a meteorite streaked across the night sky, so low and bright it seemed for a moment like a man-made object hurtling to Earth. The significance of it happening on Independence Day wasn't lost on us.

My year at EcoTraining had institutionalised me. Tonight, back at camp, it was Burger Night—a tradition that rolled around once a week. It was Friday, and I found myself missing it. But my frustration quickly faded when one of The Outpost team brought me dinner: a fillet steak with potato wedges drizzled in gravy and a cold beer to wash it down.

5th July 2014

My clock read five to five when it beeped to life. I took a quick shower before picking up the Landy on my way to the lodge. It didn't take long to get the hotbox prepped. Then it was time to wake my guests.

To give the lodge a futuristic edge, they called the rooms 'spaces'—glass boxes offering uninterrupted views. My guests occupied spaces six and seven, which required a long walk down a promenade, much farther than I had expected, given the gap between each room. I suppose the spacing is for privacy, as sound travels freely in the stillness of the African night. I eventually reached their spaces and woke them as close to five-thirty as the trek allowed

Much to my relief, Ezra was up to serve their morning coffee. I hadn't a clue how to use the fancy piece of coffee making equipment except to extract hot water for a cup of tea.

I explained we were going to mission it down the tar road to the floodplain so we could drive west along the Luvuvuh. This would be a long drive but would be worth it when we got there.

After a couple of hours of driving and sightings, we stopped at Mangala. I prepared the coffee, hot chocolate and my third cup of tea for the morning. It was still chilly, so I suggested we take our drinks and some of the freshly cooked muffins down by the river.

The morning sun was warming the riverbank, and I fancied some of that sun for myself.

As we chatted over our various brews, one of my guests, Sandy, spotted impala at full tilt. They came bounding from the bush and across a dry riverbed which was a seasonal tributary for the Luvuvuh. This got our attention and at first looked promising, but nothing followed.

I busied myself showing one boy an excellent example of a leopard track on my phone. Yes, I'd gotten so desperate that I'd resorted to photos—not even of animals, but their footprints. Sandy, who had been watching the donga, suddenly announced she'd seen movement. She felt certain it was a cat. I still couldn't see it, but her next whisper, brimming with excitement, left me eager and determined to catch a glimpse.

'Lion!'

After much explaining, I finally spotted him. He moved towards us, heading down to the river, either to drink or cross it.

Not a problem, we'd jump back into the safety of the Landy and watch from there. What a great sighting it will be.

Glancing back at the vehicle, I did a double take. It wasn't as close as I'd thought or needed it to be. It was some one hundred metres behind us. We could have sat tight, concealed with the sun behind us. But if he crossed the river, there would be little we could do except hope we gave him more of a fright than he us.

We retreated to the top of the bank at the far

edge of the river's floodplain to seek cover in the shadows of a big nyala tree. That movement was enough for him. He turned tail and lumbered off into the ridges south-east of our position. No doubt, this was something special and worth the long drive. There was no reason to call it in over the radio except to show off—so I did.

CHAPTER TWENTY

'Failure is simply the opportunity to begin again, this time more intelligently.' *Henry Ford, Industrialist.*

EcoTraining, Makuleke
7th July 2014

Alan asked me to lead the walk this morning with Max as my Back-up. He said it would be a demonstration to the students as to how it should be done and would allow me to practice ahead of my Lead Trails assessment.

Today was a lesson in switching on from the moment you set out from camp. As I left the relative safety of the outer firebreak, we immediately saw signs of activity.

The imprint of the elephant's foot appeared delicate and sharp. My gut told me it was fresh. I underlined it with the toe of my boot, signalling Max to stay alert. I hadn't realised how fresh until I rounded the scrubby umbrella thorn and spotted a young bull feeding twelve feet ahead. I shot up a clenched fist to signal, *Freeze, immediate danger.*

The teenager stepped forward and stood tall in front of me.

'Stand your ground,' I hissed to my guests.

At the first opportunity, I asked Max to lead them to the safety of the ridge while I held my position. The encounter was textbook.

As we watched from our position of high ground, we saw him move on to gate crash a breeding herd's drinking party down at the Lala Palm trough. There were trumpeting elephants running all directions. Given their mood, I decided we would change course and head west, far safer than trying to negotiate an irate breeding herd.

This diversion led us through the lala palm scrub. Normally, this wouldn't have been an issue. But I missed some lion tracks and then misjudged the age of a different set. They were fresher than I had thought, meaning I wasn't taking the safest path. This contrasted sharply with my decision later in the walk when I became overly cautious, retreating from an encounter with three elephant bulls. I chose an alternative route that put us in more danger, taking us through an area where a fourth elephant, a straggler, went unnoticed by me. No one else spotted it except for one student who caught a glimpse and Alan, who heard a telltale sound.

Once back at camp, Alan informed me that it hadn't been a dummy run—it was my actual assessment. He said I nailed it with the first encounter. It was perfect. My knowledge was solid, and I got lots of information across. I was a splendid example for the students. For enjoyment, he gave me ninety-five per cent—out of principle, he never awards full marks.

But I knew a *but* would come—I could sense it—and there it was.

Alan couldn't award me full Trails. Not because of one mistake outright but the compounding effect of multiple mistakes, namely the lion tracks and that fourth elephant which resulted in me walking in an unsafe area. Looking back, it was a tough assessment with little more that could have been thrown at me, but I made some stupid mistakes. I didn't deserve to pass.

While gutted not to get my Lead Trails, which knocked my confidence and left me feeling down, I was pleased to know that Alan would not just give it to me. As it stands, I'm NYC, not yet competent. The best way to learn is from your mistakes. This is fantastic, I make so many, I'm surely learning loads. I've got another shot on Friday, so fingers crossed it's not as eventful.

8th July 2014

Back-up Trails Guide assessments continued today with students walking Hlangaluwe in the morning and Jachacha in the afternoon. As we returned to the vehicle, we noticed it parked at a different angle. We figured that Jomi, when driving past, moved it to mess with us. While having drinks, I decided to check if he'd hidden the keys—and sure enough, they were hidden well. After thirty minutes of searching, we finally found them and returned to camp.

For revenge, we decided to call his bluff. Nicole, who was leading the walk, sat up front with me. I suggested she radio him, acting tearful, claiming she couldn’t find the keys. She pulled it off brilliantly—too well, in fact, and deserved an Oscar. Hiding under her coat so we couldn't put her off, she took the two-way radio in hand, depressed the button and started.

'EcoTraining (sniff), EcoTraining Jomi (sniffle), for Nicole.'

This faked, teary voice was compelling. But no response from Jomi. We tried again but still nothing.

We figured he mustn't be mobile yet from his walk, so we drove a little further before Nicole tried again. She was now getting into it, so much so she could barely get the words out in between her blubbing. It turned out to be too convincing. First the Outpost called in offering help and then the concession manager from Wilderness Safaris. Oh shoot, we fessed up and apologised for our tomfoolery.

It turns out it wasn't Jomi after all. Prime suspects are Steve from Trails Camp and Max who is up there for two or three days. Not sure how we'll get them back, but we won't do it over the radio.

10th July 2014

This morning was chilly, less than five degrees. Fortunately, four guests braved the cold to join me on my assessment walk. It started well with leopard tracks on the outer firebreak. So, pleased I didn't miss these.

Guinea fowl alarmed to our north-west. Rather than following up with a direct approach, I chose to see if we could spot what was spooking them from the ridge. Perhaps if it weren't my assessment, I'd have been more direct with my investigation. I wish I had. It turned out to be the leopard as the students on the field observation test that afternoon saw it had walked over our tracks.

The walk wasn't as eventful as my last, but I had learned from my mistakes. Twice, I backtracked to avoid thick bush, but overall, I chose safe routes.

I had one dangerous game encounter, which came as a relief. I didn't want to redo the assessment, which might have been the case if I hadn't come across something big, hairy, and scary. Although the encounter involved an elephant breeding herd, it wasn't overly challenging.

The elephants were on the *Sporobolus* plains with the closest one being one hundred metres away. I avoided them—standard procedure when it comes to a breeding herd.'

Alan didn't give anything away; I wasn't sure. I don't think I missed anything, though I wouldn't know if I had. I certainly recognised areas where I could improve, along with some silly mistakes. I may have identified some scat incorrectly, saying it was a leopard when it might have been a lion, but to my credit, I did say it was an enormous leopard.

No news from Alan throughout the afternoon, so I figured we'd have our debrief tomorrow. Luckily, I didn't have to sweat the decision any longer. As Alan made the usual announcements after dinner, he slipped in the following.

'The end of the course is nearly here, so drinks bills need to be paid, that includes Lead Trails Guides like James.'

I breathed a sigh of relief and thanked Alan.

CHAPTER TWENTY-ONE

'If children feel safe, they take risks, ask questions, make mistakes, learn to trust, share their feelings, and grow.' *Alfie Kohn, An Educational Reformer.*

Trails Camp, Makuleke
11th July 2014

This morning's food run didn't go as planned. I arrived at the park gate and discovered that the trailer's tailgate had fallen off. This meant a trail of crates and cooler boxes was strung out along Middle Road and San Pad. That wasn't the main issue. Getting the food back in one piece and the entire load was. I jammed some crates across the back of the trailer, and then the grocer lent me a rope to secure them.

The journey back proved slow and despite my best efforts to make the trailer grocery-tight, the jolting road dislodged a crate, causing food to fall off the back. Halfway home, I bit the bullet and unhooked the trailer to nip back in the Landy to recover some carrots and mushrooms. I'd initially set off on foot, but it was too far. I'm not averse to walking—it's what

I've been doing every day for the last year. But even though I was doing the grocery shopping, I was still in Big Five country. Getting too far from the protection of the vehicle would not be wise.

To save face, I wanted to return to camp with a whole trailer. Once I recovered the overboard veg, I picked up the tailgate and brought it back. The next challenge was to hook up the trailer, but as Jomi had ordered enough booze to sink a battleship, I had to use the high-lift jack to raise it onto the towbar.

Once at camp it was an unload followed by a quick turnaround, as I was being picked up for the Wilderness Trails Camp. I left a message for Jomi on his desk detailing a few things and finished with postscripts:

'P.S. I'm hungover

P.P.S. Sarah has one packet of cherry tomatoes, one packet of button mushrooms, one packet of rice and one packet of biscuits which she found on San Pad.

Sorry.'

Trails Camp was different from usual. Instead of paying adults, the camp was full of children. I can't lie—I was disappointed. This was my last trail, and I wasn't even going to get to walk. Instead, I found myself babysitting. It's all for a good cause though; Wilderness Safaris runs an environmental education programme for local children. This week, two groups came from the Makuleke village. Our guests included eight girls and two elders, Maria and Maria. They were Gogos or, as I would know them, Grannies.

Despite my earlier reservations, it turned out to be fun. We started by crafting bracelets from beads to give to participants in a charity cycle tour. There wasn't much chatter; the girls seemed nervous around us. After lunch, we went on a game drive. Again, it was tough to get them engaged. Each girl had been assigned an animal to study and given specific questions to answer, which made it a little easier.

One thing that surprised me was how scared—no, how petrified—both the children and the Gogos felt towards elephants. I didn't expect to see any, but I followed up on a trumpet down Luvuvuh East. There, we found a bull who was soon joined by a buddy. One girl, Delight, was beside herself with worry. We stayed with them for a while, explaining that they wouldn't harm us. We only needed to give them space and read their body language.

After dinner, each person said what they had learnt during the day. Delight said she'd learnt not to fear elephants. Others repeated things I'd told them, which I found rewarding.

Steve needed to drive a staff member to the main accommodation village, which couldn't have come at a worse time for me. Landi, a Wilderness manager, not a Land Rover, had just asked everyone to think of a question they wished they'd asked earlier but hadn't. Many questions focused on the animals, leaving me as the only one to answer them.

After the Q&A, we gathered for stories around the campfire. During each story, one child would translate it so the elders could understand. Then, it was the Gogos' turn to share a story. You could tell they'd done this many times before. They told it with passion, and occasionally, they would break into song.

With a camp full of children, bedtime arrived quickly. Chatter filled the air, but once it faded, the sounds of the night could be heard. Hyenas called, a baboon occasionally coughed, and zebras let out their high-pitched alarms. I'm used to these sounds, but tonight a new one struck me — a little girl repeatedly saying:

'Ndzi chava'

Which is Shangaan for 'I'm scared.'

12th July 2014

On this trail, we get to sleep in. I was on wake-up duty this morning at a leisurely half past six. There was no game drive first thing; instead, we started with some energising exercises before sitting down with the children to enjoy sweet and warming porridge, perfect for combating the morning chill.

When we took the girls out for a game drive, we enjoyed a decent sighting of a pair of hyenas and some wildebeest. The strangest moment, however, might have been when I was running through the bush after retrieving my toothbrush from EcoTraining. All the girls had cameras out, snapping photos of the odd sight—a white man dashing through the wilderness.

Once back at camp, the girls had quiet time, allowing them to work on their projects while I read my book and dozed. Occasionally, one of them would come to ask about their animal. When and where do they sleep? How many young do they have? How can they be conserved? How big is it? I could answer most, but to be absolutely sure, it often became a case of,

'Shall we look that up in the book?'

In the afternoon, I did a thirty-minute tree tour around camp. This was harder than I thought it would be, as I couldn't overcomplicate things. I also relied on one girl to translate for the elders. We covered five trees—though I'm not sure how much the children learned from me. However, I certainly gained a wealth of knowledge from the elders about the medicinal uses of trees.

Georgina, a young volunteer, gave a talk about following your dreams, working hard for them, and overcoming obstacles. Her story of trekking to Everest Base Camp captivated both the children and me. I'm confident the children will get plenty out of this trail, but if they only take one thing away. I hope it is that they should have a goal, and if they work hard enough, they can achieve it.

13th July 2014

Our morning drive had a couple of highlights. The first was the massive baobab, which one girl climbed. She, Jessica, was chuffed, and so were her friends, proud of her achievement. Then, the real highlight was paddling in the Limpopo. The area we picked was shallow enough for there not to be any crocs. The children and I loved it; it was such a fun thing to do, especially the impromptu long jump competition in the sand.

Once back at camp, we had quiet time for the kids to work on their presentations for the afternoon. During this, one child pointing into the bushes caught my attention as I reclined on the sofa. There, just thirty metres away, stood an elephant bull. I joined the children and crouched down on my nearly forty-year-old runner's knees that screamed for mercy. We watched in awe as a second gigantic beast wandered in, gently feeding on the trees. While I wanted to savour the moment, I was keenly aware of the risk I was taking. But with everything I'd learned as a guide, it was a calculated risk. As we sat in the sand, a couple more children joined us, then a couple more, until all eight sat with me.

When the elephants approached us, I moved the children behind the Natal mahogany, keeping us close to a tent we could duck into if needed. The eles continued to feed, so I brought the children out from behind the tree. Now just twenty metres from the elephants, we had been joined by a Gogo who crawled on all fours to our position. For me the highlight of the experience was the transformation in the children's attitude toward elephants. On Friday afternoon, during our first encounter, some girls trembled with fear. Now, they sat cross-legged in the sand, relaxed and smiling, as six-tonne bulls peacefully fed just a stone's throw away.

After dinner, we gathered around the fire, sharing stories. I recounted the one Graham told us about his night-time walk through the bush, being followed by a lion. It went down well—I think the suspense was heightened by having to tell it through a translating child.

Going to bed was tense, as I had to walk less than two metres past an eight-hundred-kilogram sentry sitting outside my tent. Rupert, the resident buffalo, wasn't going anywhere. When I first caught him in my torchlight, he startled me as his head tracked my movements. I'd like to believe he wouldn't leap up and charge, but I wouldn't stand a chance if he did. While having Rupert so close was interesting, it didn't make sleeping any easier. He has a nasal snore—though, I suppose, it's better than the throaty rumble of an elephant's snore.

CHAPTER TWENTY-TWO

'We haven't inherited the planet from our parents, we borrowed it from our children.' *Author unknown.*

EcoTraining, Makuleke
14th July 2014

Twelve guests arrived for the EcoQuest course, and all seemed to be good crack. First up was lunch, followed by a conservation lecture. I say lecture, but it became more of a debate on the legalisation of rhino horn. Before this, I was firmly against the trade, but the case for it was surprisingly compelling.

The debate stretched for hours, and it wasn't hard to see why. All of us felt passionate, voiced strong opinions, and had deep anger over the rhino's plight. But could legalising the trade truly offer a solution? Those supporting trade argued that it would reduce poaching by increasing the supply. Economics 101, supply and demand. The profits from the trade could also be used to fund anti-poaching efforts and create much-needed jobs. As a counter, there was the worry that legalising the trade would fuel demand and make it even harder to monitor and regulate.

Some were concerned about farming rhinos in captivity. Treating rhinos like domestic livestock was troubling, as it could 'take the wild out of wildlife' and make the species more vulnerable to disease and genetic problems.

Then, there was the well-made point that this has all been tried before with other endangered species, such as tigers, and that it failed to stop poaching. Even with a domestic and international ban on the trade in tiger parts, China still allows tiger farmers to breed tigers, and wild tigers continue to be poached.

Yes, legalising the trade could potentially protect rhinos and reduce poaching and there are a lot of wealthy landowners who are lobbying for this. Many of them are already stockpiling rhino horn to take advantage of the potential legalisation. However, I believe that this approach will fuel demand and be challenging to regulate.

From my point of view, the most effective way of protecting rhinos from poaching is to reduce the market demand for rhino horn. For this to happen, it needs to be a concerted effort, with governments around the world cracking down on poachers, sellers and buyers and most importantly, educating their citizens on the consequences of purchasing wildlife goods.

Many people in Vietnam and China simply don't know that rhino horn won't cure cancer or provide additional health benefits. This is where the effort needs to be stepped up. There is a golden opportunity with a more independent and globally savvy generation of the population coming through in these countries. But this may be too late to save the rhino. If things carry on the way they are, rhinos will be extinct in the wild within twenty years.

Because our debate dragged on, we had little time left for an afternoon activity. In the end, we took a short drive along Middle Road. We stopped at Palm Vlei, where a breeding herd of elephants grazed in the tall grass with the Fever Tree Forest behind. The forest was bathed in the honeyed glow of the setting sun; it was a scene typically Makuleke.

Our sundowners stretched long after the sun faded, and the elephants moved on. We had plenty to catch up on with the boys. Hein returned after a month's leave, and a stint at Mashatu, and Nico, from a previous trials group, joined us as a backup.

16th July 2014

This morning, I joined instructor Brett and two of the group for a drive to Luvuvuh West Second Lookout. It became a relaxed affair, allowing me to practice what I'd learned in yesterday's photography lecture. The morning's highlight was an African harrier hawk jumping around an apple leaf tree, searching for prey. The hunter explored the tree's many nooks and crannies with its long legs and sharp talons.

No time for fitness today; we returned late and needed to prepare for the sleep-out. Our destination, my favourite spot, the site of the Bushman paintings. But this time felt different—this was not a small intermate group, in all 18 of us set out together. I walked third in line behind Sean and Nico, who carried rifles while I was armed with a cool box of food. Looking back, all I could see were people snaking through the bushveld behind me.

The sleep-out was unplanned, so not everyone had a sleeping bag at Makuleke. This posed a problem, but we found a solution—we gave them ours. I usually sleep inside two bags under one blanket, so spending the night with just a blanket and a sky full of stars didn't excite me.

I was chuffed with how well I slept. It wasn't perfect, and I woke more than a handful of times. One time, I stirred when a leopard called with its deep *ugh ugh ugh*. It was so close that it sounded like the tree I was sleeping under was being sawed down.

This sound was once described perfectly by Jim Corbett, the legendary British-Indian hunter turned conservationist, who once wrote: 'The sound of a leopard's sawing cough in the dark turns your blood to ice, no matter how many times you've heard it before.' Whilst Corbett penned those words in the early twentieth century after decades of tracking big cats through India's remote jungles, the truth of his observation hadn't dimmed. Even now, seventy years later, that distinctive call still held the power to make the hairs on my neck stand up.

17th July 2014

I woke to the comforting smell of smoke from the sentry fire. The sun hadn't yet risen, but dawn valiantly illuminated the landscape despite the cloud cover that had kept us warm through the night. It was six o'clock—relatively late for getting up, especially by sleep-out standards, when everyone's usually cold, uncomfortable and desperate for a cuppa by the fire. But there was only Patricia, finishing the last watch. I joined her at the fire to make sure the kettle was on.

In the afternoon, I walked with Sean and eight guests. It was my hundredth walk since qualifying as a Back-up, and it was a good one. I had my first-ever sighting of a porcupine. The porcupine strolled along the path in the afternoon sun without a care. But it must have heard us as it glanced over its shoulder, raised its quills, gave them a rattle, and trotted off.

As we crossed the floodplain, we bumped some buffalo in the lala palm scrub. We saw three or four who moved off when they saw us, promptly followed by a bull, and then we flushed the rest of the herd. There must have been thirty.

After enjoying drinks and nibbles at the lookout spot on Mangeba Road, we returned to camp for dinner, followed by more drinks around the fire. The guests had planned a surprise, each taking a turn to thank an instructor or Back-up. Kiwi Vanessa had the dubious honour of addressing me. During her speech, she described two versions of James Bailey:

'There's the fun, Happy Christmas James...'

One evening around the fire, I'd told her that my middle initials H and C stood for Happy Christmas.

'Who jokes around camp,' she continued, 'and then there is Rifle James, who I experienced for two-

and-a-half hours this afternoon. He is on it and incredibly mature when out on a walk.'

It was a late one. I didn't put the cover over the glowing coals until midnight. However, the company made the late night worthwhile, a lovely way to finish my stint as Back-up here at Makuleke. Tomorrow morning it's a five o'clock wake-up to take the guests to the gate. And in the afternoon, my original course mates come back for Advanced Birding and the start of my last thirteen days in Africa.

CHAPTER TWENTY-THREE

'Nothing but breathing the air of Africa, and actually walking through it, can communicate the indescribable sensations.' *William John Burchell, Explorer & Naturalist.*

EcoTraining, Makuleke
18th July 2014

I was like an excited puppy to see everyone; it had been six months since we'd been together. I say everyone, but not all returned. We started with fifteen, but unfortunately there are only nine of us reunited. I've not heard from Ben, but I think he's struggling with either his English girlfriend or his visa. By all accounts, getting the near impossible right-to-work visa may be easier than getting his girlfriend to let him come.

19th July 2014

After a week of not many elephants, they appear to have returned in force. At two o'clock this morning, we were treated to a moonlit view of one feeding on the *Croton* outside our tent. Despite the early hour, it was well worth getting up to watch. My days of watching elephants from my bedroom are numbered.

Our birding course took us to Reed Buck Vlei. We got out of the vehicle to skirt around the edge of the water. But it wasn't walking as I know and love. I passionately want to be out there walking, tracking elephants and lion, making approaches on buffalo, and having the luck of bumping a leopard. Above all, now that I have my Lead, I want to be doing all the above with guests. I'm going to have to get out for a few sneaky walks in between activities. I do want to improve my birding, but I don't think I've got what it takes, namely the patience.

On the drive there, we found Steve's vehicle. He's been sabotaging our vehicles in one way or the other, so we found where he'd hidden his own keys and moved the Land Cruiser one hundred metres down the road behind a bush. We were content with this plan until we found out he intended to walk back to camp, leaving someone else to pick up the vehicle.

20th July 2014

A successful morning's birding at Banyini Pan included racket-tailed rollers on the way and once there, white-backed duck, pygmy geese and a lifer for me, lesser jacana. This morning, I had to crack open my survival kit. It's not an extensive one, but it came up trumps today. It contains a bit of paracord, a flint and steel, and some tea bags. It was the latter that were required as the duty team hadn't packed English Breakfast tea, only rooibos. Disaster averted.

In the afternoon, our birding led us to Luvuvuh West. I suspect it was no coincidence that this allowed us to look for the leopard spotted earlier. We found him lying in the shade of a Natal mahogany just west of Second Lookout. He was an old warrior, battered and bruised from countless catfights. His eyes were deep-set, and his brow heavy. Though he was a magnificent specimen, he wasn't what you'd call pretty. They say beauty is only skin deep, and it's about personality—well, I'm afraid he wasn't winning there either. He bared his teeth and growled at us; we didn't overstay our welcome.

21st July 2014

We headed to the old western boundary for a session of birding. Rather than a full-on morning with eyes glued to the binoculars, we took it easy as we explored a new area on foot. It was a place I've always wanted to walk, so Alan suggested we go for it. I led the walk but with Alan and Horst carrying the rifles.

Walking up front with no rifle felt liberating. The walk lived up to my expectations. I followed the drainage line from Matafila down past Tshikuyu Spring. We didn't come across any dangerous game. That said, it wasn't hard to imagine the place teeming with elephants and buffalo with the occasional leopard padding along the soft sand of the parched riverbed. These magnificent beasts would have looked a picture amongst the cathedral style leadwood, apple leaf and umbrella thorn.

24th July 2014

There's no need to leave camp to see elephants, as they often make house calls. This time, Dave and his buddy dropped by to say hello. Since he chose to come into our territory, we could get closer than we would on a walk. We sat in the dirt and watched the two from just ten metres away.

However, we accidentally blocked the route he wanted to take, leading to a five-minute standoff where he and his sidekick ensured we knew who was in charge. It wasn't the first time my heart had been in my mouth, but this time, it felt like I'd be unable to swallow it down again.

To round things off, we spent the afternoon on the beach, well the shore of the Limpopo. We swam, played cricket, touch rugby, and tossed a frisbee. The best part being we weren't chomped by any crocodiles and even better, we found some otter tracks. I can also say I've visited Zimbabwe, having crossed the river into their sovereign territory with a tinnie in hand.

25th July 2014

Only a handful joined this morning's walk—Duncan, dependable Will, and Brian, who accompanied me as my backup. As the instructor, Brian is the grown-up responsible for us during this final week, which includes our graduation. He was content to let the walk be mine and told me to lead the way.

It would be a long trek, walking from camp to Mapimbi. The distance was twelve kilometres as the crow flies, but since we didn't have a pair of wings between us, the trail became much longer with all the obstacles we had to navigate.

Straight off the bat, we found lion tracks outside camp. We thought about following them as they were fresh, and as it turned out, the spoor was also on the camp driveway. But we ploughed on with our original plan, which quickly led to our first detour: navigating around a breeding herd of one hundred elephants.

While diverting, I heard vervets sounding the alarm nearby, so we quick-marched towards them. I felt sure we'd find a leopard, as we arrived immediately, had a clear vantage point, and the ground cover was sparse, with the monkeys still going nuts. The culprit, however, turned out not to be a leopard but a crowned eagle. Disappointing, but Brian put a different spin on it.

'I've seen many more leopards than crowned eagles, so this sighting is special.'

Crossing the floodplain, we had our second encounter. Initially, I was completely unaware of what was heading our way. I was too engrossed in the brilliant substrate that made every track stand out like billboards at Piccadilly Circus. I failed to notice the small breeding herd of elephants moving down the kopje towards us. Thanks for the heads-up, Will.

We reached the safety of high ground, where we watched the elephants while snacking on some rusks.

With no tea to soften the teeth-breaking biscuits, we gnawed on them like rats, uncovering the odd juicy morsel of fruit.

I called Jomi over the radio to confirm our ETA, but the real reason was to cover up my mistake. I needed him to sign out my rifle and rounds, as I'd forgotten to do it myself. This oversight wasn't smart, and it weighed on my mind. I'm sure he understood, but he made me repeat myself again and again.

'Jomi, I forgot to sign something this morning can you do it for me?'

'Sorry, James, what do you mean?

'Jomi, I forgot to sign something important this morning. Can you do it for me?

Again, he said,

'I don't copy. What are you saying?'

Finally, and close to not seeing the funny side — uncertain whether I was breaching good practice or even the law—I simply said,

'Jomi, I forgot to sign my rifle out this morning can you do it for me?'

'Yes, of course, no problem at all James, I'll sign out your rifle for you, enjoy the rest of your walk.' he said.

This was a long walk, seven and a half hours covering twenty-two kilometres, so plenty happened along the way. The next encounter involved a herd of buffalo in the adrenaline grass. The only way around them was to move downwind and carefully pick our way through the equally tall grass. To do this, we had to stop frequently and stand on logs to ensure we wouldn't stumble upon any stragglers.

I love encounters, they're addictive. There's always another encounter out there, a new one to chase, ever closer and always better. I'm desperate for a rhino encounter and for some up-close lion action. Do I want to be charged by a lion? No, but it would be one hell of a story to tell, especially as the lion is unlikely to follow through all the way.

We had lunch overlooking the Limpopo, shaded by apple leaf trees. It wasn't fine dining, but we were hungry enough to wolf down the bully beef after the walk. The meal didn't look much better than dog food, and the canned chicken was suspiciously like cat food.

Our next destination was the Jackal Berry Forest. This had been on my to-do list for some time. I'd barely taken in the sights of the tall, dark giants when I saw an impala ram one hundred metres to the north acting strangely. I turned to Brian and whispered,

'There's an impala ram that appears to be snared'.

The impala was struggling to free himself, and in the process, he had broken one of his powerful back legs. We backed off to give him space and radioed camp to contact the Section Ranger. Then, it was just a matter of waiting for instructions. It didn't take long before we received the message confirming what needed to be done.

Will offered to do the deed for me, but this was my walk. I was the Lead, and I should take the responsibility. Duncan passed me a pair of earplugs, which I put in straight away. The whole affair became muffled, creating a strange and eerie atmosphere.

I walked up to the impala as it struggled, but as I

chambered the round, it froze and looked directly at me, its large dark eyes staring straight into mine. With the impala no longer struggling, I should have taken that moment to change my plan and shoot him through the brain for instant death. I didn't. Instead, I continued the original plan. I didn't think. I took aim and pulled the trigger. The round found its mark, the central body mass, hitting either a lung or the heart. Immediately, his front knees buckled, but he was far from dead. To speed his death up, I tried cutting his throat, but my knife wasn't sharp enough. He was dead within a minute, though that minute felt like an eternity.

We moved the body from the cover of the forest into the open. The hope was that the poachers would lose out to the vultures and the numerous scavengers of the veld. To speed up the process, I cut open his belly so there would be no need for a lappet-faced vulture to open it up for other species. The ram was a bulky chap. How a leopard can carry something like that up a tree is beyond me. Their strength-to-weight ratio must be among the greatest in the animal kingdom, assuming you don't factor in insects like the dung beetle.

We did a sweep of the area to check for more snares. We found one which I'd inadvertently stepped around. It looked fresh; the grass that had been used to tie it into position was not old at all. We removed these heavy-duty wire snares and logged the coordinates before continuing on our way.

Despite the walk turning into an anti-poaching patrol, the forest did not fail to amaze. I walked open mouthed in awe of the imperial sycamore figs, sausage trees, and fever trees amongst the jackal berries. This appeared to be a wonderland. Why did it have to be spoilt by poaching?

After a long hot walk in the sun, we reached our destination. Rather than jump straight into the Landy we stripped down to our boxers and jumped into the Limpopo. The freshwater soothed our scratched and bettered shins from a day of walking through the thorn-veld.

28th July 2014

The graduation guests arrived today. For me, my aunt and uncle, Paddy and Peter, who travelled up from the Western Cape. I picked them and a few other guests up from the main gate. Disappointingly, we didn't spot any game on the drive to camp. Still, I wasn't too concerned, given the number of elephants making their way back to Makuleke.

In the afternoon we went to Reed Buck Vlei for a walk, but as 'Tambookie' was playing up, we never made it. Instead, we limped to Jachacha and walked around the kopje. I led what were my first official guests as a Lead Trails Guide. The main aim for the walk being, not to let my Mum's sister be squashed by an elephant.

There were several encounters, starting with an elephant bull feeding on a fever tree. As we continued the walk, Will, my backup, spotted another elephant appearing from behind some lala palms. This caught both the ele and me by surprise. He approached us with an inquisitive, slightly agitated swagger. Our positioning was perfect, and I only needed to ask everyone to stay still. When the elephant gave us the chance, I had Will lead the guests up the pebbled slope of the ridge to safety.

29th July 2014

My last walk, walk number 106, was an exclusive affair. My aunt and uncle with Jomi as Back-up. Leading a bush walk through the African savannah navigates an emotional tightrope. It can be exhilarating and soothing, self-affirming and confidence shaking. But it is always special in such a wilderness area. The icing on the cake is when you're sharing it with family and a good friend.

We walked my favourite, the Fever Tree Forest, but this time from Hlangaluwe back to camp. It was a tame affair, peaceful, just right for my guests. Along the way, we encountered an ele bull feeding on a fever tree in the floodplain, and later we circumnavigated a breeding herd being harassed by the same bull.

In the evening, we gathered for the boma dinner. It looked better than I'd ever seen it; the team that stayed behind had done a superb job setting it up. It was even more impressive, considering they cracked their first tinny as our departure was signalled by the cloud of fine, powdery dirt we stirred up when pulling out of the drive as we headed off on our final game drive.

After dinner, both staff and students gave speeches. I excused myself for speaking longer than most. After all, this was my placement leaving do and graduation combined.

With the formalities completed, we got down to serious business, Fines Night. This time a mutiny broke out. Not everyone wanted to drink out of Hein's boot. To be fair, I don't think they wanted to drink out of anyone's boot. I chaired the session with all taking their punishment.

I fined Pieter and Julia for missing the last Fines Night, but funnily enough, they didn't show up for this one either. I also fined Lex, the EcoTraining Director, for selling us all a yearlong course that lasted eleven months.

A few of us lingered around the fire, talking shop, when the sound of impala snorting their alarm on Middle Road caught our attention. We jumped into the beige Landy and set out in search of a leopard. Though we found the skittish impala on the edge of camp, no predators appeared. No fairy-tale ending this time.

CHAPTER TWENTY-FOUR

'We never know the worth of water till the well is dry.' *Thomas Fuller, Churchman & Historian.*

Thirty-six thousand feet somewhere over Africa
30 July 2014

I'm excited at the prospect of seeing friends and family, with cuddles from my nieces. The latter depends on me picking up soft toys at the airport. Then there's tea, as much tea as I'd care to drink—or more precisely, Yorkshire Tea. That all said, I'll be longing for the veld in no time.

With my possessions crammed into Baby Elephant, I headed home. My journey started with a seven-hour trip aboard the Bush Bus.

On arriving at the airport, I discovered seeing family as planned and not twenty-four hours later was worth more to me than the £250 offer for being bumped onto the next flight.

Seated at the back of an Airbus, with a complimentary Castle Lager in hand and eleven hours ahead, I reflected on my year in Africa…

They say, although I'm not sure who *they* are. Anyhow, they say, you should never have regrets. But you always do.

I have plenty—not about taking the year out or doing this course, but about not fully making the most of it. I regret not trying to learn the lingo, not doing more, not exploring more of the country. I wish I'd used my time off better and said yes to more opportunities than I did.

Then there's my placement. Would I have liked to have worked full time in a commercial lodge? I've mixed feelings here. I enjoyed my shifts at the Outpost and my trails with Wilderness Safaris. But my peers who worked at regular lodges day in day out complained of having to answer the same inane questions repeatedly. For me, the learning environment of EcoTraining meant it exposed me to expert instructors daily. I benefited from challenging questions from the type of people whose holidays came with lectures. No regrets on that count, I chose correctly.

What else? I was often in a rush and drove too fast. So much so that I missed things, not least the policewoman who caught me speeding. Getting that fine in Kruger Park, of all places. Not my proudest moment. A symptom of me becoming complacent. I'd taken my surroundings for granted. I should have known better. I've been there before, given the iconic attractions for which I've worked.

Then there was the phase when I got sucked into the gun-toting macho guide stereotype. I carried a military-grade backpack, wore a bandolier for my ammunition, and drank from a boot. Fortunately, this didn't last long. No matter how many rocks I carried while running along the riverbed, I would never beat Rambo in an arm wrestle. In my defence, the ammunition pouch was standard for a Trails Guide and integral for advanced rifle handling.

I sound like I'm having a whine. I'm not; I'm just being myself. I'm always looking to learn from my mistakes and missed opportunities. Overall, the experience was incredible. I can't imagine many things that could rival leading a bush walk through the African savannah. I got to do that several times as a fully trained guide where the responsibility for the guests was entirely mine.

Of my whole foray, it was the walking safaris where I grew as a person. If there's one learning I can pass on, it's to walk with your head up. In the literal sense, so you don't walk into an elephant. But also, figuratively, walk with confidence. Trails guiding has given me confidence to not just talk about something but to have the belief to get on and do it.

If something goes wrong, don't dwell on it, don't doubt yourself, don't let the rot set in. Instead, learn from your mistakes, grab a rifle and head back out.

I learnt about real responsibility. If you're a Lead or a Back-up Guide, you can't switch off, take unnecessary risks or cut corners. You have a responsibility, a duty of care to keep the people in your charge safe and to ensure that the animals come to no harm. The stakes are high when walking in the bush.

I'm not sure how I would have reacted if I had to

pull the trigger. I believe I could have done it. Competently? I'm not sure. Even the instructors with their thousands of hours' experience have come unstuck under such circumstances. There are examples of this with their round not finding its mark first time, their rifle snagging on a branch when they needed it. One instructor could not load a second round because his rifle's chamber filled with a buffalo's blood as it pinned him to the floor.

If I found myself in such a situation and survived, that is where my troubles would start. Coping with the fallout, guilt and blame for something gone terribly wrong.

Walking trails is about taking calculated risks based on interpreting the animals, land and situation. This is not achieved through training and experience alone but through a primitive part of you being awakened. The tracking, stalking and walking unnoticed has served our species over millennia. It brings your senses alive, and you rely on them to stay alive. By sharpening this ancient art form, you become more observant, and you appreciate the smaller things.

As a Trails Guide, or at least as a student in the bush, you ask why again. Not just of those around you, but of yourself. You look things up. But this is the wilderness, there's no Google, only reference books. And that's what you do in the evenings. In camp, you're not tied by a TV schedule. There's no TV and therefore no lost time to mind-numbing serials. I adored camp life. My favourite part was sitting by the fire after dinner, with a blanket of stars for comfort.

An experience best shared with friends and a cold beer but equally fulfilling when enjoyed alone with one's thoughts.

They encouraged us to ask our guests about the highlights of their day. For me, there have been many, but sleeping under a star-filled sky with ancient man's rock paintings for wallpaper and wild animals calling out in the dead of night sits top of the list.

I will never forget one transformational moment—the realisation that conservation isn’t just about animals. This struck me during my last trial as I sat in the sand, surrounded by smiling children, watching elephants feed in camp. For those children, their time in the wild had completely reshaped their perspective. For conservation to truly succeed, we must prioritise a people-first approach.

With the relentless pace of work, I realised that a change could be just as refreshing as a break. After a three-night trail, I'd been utterly exhausted, only to return to EcoTraining for less than twenty-four hours. There, I enjoyed a lively evening around the campfire and headed back feeling revitalised. This doesn't mean the people you're spending time with need to be super bubbly to transfer that energy to you—it's more that they shouldn't suck energy from you.

The bush gives you time to think. It might be during a moment of organised solitude. Or perhaps whilst switching off from the world and losing yourself in the dancing flames of the campfire, as others cackle like hyenas over juicy morsels of gossip.

Having time to stop, think, and invest in myself was... what exactly? It wasn’t enlightening. I suppose it allowed me to see myself as other people did. Did I discover myself? Did I find what I was looking for? In a word, maybe. But it had been right there in front of me all along.

Family and friends are essential. For friends, I've taken them for granted in the past, selfishly in fact. Always expecting them to be there when I needed them, hoping to pick up where we left off, even if it was years earlier.

And family, well, being with family is the reason I'm coming home. I am who I am because of my family and where I come from. I'll always be grateful for the upbringing Mum and Dad gave me and the opportunities they provided. They have supported me with my crazy ideas. Not least this one, the craziest of them all. It meant the world to me when I chased the prospect of a leopard around the bush with them.

I need to give people more time, enjoy the time and not be beholden by time. I've developed an understanding of this precious commodity. You can't get it back. Knowing this shouldn't cause stress but focus the mind on enjoying the moment. There's no need to rush to get onto the next thing or the next place. As Bruce would say,

'Everything will happen at the right time.'

Of course, this sounds cheesy, well it is cheesy, but it's true.

I've not always wanted to rush onto the next thing, but I am guilty of trying to make things perfect. If I keep chasing that perfection, I cannot enjoy the perfect moment that I'm already in.

This can apply to jobs. In the past, I've chased

promotion from employer to employer. I should have stuck it out, particularly at ZSL. I should have stayed there longer and moved up the ranks. Such an approach would be like getting in the perfect position at a watering hole and letting amazing elephant and buffalo encounters come.

I've had many teachers in Africa, but the best are the animals themselves. Animals will do anything to avoid confrontation. They will mark their territories and advertise their presence through calling. They will go to great lengths to stop the need for violence. In human animals, this is not the case. Some people go out looking for trouble. Whether it's on a Saturday night or at work by being argumentative for augment's sake.

On this African odyssey of mine, there have been only a few occasions when I have feared for my life. Each time, it was an elephant encounter. In these situations, I questioned my significance with the six-ton animal towering above me. But at the same time, I couldn't help but be in awe of such an animal—so intelligent, so sensitive.

My learnings will change nobody's life but mine. The journey I've been on isn't earth shattering, it wasn't climbing Everest or trekking to the North Pole. Nonetheless, it was a rewarding part of my life.

Having spent the last year living from tent to tent, I'm longing for my own place to unpack and make a nest. It would be even better if I could do this with somebody I love. I've realised that this is my actual dream. Unfortunately, it's not as easily solved as buying a ticket to Africa.

I can't see myself living in London again. This is an issue as that's where my flat is, and the jobs are. I'd like to say I don't want much, but I do. I want an idyllic country life. In fact, I long for one. I want a chocolate box village with a local pub and shop as well as a cricket club as the focal point of the community. The house — actually the cottage — should have outbuildings for a dedicated 'work from home' space. Fields are essential. The cottage should back onto them and woodland so I can hop over a fence and run off into the countryside.

My memory is terrible. I've had the most fabulous year, and I'm worried I'll forget it all. Luckily, I have this diary, so I can relive each day until I get bored. I imagine that moment will come well past the date my friends and family become tired of any sentence that begins, 'When I was in Africa...'

I'm bringing home a collection of notebooks. My writing is illegible and my drawings are dodgy. Yet these notebooks are items I'll treasure forever. The ones I cherish most contain pressed flowers, leaves and grasses from my beloved veld.

While my memory may fade, my newly awakened instincts may not. In years to come when walking in an English park, my heart may stop with a breaking twig or the rustle of a bush.

CHAPTER TWENTY-FIVE

'Eventually soulmates meet, for they have the same hiding place.' *Robert Brault, Writer.*

London
6th August 2014

Is it the fact I don't have a job to rush to or am I changed by my extended time in Africa? Whatever it is, I chose not to force myself onto the crowded tube, and amazingly my heart rate didn't spike with the frustration of missing it. I stepped back and waited three minutes for the next train.

Life on the underground is busy and chaotic. There's so much visual noise, all assaulting my newly honed senses. I'd never noticed it before, but suddenly the adverts felt intrusive—a surprise, considering marketing is my field. Over the years, I've spent millions on advertising.

Everyone rushed—rushing home, to the pub, or the theatre. Despite their impatience, they remained glued to their screens, whether sitting, standing, or walking. No eye contact just faces lost in their digital worlds.

As I was waiting for the sardine-packed train to depart, the dispatcher tried to lighten the mood by wishing everyone a good evening, and then in an overacted voice said,

'Driver, on your marks, get set, go!'

My favourite part of this was watching those around me. I'd spot the crack of a smile breaking out, whilst they tried with all their might to hide it.

Despite blowing a day's trail guiding wages on my ticket to London and then thousands of rand on drinks and dinner, it was worth every cent. Not only did I catch up with the likes of Marc, Amy, Stuart and Laurie but I got to play touch rugby for my old team, Museums Inc. An ensemble of men and women from the Natural History Museum, V&A, Science Museum and British Museum. We won a closely fought match, four tries to three and I was player of the match. Call me suspicious, but the award may have been my welcome home present.

25th October 2014

Since getting back, I've been trying my hand at internet dating. I've been on a handful of dates, all have been conventional, heading to the pub, an art gallery, the usual thing. Today I was going to try something different, dogging. But I may be using the wrong phrase here.

For the last week, *Taking Chances* and I have been exchanging messages, and today we met for the first time. All thanks to my sister Emma's dog, Bramble.

Emma and the family were at a Christening in Southfields before heading to my parents in Yorkshire for half term.

I'm looking after Bramble while they attend the Christening. This was the perfect opportunity to see if *Taking Chances*, aka Hannah, wanted to meet up along with her dog, Percy.

We met outside the tube station—a surprising coincidence that Hannah had also lived in Southfields for the past ten years. We could have crossed paths countless times. A sliding doors moment. I'm convinced we never did. I would have noticed, especially if she were with Percy, her cute Havanese. A cuddly size dog with expressive eyes initially bred as a companion dog to the Cuban aristocracy in the 1800s.

Even without Percy, I'd have noticed Hannah. She was striking in her dog-walking attire—shapely black jeans, a tight-fitting blue gilet, long blonde hair, and green-brown eyes that were soft yet fearless. I really lucked out here. For a shot at seeing her again, I needed to keep her interest for three hours. With no pub on the agenda and no alcohol to help ease things, this would be challenging. Damn, I should have gone down the conventional date route.

After we greeted with a bit of bum sniffing and an awkward cheek peck, we walked towards Wimbledon Common via the long steep Augustus Road. On the way we passed three places I'd lived with a fourth not a million miles away. I didn't point them all out as they were all tied to something going wrong in my life. Probably not best to highlight two failed relationships in the opening moments of our meeting.

The dog walk turned out to be a stroke of genius. The date was fantastic, or at least I thought so. We talked endlessly, mostly about our travels and families. We hadn't visited many of the same places, but Africa was a mutual favourite, which suited me perfectly. Our bucket lists lined up, too—the Amazon and Yosemite were at the top.

I loosely shared my idea for a business to get me back to Africa. I wasn't sure she was entirely convinced. Still, she reassured me that passion is essential when starting a business—and that was something I clearly had in spades.

We walked to Wimbledon Village, quite a walk in the unseasonal heat for two dogs with short legs. We rested up at Caffè Nero. On asking Hannah what she wanted, she said a tea and a slice of lemon. I mistook this for a slice of lemon cake. My misunderstanding left me feeling awkward. Should I get myself a cake too? I am not massively into cake, especially from a café at £3 a slice. I ended up with a rocky road and brought it out. Hannah's face was a picture. She wanted a piece of lemon for her tea, not a cake.

We sat on the pavement, soaking up the autumn sun, enjoying the company and, of course, our cake, when my sister pulled up. Emma had tracked me through my phone and immediately noticed Hannah.

Now, this was awkward. I hadn't mentioned Hannah to Emma, so she was clearly bursting with questions. Instead, she had to settle for a minute of polite small talk with Hannah as we handed Bramble over.

I couldn't tell if I'd won Hannah over or lost her when I started rambling about African giant land snails firing love darts at each other. A few other things didn't help my cause. Pulling out my notebook to jot down an idea during the date was a bad move. Then there was the story about the black-tie dinner. From the table plan, I'd learned I was seated next to Lady so-and-so. I'd imagined she'd be elderly. Instead, she turned out to be a genuine hottie, mixing at the top of British society. Had I put Hannah off? Only time would tell. I certainly hoped not.

20th November 2014

My business idea is to create a community of like-minded individuals and set myself up as a tour operator and agent offering wildlife courses in Africa. My flagship product is going to be a two-week safari field trip for £1,500 excluding flights. The maiden trip is set for Easter. The first step towards this was launching my main route to market, a content-rich website, which I did today, fascinatingafrica.com.

This project will not make me a millionaire, it's to provide me with a vocation. But there is quite a significant problem, I've run out of money. Luckily, I have a lifeline and one that I'll be eternally grateful for. The Zoological Director and Director General at the Zoological Society of London have asked me to do two days' consultancy each week for the next six months. And the project, well, it's spectacular, but top secret.

I'll be able to celebrate my first week of gainful

employment in style. Hannah has invited me to a black-tie do at the five-star St. Pancras Renaissance Hotel. The highlight is that we'll be put up in a suite at the top end of their offering. I think she's a keeper.

19th May 2015

Fascinating Africa isn't going to cut it. It's becoming clear that I can't have my cake and eat it too. That fairy-tale life of one foot in the UK and the other in the African bush isn't going to happen. If I truly wanted it and threw everything I had into it, I could probably scrape by. But the drive simply isn't there. I'm used to comfort, conditioned to be responsible with a mortgage and pension. I'm not a risk-taker—I've always had it easy and never faced real struggle. Maybe if I had, I'd be more entrepreneurial. That's the incredible thing about Africa: poverty fuels innovation.

Things are getting serious with Hannah, we've been together for six months, and I can see the relationship going the distance. If I want to be Mr Family Man, then I need to get a stable job, need to be able to provide. This realisation didn't hit me out of the blue, I've known it for a while, and I've been doing something about it. Hannah and I have been working on it. Hannah searches for jobs she thinks will be suitable and pops them onto a spreadsheet sorted by deadline.

It was a numbers game, with Hannah supplying the leads so I wouldn't waste time searching. This was my introduction to the concept of a sales pipeline—

and I was the commodity for sale.

The strategy was working, and there were jobs out there. I'd made it to the final two for General Manager at Cliveden, the National Trust property famed for the Profumo affair. Then there was a position at a Wildlife Trust, another at the Wildfowl and Wetlands Trust in Barnes. A marketing lead role had opened up with a new arts organisation, established to celebrate the hundredth anniversary of World War One.

It's the pure wildlife visitor attraction job that I want. If my year out is to serve its purpose, I must stay focused on becoming the Chief Executive of a zoo. I turned down a job I'd interviewed for, even after they requested my references. The role was Director of Marketing, but the organisation wasn't of the right calibre. Hannah's words from our earlier discussions echoed in my mind: 'Would I feel proud doing the job?' The answer was no.

Money is becoming an issue. Cash is king, and I have none. My cash flow is rubbish. I'm not earning what I did before Africa, but my spending has remained the same. Hannah is something special, and I'm trying to keep up appearances and match her aspirations. I don't want to lose her.

I've never suffered from anxiety before, but with money worries and looming job application deadlines, I think I'm dealing with it now. Last night, I genuinely thought I was having a heart attack—my heart was racing, and my chest felt tight. I didn't let Hannah know what was happening. Instead, I turned inward, which wasn't great for our relationship. She knew something was up but also knew not to pry. She snuggled up. I can't tell you how much that helped.

Over the last month, I've been going to the Starbucks in Camden Town to do an hour's worth of job applications before the short walk to the Zoo each morning. As a regular, I'm recognising familiar faces who have the coffee shop as part of their daily routine. There's an old man who reads the racing independent, an overnight worker who falls asleep on the table, a yummy American mummy with two bratty kids and a cab driver with a cockney crush on a waitress.

I'm finding it tough to get my career back on track. I should never have given up my job. It was a privileged position I had worked hard to achieve, though I imagine luck played a part, too. Looking back, I realise I was arrogant to assume I could walk straight into a similar role whenever I decided to return.

The job search left me shattered. The early starts, the full-time interim work, lunchtime applications and draining interviews left me exhausted on the sofa each night. Running away to Africa sounded tempting—this time with Hannah—but I'd already promised myself I wouldn't. In fact, someone asked me about it just last month.

'So, James, have you got this Africa thing out of your system?'

Caught off guard, I replied,

'Err, yes, definitely a great time in my life and has given me memories that will last me forever. But, yes, totally out of my system.'

Am I over Africa? Probably not. I'll undoubtedly

murder Toto's Africa the next time a karaoke opportunity presents itself. But what is it about Africa I find so intoxicating? Perhaps it's the spirit of adventure, the sunsets and sundowners, the people and their hospitality, the animals, the scenery or the smell of the sun-baked dust? Once it's in your blood, like malaria, it's near impossible to shake.

30th June 2015

Into my forty-seventh week since returning from Africa and I got the call I was desperate for. The offer of a job. One linked to science, so a bonus. It is to become Head of Marketing for the Epilepsy Society as they embark on an exciting new direction of research through whole-genome sequencing. It wasn't a visitor attraction, but it was for a fundraising charity which would aid my career goals further down the line.

I was excited, elated, and relieved. It means Hannah and I can start the life we'd dreamed of. I can ask her to marry me.

After just a matter of months with Hannah, I had already told Johnny she was the one—I knew I would marry her. I feel incredibly fortunate that Hannah took a chance on me and stood by my side during this transition into society.

I am proud of her and to be with her. She's beautiful and successful, negotiating contracts with top five-star hotels around the world. Hannah has a kind heart and sentimental soul, the type of person who saves a leaf from the privet hedge after our first kiss. She laughs at my bad jokes which I hope one day will become dad jokes; she gives me confidence by believing in me. Like me she is tea, not coffee and never full fat, always skimmed milk. Hannah adores the niblings and inspires me to be the best person I can be.

Hannah is a companion. A soul mate. Someone who values the same things in life, someone who knows what I'm thinking, someone to make a home with. I didn't realise it, but Hannah was the reason I came back from Africa.

Wiltshire, England
5th June 2017

Since the sixteenth of January when I saw a job advertised, I have been waiting for the possibility of this moment. I'd driven eighty minutes from our little country cottage in Hampshire. The cottage backing onto open fields with a peaceful view felt extra special this morning when I woke to see deer grazing in the delicate mist of the sunrise.

It's ten o'clock and I'm sitting in the office of a country estate. A metal spiral staircase winds up to the mezzanine floor. There's a buzz about the place, with people rushing back and forth. Stunning photographs of lions and tigers adorn the walls in reception.

I'm in the offices of the first stately home to open its doors to the paying public. That was in 1949. The estate then made history again by creating the first safari park outside Africa, introducing lions to its grounds in 1966.

The estate is Longleat, the most visited safari park in the UK, and I am its new Head of Marketing.

Am I about to start the most perfect job ever?

Thank you for reading! If you enjoyed this book, please consider:

- Leaving a quick review on Amazon
- Sharing a photo on social media with #TheRookieRanger
- Checking our directory of African travel specialists to help plan your dream safari

Your support helps others discover these resources and makes a real difference.

ACKNOWLEDGMENTS

Writing this book has been a journey of reflection, inspiration, and countless cups of tea. It wouldn't have been possible without the support of many incredible people.

To all the instructors I met during my time with EcoTraining, thank you for not only teaching me but also inspiring me. You didn't just teach me how to interpret the behaviour of animals; you instilled in me a deep love for the entire ecosystem and what makes it tick. You taught me that a safari is about more than wildlife—it's about the value of time, the greatest gift anyone can give. We owe it to whoever turns up on our trail to make their experience extra special so that their time is well spent. And we owe it to the planet to use our guests' attention to champion the cause of conservation. We only have one shot at getting Earth right. It's up to all of us to protect it and everything on it.

To Bruce and Dee, thank you for giving me the opportunity to do my placement as a Back-up at Makuleke. What an incredible place to learn and grow. You were fantastic mentors for walking trails and running a camp. Your mentorship extended beyond work. You were welcoming hosts, tolerating guest after guest of mine who came through Makuleke.

To Alison, for reading the first draft. The feedback you gave was invaluable. Even more so was the encouragement. Without it, I don't think I'd have pushed on to complete this project.

To Jomi, for being the first person to read this book cover to cover who was actually there. Your feedback meant everything. It was validation that this story was worth telling. The fact that you didn't say it was all buffalo poop gave me the confidence to put it out there.

To my friends, I owe you all an apology for the many times I've started a conversation with, "When I was in Africa…" Though, to be fair, at least 50% of the time, I'm doing it to get a rise out of you.

And now, to my family—the people who mean the most to me.

Paddy and Peter, Alison and Graham, your generosity with your time and hospitality, as always, made me feel as though I had never left home. Whether in the Western Cape or Gauteng, I was truly grateful for your support. Thank you.

Emma and Johnny, my sister and brother, thank you for always being my biggest ambassadors. You think I'm more capable than I actually am. That belief is a source of strength.

Brother-in-law Mike, I really appreciate how you welcomed me into your home on my return, and I hope I didn't outstay my welcome, although I'm sure I did. Thanks for giving me the time to acclimatise back into civilisation.

Mum and Dad, I now understand, as a parent myself, the sacrifices you made for me. The unshakable love you've shown is something I carry with me. Thank you for everything—for your guidance, your belief in me, and for setting an example of what it means to support someone unconditionally.

To my boys, Zach and Archie, you are my greatest inspiration. I hope this book serves as a reminder of how important it is to chase your dreams. So, let's get that in writing. Zach, aged seven, your dream is to become a TV star like Bear Grylls. Archie, at five, you want to become the world's best professional cricketer. I couldn't be prouder of you just for having those dreams.

To Hannah, my rock, my wife. Thank you for tolerating an empty bed when I rise in the early hours to get some writing done before the day begins. Your first question, after the ribbing for waking you—"Was it work or the book this morning?"—always makes me awkwardly smile. Without your love, patience, and support, this book would still be a dream.

To me, a promise: I will be back. My boots will once again tread the ancient paths of Makuleke, where fever tree forests swelter in the African sun, baobab branches cradle lounging leopards, elephant bulls full of musth meander unhurried through the mopane, and buffalo graze the floodplain.

And to Africa, Thank you.

AMAZING PEOPLE & COMPANIES

Alan McSmith Safaris: (w) alanmcsmith.com

Ben Talpade: (w) carnivoresandconservation.wordpress.com/bentalpade

Brett Horley: (w) bhs-safari.co

Brian Kelly: (w) pathofthepanther.com

Bruce Lawson: (w) linktr.ee/brucelawsontrails

Cliff Olin (ig) @cliffovesai

Durham County Cricket Club: (w) durhamcricket.co.uk

EcoTraining: (w) ecotraining.co.za

Enkosini: (w) enkosini.org

Epilepsy Society: (w) epilepsysociety.org.uk

Fascinating Africa: (w) fascinatingafrica.com/

Graham Cooke: (w) hlatiniaafrica.com; (book) My Life With Leopards

Hein Myers: (w) african-origins.com

Henry Parsons: (ig) @painted_wolves

Innocent Ngwenya: (Vid) youtube.com/watch?v=8URTjvXChFg

James Bailey: (w) james-bailey.ueniweb.com

Jean-Pierre Le Roux: (w) inspirationalnatureguiding.com

Jomi Krobb: (w) trunksandtracks.com; (pod) trunksandtracks.com/podcast

Lapolosa: (w) lapolosa.org

Margaux Langley: (w) hyltonlangleysafaris.co.za

Massimo Rebuzzi: (w) africanbushco.com

Odycy: (w) odycy.com - Find, Compare & Book Healthcare

Pafuri Collection: (w) returnafrica.com

Rhodes Bezuidenhout: (w) shanganitrails.co.za

Roger Highfield: (w) rogerhighfield.com

Science Museum Group: (w) sciencemuseumgroup.org.uk

Sean Patrick: (book) Game Ranger in Your Back Pack

Siyafunda Wildlife & Conservation: (w) siyafundaconservation.com

Steve Faulconbridge: (ig) @faulconbridgesteve

Stuart Barnes: (w) stuartbarnesconsulting.com

The Outpost: (w) rareearth.co.za/properties/the-outpost

Ulrica Vilen-Letts: (ig) @ulricasnaps

Wilderness Safaris: (w) wildernessdestinations.com

Zoological Society of London: (w) zsl.org

REFERENCES

Animal People Forum. 'Rescuers Send Lion to Canned Hunt Supplier', *Animal People Forum*, 2 March 2006, https://newspaper.animalpeopleforum.org/2006/03/02/rescuers-send-lion-to-canned-hunt-supplier/

Apple Podcasts. 'Episode Twenty-Two: Walking from Cape Town to Cairo with Bruce Lawson', *Apple Podcasts*, 2024, https://podcasts.apple.com/ph/podcast/episode-22-walking-from-cape-town-to-cairo-with-bruce-lawson/id1509032518?i=1000500805426

Carnivores and Conservation. 'Elephant', *Carnivores and Conservation*, n.d., https://carnivoresandconservation.wordpress.com/category/south-africa/elephant/

EcoTraining. 'Henry Parsons: The Bush, EcoTraining and I', *EcoTraining*, 2024, https://www.ecotraining.co.za/blog/henry-parsons-the-bush-ecotraining-and-i/

Fascinating Africa. *Fascinating Africa*, n.d., https://fascinatingafrica.com/

Ramsay, S. 'Bruce Lawson Interview', *Scott Ramsay*, 20 January 2023, https://scottramsay.africa/bruce-lawson-interview/

Ramsay, S. 'The Buddha of the Bush', *Getaway*, n.d., https://www.getaway.co.za/wildlife/the-buddha-of-the-bush/

Save the Rhino. 'Shoot to Kill', *Save the Rhino*, n.d., https://www.savetherhino.org/thorny-issues/shoot-to-kill/

Talpade, B. 'A Sad Ending to the Story of a Six-Tonne Bull Elephant', *Carnivores and Conservation*, 3 May 2014, https://carnivoresandconservation.wordpress.com/2014/05/03/a-sad-ending-to-the-story-of-a-six-tonne-bull-elephant/

The Telegraph. 'Poacher to Tracker in South Africa', *The Telegraph*, 2024, https://www.telegraph.co.uk/travel/safaris-and-wildlife/poacher-to-tracker-in-south-africa/

Printed in Great Britain
by Amazon

59178072R00189